Collins

Caribbean
Social Studies
2

T0340492

Naam Thomas, Nicole Philip-Dowe, Lisa Greenstein,
Bruce Nicholson & Daphne Paizee

Collins

William Collins' dream of knowledge for all began with the publication of his first book in 1819. A self-educated mill worker, he not only enriched millions of lives, but also founded a flourishing publishing house. Today, staying true to this spirit, Collins books are packed with inspiration, innovation and practical expertise. They place you at the centre of a world of possibility and give you exactly what you need to explore it.

Collins. Freedom to teach.

Published by Collins
An imprint of HarperCollins*Publishers*
The News Building
1 London Bridge Street
London SE1 9GF

HarperCollins Publishers
Macken House, 39/40 Mayor Street Upper, Dublin 1, D01 C9W8, Ireland

Browse the complete Collins Caribbean catalogue at
www.collins.co.uk/caribbeanschools

10 9 8 7 6 5 4

ISBN 978-0-00-825647-0

British Library Cataloguing in Publication Data
A catalogue record for this publication is available from the British Library.

Authors: Naam Thomas, Nicole Philip-Dowe, Lisa Greenstein, Bruce Nicholson & Daphne Paizee
Publisher: Dr Elaine Higgleton
Development editor: Megan LaBarre
In-house senior editor: Julianna Dunn
Project manager: Claire Parkyns, QBS Learning
Copyeditor: Tania Pattison
Proofreader: Helen Bleck
Indexer, Illustrator, Photo researcher: QBS Learning
Cover designer: Gordon MacGilp
Cover photo: Przemyslaw Skibinski / Shutterstock
Series designer: Kevin Robbins
Typesetter: QBS Learning
Production controller: Tina Paul
Printed and bound by: Ashford Colour Press Ltd

MIX
Paper | Supporting responsible forestry
FSC
www.fsc.org
FSC™ C007454

This book contains FSC™ certified paper and other controlled sources to ensure responsible forest management.

For more information visit: www.harpercollins.co.uk/green

See also page 300 for photograph acknowledgements

The publishers gratefully acknowledge the permission granted to reproduce the copyright material in this book. Every effort has been made to trace copyright holders and to obtain their permission for the use of copyright material. The publishers will gladly receive any information enabling them to rectify any error or omission at the first opportunity.

Contents

How to use this book

These learning objectives tell you what you will be learning about in the lesson.

Each topic is divided into headings.

Each topic has colourful photographs and illustrations to add context and meaning.

Discussion features allow you to work in pairs, in a group or as a class to explore the topic further.

Try these questions to check your understanding of each topic.

Groups in society

We are learning to:

- define the term group
- identify and examine the different groups to which people belong.

Groups ❯❯

We all belong to **groups**. A **social group** is made up of two or more people who work together to achieve a common purpose or goal. For example, you can be a part of a family, a club or class at school, a church group or a sports club.

Groups allow us to:

- work towards a common aim or goal/objective
- share common interests and needs
- create a sense of **unity**
- create a sense of identity and **belonging**
- do activities together or **interact** together often
- have common rules of behaviour, sanctions or rewards.

Groups that do not have these characteristics are not classed as social groups, because they are temporary or do not fulfil all or any of the above characteristics; for example, a crowd at a sporting event.

One of the first groups you are part of is the family group, as you are born into that group. Later you will become part of a wider community group, and then as you go through life you will become part of a number of groups.

Family and community groups are the first types of group that you will be part of.

Examples of groups ❯❯❯

People can belong to many different groups. Groups can be classified in different categories. For example:

- **primary groups** – small groups which people interact with often; for example, your family

Exercise

1. Write your own definition of 'social group'.
2. Give two examples of a social group.
3. What do groups allow us to do?
4. Is a crowd of people at a sporting event classed as a group? Give a reason for your answer.
5. Name the first social group that you became a member of.

Discussion

In groups, brainstorm the definition of 'group' and think of as many different types of group as you can.

Leadership

We are learning to:

- define the terms leader, leadership, power and authority
- state the qualities of a good leader.

What is a leader?

A **leader** is someone who leads or guides a particular group, and who is in overall charge of that group. A leader is someone the rest of the group follows.

Leadership is shown when the leader (or leaders) influence the group to achieve a common objective. Leadership has a direct impact on the way in which a group functions. It is important to have effective leadership that encourages cohesion within groups. When we talk about **leadership qualities,** we mean those personal qualities that make someone good at leading others.

Leadership qualities

Good leaders must have good leadership qualities. A good leader should be able to:

- *communicate well* with the members
- be able to *deal with people*
- *set goals* for the group and *put members' needs* first
- *allocate resources* to achieve the group's goals
- *motivate and persuade* other members to achieve the group's goals
- be *honest*, *reliable* and *fair*
- be *responsible*
- *command respect* of the members and be *respectful* towards them
- be *open to and apply good ideas* from members
- be *influential* on how people think and act.

Exercise

1. Explain in your own words the terms leader and leadership.
2. Write a list of the qualities that you believe people need in order to become leaders.
3. Decide on the three most important qualities in a leader. Use the word cloud to help you.

Discussion

In groups, discuss the difference between power and authority.

honest
trustworthy
reliable persuasive
disciplined
having integrity selfless
fair
hardworking
respectful responsible
kind calm
good communicator
tolerant

Activity

Describe qualities a good leader should have. Write about 150 words.

Key vocabulary

leader

leadership

leadership qualities

honest

responsible

respectful

Activity features allow you to do practical activities related to the topic.

These are the most important new social studies words in the topic. You can check their meanings in the Glossary at the end of the book.

This page gives a summary of the exciting new ideas you will be learning about in the unit.

These lists at the end of a unit act as a checklist of the key ideas of the unit.

This is the topic covered in the unit, which links to the syllabus.

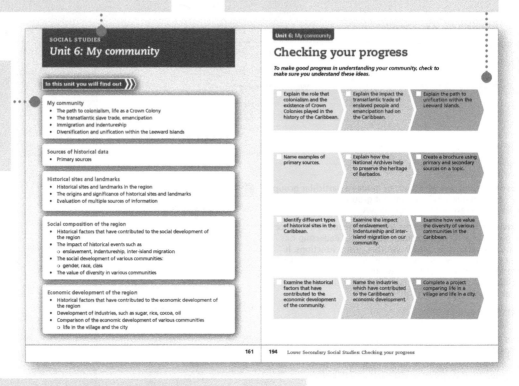

These end-of-unit questions allow you and your teacher to check that you have understood the ideas in each unit and can explain social studies using the skills and knowledge you have gained.

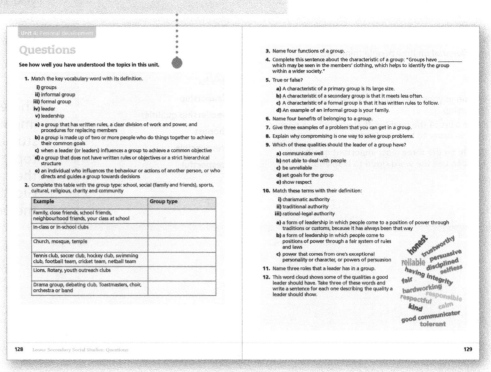

Unit 1: Economic growth and development

Earning a living

- Explain the terms and concepts: wages/salary, employers, employees/workers, work ethics
- Identify different ways that people earn a living: types and classification of careers

Employment

- Explain the terms and concepts: career, employment, unemployment, self-employment, brain drain

Labour force

- Explain the terms: primary, secondary, tertiary and quaternary
- Classification of the labour force
  - ○ primary, secondary, tertiary, quaternary
  - ○ unskilled, permanent, temporary, labour force
- The importance of each category of worker to economic development of the country

Financial responsibility

- Define relevant terms: money, need, want, saving, precautionary, transactionary, speculative
- Distinguish between a need and a want
- Reasons for saving, classification of savings, benefits of saving
- Identify factors that may hinder a person from saving

Managing income earned

- The importance of a budget
- How budget planning can assist with financial stability
- Ways in which individuals and families manage income

Earning a living

We are learning how to:

- define relevant terms and concepts: wages/salary, employers, employees/ workers, work ethics.

Wages and salaries

The term earning a living refers to the many ways through which a **wage** or **salary** may be earned. A wage is a payment to a worker for work done in a particular time period. Payment may be calculated as a fixed amount for each task completed (known as a piece rate), at an hourly or daily rate or based on an easily measured quantity of work done. A salary is where the employer pays a prearranged amount at regular intervals (such as weekly or monthly), often regardless of hours worked.

Large companies, such as Caribbean Alliance Insurance, based in Antigua, pay workers a basic wage, as well as non-salaried benefits called perks. These are benefits such as paid vacations, company vehicles, company medical benefits or free housing.

An employer at work in the Caribbean.

The employer and the employee

An **employer** is a person, or organisation, who employs someone to do a particular job. Employers have a responsibility to workers, such as ensuring safe working conditions, and a responsibility to the government to operate lawfully.

Employees are people who work for a company. They are hired to do a job, and are usually paid on a monthly basis. For example, a cashier is paid to sit at a cashpoint and ring up the goods at a shop. Other examples include teachers, nurses, police officers and fire fighters, who are employed by the government to work in schools, hospitals, police stations and fire stations.

Activity

Write about 100 words explaining the role that ethics can play in the life of the worker outside the workplace. Then write down a list of the changes you think you ought to make in your life in order to be a diligent person.

Exercise

1. In your own words, define the terms employer and employee.

2. Compare the roles of the employer with the employee.

3. What is the difference between a wage and a salary?

4. Name one responsibility an employer has to its workers and to the government.

Work ethics refer to rules and standards of conduct that are acceptable in the workplace. If rules of conduct are not observed by workers they can be held accountable by their supervisors and it can be entered in their personal record. This may adversely affect their chances for promotion. **Ethical conduct** (the moral principles people live by) is equally applicable to all spheres of life such as at home, school or places of worship.

Acceptable standards of conduct for workers include:

- **honesty** and **integrity**, requiring a worker to be truthful and not to falsify information such as claims of overtime work
- respect for the property of the company, such as to refrain from the abuse of vehicles, telephones, copier or fax machines and company materials
- to make sure that tasks are completed in an efficient and timely manner
- work as a team and cooperate with co-workers
- to be properly dressed and to respect the rights of workers or clients
- to be reliable in the course of their work.

An employee at work in the Caribbean.

Case study

At the Top Pop soft drink factory, workers were reported by supervisors for playing internet games during working hours, and using the company phone for their personal use. Four company workers were seen at a beach with the company vehicle, playing music loudly and making a nuisance of themselves. The workers were summoned to see their managers, where they admitted not acting correctly. They were all demoted for breaking company rules and also made to work extra hours.

Questions

1. What examples of work ethics have been broken in the case study?

2. Why do you think it is important to observe proper work ethics while at work?

3. Suggest three ways a company can encourage workers to conduct themselves ethically.

4. What do you think is the meaning of the word integrity?

5. Explain how a worker can demonstrate **reliability**.

Discussion

In groups, brainstorm your understanding of the terms wages, salary, employer, employee and work ethics.

Key vocabulary

wages

salary

employer

employee

work ethics

ethical conduct

honesty

integrity

reliability

9

Classifications of careers

We are learning to:

- identify different ways that people earn a living: managers, professionals, technicians and associate professionals.

The International Standard Classification of Occupations (ISCO) is an international organisation that places **careers** into different **classifications**.

Occupational classifications are used to group similar job types into categories or groups. This can help people in education and training, career guidance or human resources. In total, there are ten different categories of workers, known as major groups.

Major group 1: Managers

Managers are senior experienced personnel whose main tasks are to plan, direct, organise and coordinate the activities of their organisation. Typical tasks include:

- giving instructions to workers on how to perform their tasks
- making sure that the workers have the necessary tools and other resources to carry out their work
- making sure that all workers operate as a team and in harmony with each other.

Examples include senior government officials, as well as managers in the fields of sales and marketing, agriculture, manufacturing, health care, education and hotels and restaurants.

Major group 2: Professionals

Professionals are workers who have advanced qualifications, knowledge and work experience that are applied to their job. Examples include doctors, chemists, scientists, electrical engineers, architects, town planners, midwives, vets, dentists, opticians, teachers, accountants and lawyers.

Exercise

1. How many different types of job classification are there?

2. Why do you think jobs need to be classified?

3. What types of jobs would you do if you were a manager or a professional? Which job would you like to do?

Did you know...?

The ten different categories of workers are:

1. Managers
2. Professionals
3. Technicians and associate professionals
4. Clerical support workers
5. Sales and services workers
6. Skilled agricultural, forestry and fishery workers
7. Craft and related trades workers
8. Plant and machine operators and assemblers
9. Elementary occupations
10. Armed forces

A doctor is an example of a professional worker (group 2).

Major group 3: Technicians and associate professionals ⟫⟫⟫

Workers in this group are **technicians** and **associate professionals** who work in technical or research-related jobs and who have been educated to university level.

Examples include engineering technicians, mining and construction supervisors, air traffic controllers, medical technicians (such as people who create artificial limbs), ambulance workers, dental assistants and government officials, such as immigration and tax officials.

Major group 4: Clerical support workers ⟫⟫

This group of workers carry out tasks related to the recording, organising and storing of information. Examples of job types in this group include secretaries, telephone switchboard operators, hotel receptionists, bookkeepers, and office, payroll, bank transport and library clerks.

Workers in this group would be educated to secondary level and would receive **on-the-job training** while working in their jobs to gain experience.

A computer repair person is an example of someone who works in a group 3 occupation.

Discussion

In groups, discuss the major groups 1–4. Are there any jobs in these groups that you would like to do?

Exercise

4. Which group would the following jobs be classified under?

   a) vet
   b) assistant vet
   c) secretary
   d) office clerk
   e) tax official

5. Match the activity of the worker to their classification of job.

   a) This worker is the technical expert in the company.
   b) This worker organises, trains and motivates the workers.
   c) This worker is highly skilled, has advanced qualifications in a specialist field and has experience.

   i) technician and associate professional
   ii) professional
   iii) manager

Research

Using the internet or magazines, research two or three examples of the different jobs for each of the major groups 1–4. Try to find examples in your country. Create a portfolio which gives the job title and, if possible, add a photograph for each job.

Key vocabulary

career
classification
manager
professional
technician
associate professional
on-the-job training

Classifications of careers

We are learning to:

* identify different ways that people earn a living: sales and service, skilled agricultural, forestry and fishery workers.

Major group 5: Sales and services workers

This group includes occupations related to the **sales** and **service industries**, such as travel, housekeeping, catering, personal care, working and selling in shops or retail and public services.

People who work in the sales and service industries are known as **tertiary workers**. The **tertiary sector** involves services rather than physical goods. Examples of people in service industries include waiters, shop assistants and porters in hotels.

Examples of job types in this group include:

* cooks, waiters, bartenders
* hairdressers, beauticians
* cleaners and housekeepers in offices and hotels
* street and market sellers, shopkeepers
* sales workers, such as door-to-door salespeople, service station attendants, food counter workers
* home health-care assistants, doctors
* public services, such as the police, firefighters, prison guards, security guards.

Workers in sales and services would typically be educated to secondary school level and would receive on-the-job training while working in their jobs to gain experience.

A sales worker is an example of someone who works in the sales industry (group 5).

A cook is an example of someone who works in a service industry (group 5).

Exercise

1. In your own words, explain what type of workers belong to the group 5 classification.

2. What is the tertiary sector?

3. What types of jobs would a group 5 worker do?

4. Identify whether these job types belong to a group 5 classification:

    a) hairdresser b) taxi driver
    c) accountant d) porter

Major group 6: Skilled agricultural, forestry and fishery workers

Workers in this group work in the agricultural sector. Their tasks include:

- growing and harvesting field or tree and shrub crops
- gathering wild fruits and plants
- breeding, tending or hunting animals
- producing a variety of animal husbandry products
- cultivating, conserving and exploiting forests
- breeding or catching fish.

Examples of job types in this group include:

- market gardeners and crop growers
- animal producers, such as livestock, dairy and poultry
- crop and animal producers
- forestry workers
- fishery workers
- subsistence farmers.

Workers in this group tend to be self-employed and provide income for themselves and their households. Like workers in group 4, workers in this group would typically be educated to secondary school level and would receive on-the-job training.

A fisherman is an example of someone who works in a group 6 occupation.

Activity

In groups, each person chooses a worker employed in a sales or service job. As a game of charades, every person acts out the person's role and asks the group to identify the worker's occupation.

Exercise

5. What type of tasks would someone employed in a group 6 job be required to do?

6. Which group would the following jobs be classified under?
   a) chef
   b) market gardener
   c) taxi driver
   d) doctor
   e) fisherman
   f) barber

7. Using the internet or magazines, research two or three examples of the different types of jobs for groups 5 and 6. Try to find examples in your country. Add to your portfolio, giving the job title, and add a photograph for each job.

Key vocabulary

sales industry

service industry

tertiary workers

tertiary sector

Classifications of careers

We are learning to:

- identify different ways that people earn a living: craft and related trades workers, plant and machine operators and assemblers, elementary occupations.

Major group 7: Craft and related trades workers »

Workers in this group work in the building, or construction, industry or in related industries, such as masonry, carpentry, roofing, plumbing, electrical work or welding. The type of work generally includes:

- building and maintaining buildings
- making and maintaining machinery
- printing work
- processing food, textiles, metal or wooden products
- making hand-crafted goods.

The work in this group is usually carried out by hand or with hand-powered tools. Examples of job types in this group include:

- building workers, such as bricklayers, stonemasons, carpenters
- other building trade workers, such as roofers, plasterers, plumbers, pipe fitters, painters and floor layers
- metal workers, including welders, sheet-metal workers, blacksmiths, toolmakers
- machinery maintenance and repair workers, such as car and aircraft mechanics, agricultural machinery repairers
- handicraft makers, such as musical instrument makers, jewellery makers, glassmakers, potters
- printers and binders
- butchers, bakers, cheesemakers, tobacco workers.

Workers in this group are educated to secondary school level and receive on-the-job training.

A bricklayer is an example of someone who works in a group 7 occupation.

> **Did you know...?**
>
> The International Standard Classification of Occupations (ISCO) lists armed forces occupations as major group 10. This includes all jobs held by members of the armed forces.

Exercise

1. In your own words, explain what type of workers belong to the group 7 classification.

2. What types of jobs would a group 7 worker do?

3. Identify whether these job types belong to a group 7 classification:

    a) baker **b)** receptionist **c)** jewellery maker **d)** chef

Activity

Draw a mind map to show what type of job in group 7 goes with the type of work they do. For example, a bricklayer would build buildings.

Major group 8: Plant and machine operator and assemblers

Workers in this group operate industrial and agricultural machinery and equipment. It can be a specialised sector to work in and people who work in these jobs need to have experience and understanding of the machinery, as well as an ability to keep up to date with the technology. The types of jobs in this group include:

- mining and quarry machine operators
- metal and chemical machine operators
- textile machine operators, including weaving, knitting, sewing, bleaching, dyeing and shoemaking
- food machine operators, including meat, seafood, dairy, fruit, vegetables and cocoa processing
- assembly line workers
- drivers, including train, motorbike, car, taxi, van, bus, truck and earth-moving machinery
- ship workers and crew.

Workers in this group are also educated to secondary school level and receive on-the-job training.

An assembly line worker is an example of someone who works in a group 8 occupation.

Major group 9: Elementary occupations

Elementary occupations cover jobs which perform simple tasks using basic equipment and some physical effort. They are not regarded as skilled labour. The types of jobs in this group include:

- domestic, hotel and office cleaners
- agricultural, forestry and fishery labourers
- construction, manufacturing and transport labour
- fast-food workers and kitchen helpers
- messengers, odd-job people, rubbish collectors.

Exercise

4. Identify the classification of the following workers:

   a) train driver **b)** hotel cleaner **c)** cheesemaker

   d) car mechanic

5. Make a list of workers in the craft and related trades group that may have been employed to build your school.

6. Using the internet or magazines, research two or three examples of the different types of jobs for each of groups 7–9. Try to find examples in your country. Add to your portfolio, giving the job title, and add a photograph for each job.

Activity

Look back over Units 1.2–1.4 and the types of jobs in each classification group. Create a graphic organiser which summarises the information for all of these groups. You could include the group type, the type of tasks and job examples.

Project

In groups, make a list of all the teaching, clerical and support staff jobs at your school. Match each one to the job classification system. Create a report of your findings and report back to the class.

Key vocabulary

elementary occupations

15

Employment

We are learning to:

- define and explain the terms and concepts: career, employment, unemployment, self-employment.

Careers

A career is the job or profession that someone works in during their working life. The type of career someone takes is determined by several factors.

- Natural talents, abilities and interests can lead to a particular profession – for example, car mechanic, athlete, dancer, sculptor, doctor or teacher.
- The skill level and previous experience gained from being guided by a skilled senior person lead us to our life occupations – for example, car mechanic.
- Our level of education provides us with the knowledge and skills to perform a job – for example, technical training may lead a person to become a plant supervisor.
- The influence of role models inspires us to select our careers. Olympic gold medallist Kirani James may inspire young athletes to become sprinters.
- Your parents will know your natural strengths and advise and guide you in your career choice. They may also influence you according to family tradition.
- Many people consider job satisfaction before choosing a job, because if it is enjoyable people tend to think that they are actually not working.
- The level of wages offered by an employer may be more attractive in a particular career, because some people often rate financial rewards more highly than other factors when choosing a job.
- We may choose a career based on future industries, such as solar and wind power, so that when we qualify as a solar engineer we can find a job in this industry in the future.

Job satisfaction is a factor many consider before choosing their career.

Discussion

In groups, discuss the terms career, employment, unemployment and self-employment and explain the differences between them.

Exercise

1. In your own words, define the term career.

2. Write down three factors that you would consider before deciding on a career.

3. Identify a skill you consider to be your natural ability.

Most adults need to work in order to earn a living. For most people, this means using their skills to find **employment** within the economy. For example:

- Employees are people who work for a company. They are hired to do a job, and are usually paid on a monthly basis. For example, a cashier is paid to sit at a cashpoint and ring up the goods at a shop.

- **Self-employed** people provide goods or services, and work for themselves. Someone who starts a business, whether it is a shop or a business that provides a service, such as sewing and fixing garments, is self-employed.

Many countries have a problem of **unemployment**. This is the situation where someone is looking for work, or is able to work, but cannot find a job or employment opportunity.

In the Caribbean, we have plenty of employment opportunities, but the jobs available do not always match the levels of training and expertise of our human resources. This causes **underemployment**. You can read some examples of this below. A highly qualified person may be underemployed in a job that does not use their skills or training. If someone feels they are underemployed, they may leave the country to find employment elsewhere. This is known as **brain drain**.

There are plenty of job opportunities across the Caribbean.

Activity

Make a list of some jobs that you and a friend can do on your own during your spare time in order to earn money.

Case study

Three friends, Shania, Kaliya and Daniel, are all interested in business. After school, they attend university to study business sciences. After they qualify, each graduate goes in a different direction. Shania applies to a bank, where she gets a job as an investment consultant. Kaliya does some research and opens a clothing importation business. Daniel wants to work in a large company, but he can't find a job. He takes a temporary job waiting tables at a local restaurant until he can find a job better suited to his skills.

Questions

1. What do the three friends have in common?

2. Which of the three friends is self-employed?

3. Which of the three friends is underemployed?

4. Two of the friends are paid employees. What is the difference between their situations?

5. What do you think is likely to happen if Daniel does not find more suitable employment?

Key vocabulary

employment

self-employed

unemployment

underemployment

brain drain

Classification of the labour force

We are learning to:

- define and explain relevant terms and concepts: primary, secondary, tertiary and quaternary
- understand the classification of the labour force: primary, secondary, tertiary, quaternary.

Classification of the labour force: primary

Today, there are four main sectors of **industry**. They are classified as **primary**, **secondary**, **tertiary** and **quaternary**.

The primary sector involves the extraction of raw materials and natural resources. Examples include farming, fishing, forestry and mining.

In Trinidad and Tobago, people who work on oil rigs, or who drill for natural gas, are primary workers. Other examples include agriculture, forestry, fishing and mining. Primary occupations are therefore farmers, fishermen, loggers, miners and oil drillers.

The oil industry in Trinidad and Tobago is an example of a primary industry.

Classification of the labour force: secondary

The secondary sector turns raw materials into finished goods. For example, factory workers, builders and dressmakers are secondary workers.

Manufacturing, refining, processing and construction are part of the secondary sector. Companies in the Caribbean working in this sector include:

- oil refining at Petrotrin Limited in Trinidad
- bauxite at Alpart in Jamaica
- sand and limestone quarrying by C. O. Williams in Barbados.

Project

In groups, research one category of worker, for example, primary. Choose one career within that classification. Research the career and find out why that job is important to the development of the economy of your country. Present your findings in a group report.

Exercise

1. In your own words, define the terms primary and secondary.

2. Identify which sectors these jobs belong to:

   a) oil refining   **b)** oil drilling   **c)** fishing
   d) sand and limestone quarrying

Classification of the labour force: tertiary ▶▶▶

The tertiary sector involves services rather than physical goods. Examples of people in service industries include waiters, shop assistants and doctors. This class of worker is engaged in the provision of **direct** and **indirect services**. A direct service sells a service direct to customers for their individual benefit. Direct services include:

- services linked to well-being and health – for example, by hospitals and health centres
- education services provided both by the government and private sector from early childhood education to primary, secondary and tertiary university level free of charge
- shoe repair, domestic help, house painting.

An indirect service is one that sells a service to many customers at the same time. Indirect services include:

- banking, to pay workers and suppliers, make cash and cheque deposits, automatic teller services
- transport, such as taxis, buses, trucks, ferries, air travel
- food processing services, bottling and packaging
- advertising and promotion of goods and services on the television and radio, and billboards along the nation's highways.

A health care worker is an example of someone who works in the tertiary sector.

Classification of the labour force: quaternary ▶▶

Quaternary industries provide knowledge and skills, such as information technology, research and development, innovation industries and the media. Examples of people who work in quaternary industries include those in research and development, science, information and communications technology, and business consultants. A quaternary media industry in the Caribbean includes the newspapers – for example, the *St Kitts & Nevis Observer*, the *Barbados Advocate* or the *Guyana Chronicle*.

Project

Working in groups, recall from previous lessons some examples of career types. Your teacher will write responses on the board. Create a table that categorises responses into: types of workers, examples of career/job types, the industry to which the job is aligned and the resulting product/service.

Exercise

3. In your own words, define the terms tertiary and quaternary.
4. Identify which sectors these workers belong to:
   a) teacher **b)** scientist **c)** bus driver
   d) newspaper writer
5. Create a mind map to help explain the terms primary, secondary, tertiary and quaternary.

Key vocabulary

industry

primary industry

secondary industry

tertiary industry

quaternary industry

direct services

indirect services

The labour force

We are learning to:

- define and explain relevant terms and concepts: unskilled, permanent, temporary, labour force.

Unskilled workers ⟩⟩

Unskilled workers are workers who follow primary, secondary, tertiary and quartenary workers and who have no formal training, education or skill. Unskilled workers are usually employed as domestic helpers, cleaners, messengers, sanitation workers or labourers.

The unskilled sector provides services that do not require special skills or heavy physical effort. Usually, a worker in the unskilled sector only has a primary level of education. Examples include sanitation workers at your school, porters at the airport and delivery drivers.

Some of the reasons workers can only find work in the unskilled sector include:

- a lack of basic education, vocational or craft training
- a lack of motivation due to negative effects of a broken home
- an inability to read, write, compute or communicate.

A street hawker is an example of an unskilled worker.

Permanent workers ⟩⟩⟩

Permanent workers are workers whose job is on a full-time basis. They can often be employed in the same job until they retire – for example, a personnel manager. Some of the advantages of permanent work include:

- The jobs can be highly skilled and of great value to their firms.
- Benefits include retirement benefits, health insurance, paid holidays and company vehicles.
- These jobs provide opportunities for promotion and higher salaries.
- The jobs are long-term and employees are paid every month.
- There is a higher level of commitment between employer and employee.

Exercise

1. In your own words, define the term unskilled worker.
2. Why are some people only able to find unskilled jobs?
3. In your own words, explain the benefits of having a permanent job.

Temporary workers >>>>

Temporary work, or temporary employment, is when an employer offers short-term employment, perhaps to fill a temporary absence or a staff shortage.

Instead of offering a permanent position, the employer may offer a **contract** so that they can pay someone to complete a particular set of tasks.

Once the contract is finished, the worker must find other work. Temporary work is often accepted because it:

- is preferred to no work at all
- may lead to a permanent position
- may open a door to future opportunities
- may provide a young worker with a work history
- maintains production if someone is absent.

One advantage of temporary, part-time work is that workers may work around other projects. Workers can take on more work if they need to earn more money. They can also work from home.

A police officer is an example of someone who works in a permanent role and often is in the job until they retire.

The labour force >>

The **labour force** is the part of the population that is able and available to work. The characteristics of the labour force are different for every country. In Barbados, the labour force is made up of people between the ages of 16 and 67. The labour force therefore comprises both persons employed and unemployed.

In 2016, it was estimated that the total labour force in Barbados was approximately 147 200 persons. Approximately 50 per cent of these are male and 50 per cent female. Of those persons employed, approximately 78 per cent are employed in service industries, and 2.7 per cent in agriculture.

Over time skilled members of the labour force have left the Caribbean to reside in the UK and the USA in search of better opportunities. This phenomenon is called the brain drain.

Activity

Scan magazines and newspapers, and clip out pictures of unskilled, permanent and temporary workers. Then make a collage showing what you have learned. Ask your teacher to display it in the classroom.

Exercise

4. In what situation might an employer need some temporary workers?

5. Why do people sometimes take on temporary work? What advantages does this offer?

6. Produce a mind map comparing the advantages and benefits of being **a)** a permanent worker and **b)** a temporary worker.

Key vocabulary

unskilled workers

permanent workers

temporary workers

contract

labour force

The labour force and economic development

We are learning to:

- explain the importance of each category of worker to economic development.

Primary sector workers

Trinidad and Tobago is the largest oil and natural gas producer in the Caribbean. It is a wealthy and well-developed state with a high **per capita** income. The oil and gas companies, in the primary sector, make a significant contribution to the economy of Trinidad and Tobago. Companies include Atlantic LNG, National Gas Company, Petrotrin, Amoco, Trinmar, Enron Oil & Gas, British Gas, Texaco, Royal Dutch Shell, Repsol SA and Elf Aquitaine. The government of Trinidad and Tobago has identified **growth poles**, or areas, of the country where investments should be made in order to promote **diversity**.

Sugar cane fields in Guyana.

In Guyana, primary industries such as agriculture and gold and mineral mining are the country's biggest earners and employment sectors. The state-owned sugar company GUYSUCO produces sugar, while the Guyana Rice Development Board offers essential support services to rice farms. Bauxite mining occurs in the Demerara and Berbice River basins. Guyanese bauxite is of very high quality, but it is expensive to mine due to transport costs.

Secondary sector workers

The value of the secondary sector to economic development is related to the satisfaction of human needs from products that are created by the manufacturing sector.

For example, gasoline and aviation fuel enable road and air travel. Lumber, steel and cement are key inputs in facilities for educational, health, cultural, commercial and residential construction.

Electricity enables the use of labour-saving devices such as washing machines, water pumps, ovens and other small appliances, while manufactured goods earn export **revenue** for the country.

> **Did you know...?**
>
> Sugar cane fields in Guyana are irrigated by an extensive network of canals. The canals are also used for pest control and the transport of harvested cane to sugar factories.

> **Project**
>
> Make a list of products your family uses that require, or are made from, the gas or oil industries. Also list any products made from local materials, like furniture items and foods.

Tertiary sector workers >>>>

The value of the tertiary sector to economic development includes personal services such as medical, dental and optical services, private transport, domestic help, food delivery and internet and telephone services. These all enhance the quality of life of the citizens of the country.

Services to trade – such as banking, transport, canning, labelling packaging, delivery, machine repair, toolmaking, security, cleaning and maintenance are key elements in infrastructural services to industry, and to economic growth and development generally.

An oil refinery belonging to Atlantic LNG.

The quatenary sector >>

The quatenary sector is important in terms of economic development because the information, or knowledge, industries accelerate decision making at all levels of human endeavour. Education guides us to wise decisions in our everyday life, such as the careers that we will choose.

Technology has assisted the invention of labour-saving devices in the home. Research, development and innovation combine to create artificial intelligence, which is expected to change our lives dramatically in the future.

Life expectancy has been given a boost through modern technology in medicine, and someone living in the Caribbean is now expected to live into their seventies. The media keep the nation informed daily, and are a major source of information for everyone in the country.

Activity

Compose a poem about the contribution of workers from the four sectors. Then ask the class musician and calypsonian to sing it for the class.

Exercise

1. Which primary sectors are important to:
   a) Trinidad and Tobago
   b) Guyana?
2. Choose a worker from the agriculture or mining industries and identify the contribution they each make to your family's quality of life.
3. What contribution to life in the Caribbean do tertiary sector workers make?
4. How does modern medical technology in the quatenary sector improve life expectancy?
5. In simple terms, why is it important for any country to have a diverse economy?

Key vocabulary

per capita

growth poles

diversity

revenue

Financial responsibility

We are learning to:

- define relevant terms: money, need, want, saving, precautionary, transactionary, speculative.

Money ▶▶

Money is anything widely regarded as valuable that is acceptable in a transaction between two or more parties. Cash, credit cards, cheques, gold, scarce commodities and salt are different forms of money that have been used over time. A new type of money called **bitcoin**, or virtual money, is beginning to attract attention. It may become the money of the future.

Money must have certain qualities:

A bank in Antigua.

- It must be acceptable to all parties, meaning that the parties to a transaction must agree to accept it as a means of payment.
- It must be scarce for it to have value. We cannot use leaves for money, as they have little value.
- It must be durable and not deteriorate, because people will lose confidence in it. Would you accept a torn crumpled dollar?

The Eastern Caribbean 20 dollar bill.

- It must be in different sizes or divisible to enable small transactions. This is the reason for large and small bills and coins.
- It must be portable in order for it to be easily carried around.
- It must be difficult to copy, to prevent people from reproducing it illegally.
- It must be uniform – all bills and coins of equal value must look exactly the same.

The functions of money include:

- It can hold its value over time (store of value).
- It enables transactions (medium of exchange).
- It rates the value of goods to each other (measure of value).
- It allows payments in the future to repay credit given (standard for deferred payment).

Exercise

1. In your view, what are the five most important qualities that money should have?

2. In your own words, explain the functions of money.

Needs and wants ⟩⟩⟩

Human beings have many needs and wants that together contribute to a satisfying standard of living.

A **need** is a necessity that sustains basic life, and having to do without it will cause suffering or in extreme cases even death. For example, food, water, shelter, clothing and good health are basic bodily needs. We can live without food for two weeks. but we will die if we do not have water for two or three days.

A **want** is a human desire not considered necessary to sustain life, but which human beings desire to fulfil their lives – for example, a new pair of shoes or trainers, or a new mobile phone.

Savings refers to money that is set aside and not spent in the present but which may be used in the future. For example, you may have a piggy bank which you use to put away money for a future use. Many people have savings in the bank or other financial institutions.

Project

Working in groups, find five pictures in magazines or catalogues of items that you want and five pictures of items that you need. Then order them from 1 to 10 the most essential (1) to the least essential (10).

The need for money ⟩⟩⟩⟩

- The **transaction need** for money is simply to make everyday purchases such as buying a soft drink or paying for a taxi.
- The **precautionary need** for money is for unexpected events such as sudden illnesses or a leaking roof.
- The **speculative need** for money is wealth held in a different form. For example, a good substitute for money is a house, land or gold coins, which can be converted into money.

Activity

Write a reflective piece in which you discuss your needs and wants. How badly do you need both?

Exercise

3. Explain the difference between a need and a want.

4. Name two everyday items that you consider a need.

5. Name two items of your own that you consider a want.

6. Why should people save their money?

7. In your own words, explain the difference between transactional, precautionary and speculative needs for money.

8. Identify three examples of a transaction, precautionary and speculative need for money.

Key vocabulary

money

bitcoin

need

want

savings

transaction need

precautionary need

speculative need

Needs and wants

We are learning to:

* distinguish between a need and a want.

Distinguish between needs and wants »

The difference between a need and a want can be summarised as follows:

* A need relates to human requirements that nurture the body and mind. These determine a basic quality of life. For example, food, water, clothing, shelter and health care are basic human needs.
* A want is a human desire that increases satisfaction of life beyond basic bodily needs. For example, we would like to have holidays, swimming pools and jewellery, but they are not essential to our basic needs.

Factors that influence our wants and needs are determined by several factors:

* We make personal choices – for example, we buy a certain brand of footwear.
* Peer pressure can create want - we may buy something that is popular among our peers so we are part of the crowd – for example, branded clothing.
* Bodily needs cause us to buy food and water.
* Habits determine our wants – for example, if we buy something every day (say, bottled water), it becomes a habit.
* Information can help us to make better choices – for example, we may buy a bottle of water instead of a soft drink because we have been told that soft drinks have sugar and additives that may be harmful to our bodies.
* Advertising persuades us to spend on wants, because advertisers use **psychology** to influence our choices – for example, the picture of the burger that looks more appealing than the actual burger.

Having a meal is an example of a need.

Having a swimming pool at home is an example of a want.

Exercise

1. Identify whether each of the following is a want or a need:

   a) bottled water   **b)** cheese sandwich
   c) T-bone steak   **d)** pair of khaki pants
   e) designer footwear **f)** bus travel
   g) visit to the health centre

2. Why do you think peer pressure can make you spend?

3. Identify an advertisement that influenced you to make a purchase.

A **psychologist** is someone who analyses and studies human behaviour. The psychologist Abraham Maslow proposed a theory on human needs, which he separated into different categories.

The chart identifies the pyramid structure of human needs as proposed by Maslow:

- primary or bodily needs, such as food and water
- secondary needs, such as safety and security from physical harm, for example, shelter, clothing and health
- social needs, such as a sense of belonging, affection, friendship and acceptance in a group
- tertiary needs, such as self-esteem needs, for example, achievement, recognition and status
- ambition needs, such as fulfilling one's dreams and personal growth and achieving one's potential.

Maslow's pyramid of needs

Case study

Siblings Steve and Rebecca are 13 and 14 years old respectively. Both complained to their mum that they did not have the latest clothes and computer games that their friends enjoyed. They felt they did not belong to the cool crowd.

Their mum explained that they could not afford the items they desired, but they were well fed and had a roof over their heads. She said they should be thankful that their needs were satisfied.

Questions

1. Which of Maslow's needs is highlighted in the case study?

2. Make a list of six of your personal wants. Arrange the list in order of importance.

3. Select any three items from your list and explain how they can contribute positively to the quality of your life.

4. Write a short article on a need you consider to be the most important to you. Give reasons for your choice. Then do the same for a 'want'.

5. Can your education influence your purchasing choices?

Key vocabulary

psychology

psychologist

Saving our money

We are learning to:

- understand reasons for saving, classification of savings, benefits of saving
- identify factors that may hinder a person from saving.

Reasons for saving

Money is usually saved for known or unknown events in the present and future. A fund must therefore be set aside for them.

An unknown event may be an unexpected illness, such as cancer, which is costly to treat. A known event could include the purchase and maintenance of a new house or car.

Retirement income is another easily identified need, because we are going to age and retire, and will need income on which to live comfortably in our senior years. Future family needs that enhance quality of life – such as yearly holidays, servicing debts, education and special milestones, like special birthdays and anniversaries – are added needs that require savings.

The Scotia Bank Ltd in Nassau, Bahamas.

Classification of savings

Savings in the Caribbean may be placed in the formal or informal sectors.

The **formal savings** sector consists of commercial banks, such as Scotia Bank Ltd, into which we make regular deposits in a savings account to earn interest income over time. There are also credit unions, insurance companies and the stock exchanges. They all offer opportunities for long-term savings products to clients wishing to save.

The **informal savings** sector includes sou-sou, Meeting turn or Box hand, which is a form of saving in the Caribbean. This is a system where members contribute a weekly sum to a pool of money, which is paid to a different member every week or month. This payment is called a hand. Private moneylenders and saving at home are also part of the informal sector.

Activity

Identify one of your future needs and suggest a type of saving shown in the diagram on page 29 that can be used to satisfy this need.

Exercise

1. Explain in your own words why we should save money.
2. What types of saving institutions are there in the Caribbean?

The benefits of savings ▶▶▶

The benefits of savings include:

- They provide financial independence for future needs.
- They can increase the saver's standard of living, as interest can be earned off savings.
- They can act as a source of financial comfort for unplanned events.
- They can buy a need, so the saver does not have to borrow money from a bank at high interest rates.

Hindrances to saving ▶▶

Factors that hinder saving include the following:

- A lack of financial education by family members hinders saving; if parents stress the value and importance of careful spending and saving, this will form part of a child's upbringing and will persist into later life.
- With high costs of living it is difficult to save because almost all income earned is used to meet basic needs, which leaves little for saving.
- The lack of a budget and poor spending habits hinder saving – a budget is a disciplined way to make sure that planned income is equal to planned spending, with money left over for savings.
- Levels of debts leave very little left over to save – saving can only be achieved if some spending is given up.
- Although low income earners pay less tax on their earnings, they pay indirect taxes such as VAT, which reduces their spending power.

Project

Students work in groups, each person beginning with $400. Every student identifies a target amount to be saved after one month, and should record their weekly expenditures for the month. The class discusses scenarios, to determine the factors that may have hindered saving. Make a plan of expenditure and saving for your total monthly allowance, then discuss it with the class to start a debate on saving.

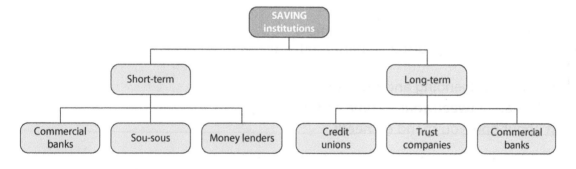

Exercise

3. In your own words, write a short article (150 words) about the importance of saving.

4. What is the difference between the formal and the informal savings sector?

Key vocabulary

formal savings

informal savings

Planning a budget

We are learning to:

- define the relevant terms and concepts: budget
- examine the importance of a budget.

The importance of planning a budget

A **budget** is an itemised summary of expected **income** (earnings) and **expenditure** (what you spend). A person, family, country or business can have a budget. A budget can also refer to how much money you have available to spend on something – for example, some clothes, a car or a house.

A budget is also a detailed financial plan of the way planned income is able to finance planned expenditure over a given period.

A family working out a budget.

Why is a budget important?

- A budget is important because it guards against unplanned spending, which causes us to spend more than we should. It further helps us to decide, in advance, how income can achieve future goals through the discipline of a financial plan.
- A budget also prevents financial instability over time. Financial instability occurs when financial debts exceed income over an extended period. A budget therefore promotes careful spending and prevents overspending.

Here are some tips as to how you could draw up a monthly budget plan:

- get organised and take your time when you plan your budget
- add up all your income
- work out your essential spending – for example, for families it will be rent/mortgage, bills, food and clothing
- work out your need spending and reduce it
- work out the gap between your income and spending
- be honest about how you spend on needs.

Exercise

1. Explain what a budget is. Who can have one?
2. Why is it important to have a budget?

Case study

Daniel decided that he wanted to create a monthly budget, as he found that he did not have enough money at the end of each month. Here is the budget Daniel came up with.

PLANNED INCOME	END OF MONTH
Monthly salary	$14 000
Other earnings	$ 2 000
Total income	**$16 000**

PLANNED EXPENSES	
Utilities and rent	$6 000
Food	$5 000
Auto Fuel	$2 000
Other	$2 000
Total planned spend	**$15 000**

DISPOSABLE INCOME	
Going out/leisure	$200
Phone	$250
Clothes	$300
Total spend	**$750**

UNPLANNED EXPENSES	
Plumbing repairs	$500
Total expenses	$16 250 ($15 000 + $500 + $750)
Net income	**−$250** ($16 000 − $16 250)

Questions

1. How much money does Daniel have left over this month?

2. What could he save on to make sure that his monthly budget worked?

3. Of the disposable income items, which one do you think Daniel needs to keep? Why?

4. What do you think Daniel should do **a)** for this month and **b)** for future months?

Activity

In pairs, do a role play, where one of you is Daniel and the other is Daniel's friend. Act out what his friend would advise him about his spending and budget.

Activity

Copy a blank version of the budget plan and create a personal budget.

Add your income (for example, your allowance, birthday money, chores money and school allowance) and spending to the budget.

Compare your budget with a partner's and then share with the class.

Key vocabulary

budget

income

expenditure

Planning for the future

We are learning how to:

• examine how budget planning can assist with financial stability.

Financial stability ≫

Financial stability refers to the prudent use of our financial resources to meet our future goals over an extended period without becoming indebted.

Financial stability is therefore achieved when, over time, our income is equal to, or exceeds, expenditure in a sustained manner and our goals have been achieved.

Budget planning and financial stability go hand in hand. A budget plan matches planned spending to planned income, preventing the creation of large debts over time. It also helps to identify savings that may be used to reduce debt and maintain financial stability.

It further creates a pool of savings to fund emergencies and unplanned events, as an alternative to costly borrowing from the bank. Financial stability is achieved through the discipline provided by a budget.

Saving over a long period of time can help meet our future goals, such as going to university.

The benefits of planning a budget ≫≫

The benefits of having a budget include:

• It provides financial stability over a long period.
• It can identify ways to save income, which over time can be used for investment, and to pay medical bills and finance unplanned events.
• It enables us to pay debts on time and avoid the stress caused by debt creation.
• It leads to the achievement of financial independence (this can apply to an individual, a family, a business or a country).

Research

Conduct research to identify what type of saving/investment is needed to earn income to finance future needs.

Exercise

1. Define in your own words the terms budget planning and financial stability.

2. How may budget planning achieve financial stability?

3. What are the benefits of planning a budget?

4. Why do you think it is important to be able to achieve financial independence?

Planning for the future ▶▶▶

We all wish to be successful in the future. Importantly, we possess the ability to influence the quality of our future by devising a plan to achieve this goal.

Planning for the future is a roadmap for future success for the short term (five years), medium term (ten to fifteen years) and long term (fifty years).

Needs planning ▶▶

Perhaps the best way to plan for the future is to conduct **needs planning**. Needs planning identifies our future needs and the source of future income to pay for these needs when they arise. Some of our future needs include:

House repairs are often costly – money should be set aside to pay for these needs.

- Basic physical needs such as food, shelter, clothing and health, which persist well into our advanced years. We must therefore have money planned for meals, a place to live, clothes to wear and a health plan for medical care.
- Primary, secondary and tertiary education in the present and future. We should have the income in place to finance these important future needs.
- Special occasions in the future, such as landmark birthdays, anniversaries, weddings and family vacations. We must carefully plan to avoid borrowing for these needs. A savings plan for these occasions is therefore necessary.
- Building renovation and maintenance. Since it is costly to carry out house repairs, a separate fund should be set up to finance these needs.
- Saving for our retirement years. This is a critical need, since our income from employment will cease. This predictable future need can be achieved by saving throughout our early working years.

Discussion

Ask your teacher to select groups of five students to choose a benefit of budget planning and consult their parents to help them understand how it contributes to financial stability. Use the information for a class discussion.

Exercise

5. Define in your own words the terms short-, medium- and long-term goals.

6. In your own words, explain the term needs planning.

7. Why is it necessary to plan for the future?

8. State three benefits related to future planning.

9. Place the following needs/wants into the short-, medium- or long-term periods:

   a) retirement
   b) tertiary education
   c) silver anniversary
   d) wedding
   e) food

Key vocabulary

financial stability

needs planning

How to manage your income

We are learning how to:

- investigate ways in which individuals and families manage income.

Managing your budget ›››

We have learned from previous lessons how planning for the future, and careful budgeting, can contribute to financial stability and a life well lived for an individual or a family.

There are many ways individual and families can manage their income and keep to their budgets. Activities that families or individuals can engage in to control spending include:

- Preparing and eating meals at home instead of eating at food outlets. This can save a lot of money, as food from supermarkets and local producers is much cheaper than eating out.
- Resisting the temptation to make unplanned purchases (also known as impulse buying), and instead buying from a prepared list.
- Sharing household duties instead of hiring domestic help, which costs money.
- Making sure that the house, equipment and appliances are always maintained, so that breakdowns do not mean purchasing expensive new items.
- Carpooling to save transport costs.
- Turning off houselights and water taps when not in use, to reduce spending large sums on water and electricity bills.
- Shopping at outlets that give bargain coupons, price reductions and clearance sales.
- Rearing livestock and planting fruit trees in one's yard space to reduce expenditure on meat and fruits.

Sharing household duties – instead of hiring domestic help – saves money.

Exercise

1. Name some of the ways that families can cut down on spending at home.

2. Write a paragraph on some of the ways that your family controls their spending.

3. Why do you think it is important to control spending?

4. Suggest other ways you could save money at home.

Project

Working in different groups, ask your teacher to locate unused space at school to start a pot garden. Plant six-week crops such as chives, pimento peppers, hot peppers and sweet peppers. Invite other classes to start a competition and donate the crops to a nearby orphanage.

Case study

Grow Box Project

In 2005, The Ministry of Agriculture, Land and Fisheries launched an initiative to reintroduce the concept of home gardening to communities throughout Trinidad. One of the initiatives developed to achieve this objective is the **Grow Box Project**.

This project seeks to establish home gardens in urban areas where land is scarce. It encourages families to produce safe, healthy, fresh food in their own back yards.

The Grow Box Project targets households, community groups, church groups and schools used for community activities.

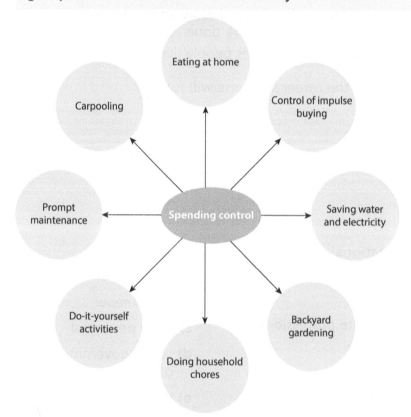

Activity

Brainstorm your own ideas on how to save money at home. Suggest what you personally can contribute to manage the income earned in your family more efficiently.

Exercise

5. What are the advantages of growing your own vegetables in a kitchen garden?

6. Who does the Grow Box Project target?

7. From the concept chart, choose five items that can most reduce expenditure in your household.

8. Explain how these items can help reduce expenditure.

9. Write a paragraph on the following activities and identify benefits other than the control of spending:

   a) carpooling   **b)** eating at home   **c)** home gardening

Project

Design and produce a brochure or flyer entitled 'Tips for Saving'. Use the chart on this page to assess the merits of your brochure.

Questions

See how well you have understood the topics in this unit.

1. Match the key vocabulary word with its definition.

   i) wages

   ii) salary

   iii) employer

   iv) employee

   v) work ethics

   vi) ethical conduct

   a) someone who is paid to work for someone else

   b) the rules and standards of conduct that are acceptable in the workplace

   c) a person or organisation that employs people

   d) a payment to a worker for work done in a particular time period

   e) a payment made to a worker by an employer at regular intervals for work done

   f) a set of moral principles people live by

2. List five factors that could determine the career someone will follow.

3. Define these terms:

   a) employer
   b) employee
   c) employment
   d) unemployment
   e) underemployment

4. Match the job types to the occupational classification.

   i) Group 1 Managers

   ii) Group 2 Professionals

   iii) Group 3 Technicians and associate professionals

   iv) Group 4 Clerical support workers

   v) Group 5 Sales and services workers

   vi) Group 6 Skilled agricultural, forestry and fishery workers

   vii) Group 7 Craft and related trades workers

   viii) Group 8 Plant and machine operators and assemblers

   ix) Group 9 Elementary occupations

   x) Group 10 Armed forces

   a) ship worker

   b) bookkeeper

   c) army personnel

   d) senior government officials

   e) kitchen helpers

   f) air traffic controllers

   g) beautician

   h) market gardeners

   i) printing workers

   j) teachers

5. Complete these sentences:

   A _____ industry is an industry that provides knowledge and ideas.
   A _____ industry is an industry that harvests raw materials and natural resources.

A _____ industry is an industry mostly involved in processing and manufacturing.

A _____ industry is an industry that provides services.

6. Explain the difference between a permanent worker and a temporary worker.

7. Write a sentence to define each of these terms:

a) transaction need

b) precautionary need

c) speculative need

8. Write a paragraph explaining which factors influence our needs and wants.

9. Write an essay of about 150 words explaining the qualities and functions of money.

10. Look at Maslow's pyramid of needs. Fill in the gaps using the terms in the box.

secondary needs	self-fulfilment	primary needs
social needs	tertiary needs	

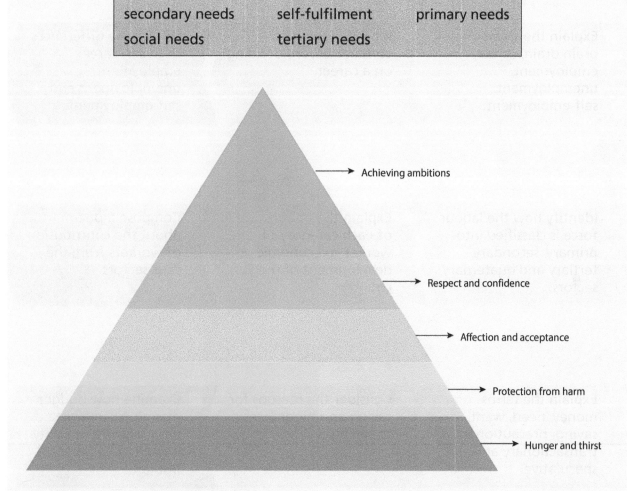

→ Achieving ambitions

→ Respect and confidence

→ Affection and acceptance

→ Protection from harm

→ Hunger and thirst

11. Name three benefits of saving.

12. Explain three hindrances to saving and suggest solutions to the hindrances identified.

Checking your progress

To make good progress in understanding economic growth and development, check that you understand these ideas.

Explain the terms wages, salary, employer, employee and work ethics.

Identify the types and classification of careers.

Create a graphic organiser that summarises the classification of careers.

Explain the terms brain drain, career, employment, unemployment, self-employment.

Identify factors to consider before deciding on a career.

Discuss the differences between career, employment, unemployment and self-employment.

Identify how the labour force is classified into primary, secondary, tertiary and quaternary sectors.

Explain the importance of each category of worker to economic development of the country.

Compose a poem about the contribution of workers from the four sectors.

Explain the terms money, need, want, saving, precautionary, transactionary and speculative.

Consider the reasons for saving and hindrances to saving.

Examine how budget planning can assist with financial stability and create a personal budget.

Unit 2: Caribbean integration and global links

In this unit you will find out ⟩⟩⟩

The Caribbean citizen

- Explain the terms national identity and Caribbean identity
- Explain the importance of a national identity and a Caribbean identity
  - ○ unity among people
  - ○ friendship
  - ○ cultural identity
  - ○ human resources

- Identify ways Caribbean citizens can show more appreciation for their national and Caribbean identity
  - ○ patriotism for country and region
  - ○ respect for our environment
  - ○ conservation and preservation of resources
  - ○ Carifesta

- Identify and categorise outstanding individuals in various fields from the Caribbean region and explain how their contributions have built Caribbean identity
  - ○ politics and economics
  - ○ sport and the arts
  - ○ entertainment and science

- Justify how the contribution of these individuals helps to create links with the rest of the world
- Value the contributions of outstanding individuals locally and in the Caribbean region

National and Caribbean identity

We are learning to:

- define the relevant terms and concepts: national and Caribbean identity.

National identity

Identity can be defined as the characteristics, style or manner that define a person and how that person is recognised. Identity can be influenced by personal choice but also by society through existing social and cultural situations.

National identity is the idea of what it means to belong to a particular country, state or a nation. Unlike identity, our national identity is not something we are born with, but instead is a common set of experiences or characteristics that people share.

Often, national identity is carried in shared characteristics such as language, national colours and symbols, the history of the nation, family connections, culture, cuisine, music and heritage. Most countries have:

- a flag, an anthem and a national emblem
- a shared history and culture
- a currency (the money used in that country)
- national holidays, customs and traditions.

We discussed in Form 1 that a **cultural background** includes things that a group of people share, such as their religion, language, music, traditions, customs, art and history.

Our **cultural heritage** consists of the cultural traditions that we have inherited from past generations. Together our cultural background and cultural heritage help to create our national identity.

Research

Research the national flag, anthem or emblem of your country. Find out its history and collect pictures using newspapers, magazines and the internet, and add this to your portfolio.

Victoria amazonica (Victoria regia), a water lily, is the national flower of Guyana.

Exercise

1. Write your own definition of national identity. Add this to your portfolio.

2. Name three ways in which national identity can be shown by a country.

3. What are some examples of national identity of the people in your country?

Caribbean identity is the idea of what it means to belong to the Caribbean region. The characteristics of this include:

- **ethnicity** – people from shared racial and ethnic groups tend to have shared characteristics, which often cut across geographical borders
- religion – the religious groups people belong to give a strong basis for identity
- history – the shared history of the Caribbean, including enslavement, indentureship and colonialism
- politics – people identify themselves based on political allegiances and these are often passed from one generation to the next
- geography – people identify themselves based on their place of birth
- language – the languages people speak, including creoles and dialects
- customs – social, religious, national holidays, etc.
- arts – the music, dance, stories, theatre and art.

Discussion

Discuss your understanding of the differences between national and Caribbean identity.

Steelpan players, Trinidad Carnival, Port of Spain.

Exercise

4. Write your own definition of Caribbean identity. Add this to your portfolio.

5. Name three ways in which Caribbean identity can be shown. Give an example of each.

6. Describe what you can see in the picture and which features of Caribbean identity it shows.

Key vocabulary

....

identity

national identity

cultural background

cultural heritage

Caribbean identity

ethnicity

People and our heritage

We are learning to:

- explain the importance of a Caribbean identity.

Identity

We have seen what it means to have 'identity', but why is it important to have an identity? It is important that within our own country, and the wider Caribbean, we are able to be **patriotic** and respect the cultures of other people and their identities. How can we show this?

Unity among people

Most communities in the Caribbean are **diverse** because people from many different cultures and ancestries live and work there. This diversity is something that creates unity and is something that we celebrate. We can take part in festivals that celebrate other cultures, which brings us together. For example:

- Eid al-Fitr is a Muslim holiday, which celebrates the end of the fasting during the month of Ramadan.
- Diwali is a Hindu festival, which is celebrated in October/November.
- Christmas and Easter are Christian celebrations.
- Carnival – many Caribbean countries celebrate carnival, and people from many different cultural groups take part.

The common history of ancestry, languages, festivals and sporting events also helps people of each country to come together. People can also unite to help care for the environment, conservation of heritage sites and shared political concerns.

Dominica Carnival, Roseau.

Friendship

Friendship is a relationship of mutual affection between people and plays an important part in shaping Caribbean society. Friendship is a combination of loyalty, affection, love, respect, trust and **appreciation** and can often last many years.

Friendship can happen in many parts of life and for different reasons – in your neighbourhood, at work, at school, at the youth club, at the sports club, at the church group, among people of your own age or with people who have common interests.

Research

Research the Barbados Crop Over Festival and the Montserrat Calabash Festival. Find out when they take place, who takes part and what events they have. Explain how they bring people together.

Cultural diversity ▶▶

For many generations, the Caribbean has been a place of great **cultural diversity**. Our people come from Africa, Europe, China and India, with many different ethnicities, languages, religions and cultural traditions. These different influences have met and mixed in the region, where we now have many subcultures.

There are competitions, festivals and events all year round. Examples include:

- music – steel bands, calypso, soca, rapso, parang, reggae, chutney, dancehall
- religious festivals – Christmas, Easter, Diwali, Phagwah, Eid al-Fitr
- cultural festivals – Carnival, Barbados Crop Over Festival, Montserrat Calabash Festival.

Pooling human resources ▶▶▶

We define **human resources** as people and their knowledge, abilities, experience and talents.

In order for the country to prosper, its people need to develop their skills and knowledge so that they can carry out the work that best uses their talents. This allows people to perform jobs in different industries. As a result, the country needs to produce its goods and services, which help the population to maintain its standard of living.

CARICOM (Caribbean Community) is an organisation of Caribbean states that promotes **cooperation** and **integration** between its member states, especially in areas like trade and transportation. CARICOM encourages working together in a united way for the greater benefit of all.

Project

Research which countries are members of CARICOM. Then, write a letter to the CARICOM Heads of Government on the topic 'One People… One Region', asking what their plan and vision is to promote unity in the region.

Dancers at the Barbados Crop Over Festival.

Key vocabulary

patriotic

diverse

friendship

appreciation

cultural diversity

human resources

CARICOM

cooperation

integration

Exercise

1. Name three ways in which people can respect the cultures of other people and their identities.

2. Name some of the different ways we can celebrate cultural diversity.

3. Organise your own Cultural Day Programme at school. Role-play ideas as a class. Think about what you can do to promote unity in your community.

4. In your own words, explain what role CARICOM has in bringing the Caribbean islands together.

Appreciating our identity

We are learning to:

- identify ways Caribbean citizens can show more appreciation for their national and Caribbean identity.

Patriotism for country and region ▶▶

Patriotism means showing a deep love for, and devotion to, your country. It means taking **pride** in what your country has achieved and it also means looking after your country and being tolerant and caring of other people who live there.

Patriotism can be shown by respect for the environment and our national emblems, conservation and preservation of our resources and participation in Carifesta.

Respect for our environment ▶▶▶

The environment in the Caribbean is at risk from

- pollution of the land, sea and air
- **exploitation** of our natural resources
- destruction of habitats and
- damage to sustainable resources.

Frigate Bird Sanctuary, Barbuda.

It is the responsibility of all citizens in the world to make sure that steps are taken now, so that our natural environment is preserved for future generations. In the Caribbean, this means taking care to look after our tropical rainforests, beaches and coastline, hills, mangroves, fishing beds, coral reefs, caves and waterfalls.

We need natural resources such as water, wood and minerals in our everyday lives. In the Caribbean, thousands of people work in the **tourism** industry. Without our natural heritage, tourists would not visit the islands.

Discussion

In groups, brainstorm the parts of the natural environment that are at risk in your country. Make a list of all the different types.

Exercise

1. Write your own definition of patriotism.

2. Which parts of the environment in your country need close looking after by the citizens?

3. In your own words, write down the main risks to our environment in the Caribbean.

Respect for our national emblems ▶▶▶

Caribbean countries often have one or more national emblems:

- a coat of arms, which represents the country
- a national flag
- a national flower
- a national bird.

National emblems are a reminder of a country's goals, values and history, and are reminders to citizens to respect the heritage of their country and ongoing development.

Conservation and preservation of resources ▶

In Form 1, we found out about the cultural heritage of the Caribbean. We also discovered the importance of conserving our heritage and resources, so that future generations will understand what it means to be part of the Caribbean. We learned that to preserve (**preservation**) something means to keep it in its original state and to conserve (**conservation**) something means that we try to protect it from harm or from being damaged.

Our cultural heritage is formed from the cultural traditions that we have inherited from past generations. It can include artefacts, such as paintings, drawings or sculptures; or buildings, historical monuments or natural features, such as rainforests. It can also include things that we cannot touch, such as stories, the performing arts and customs.

Several sites of historical and natural importance have been identified as World Heritage Sites in the Caribbean. The aim is to ensure the preservation of these sites, as they are part of the heritage of the Caribbean. Examples include the Citadel in northern Haiti and the Belize Barrier Reef Reserve.

Research

Research the history of one of the national emblems of your country. Find out the history of the emblem and where you can find it today. Collect pictures using newspapers, magazines and the internet, and add this to your portfolio.

The Citadel, a UNESCO World Heritage Site in Haiti.

Exercise

4. Name the national emblems of your country.
5. Why should we respect our country's national emblems?
6. Think about the types of cultural heritage. Have you seen one today? Write a description of it in your notebook.

Key vocabulary

patriotism

pride

exploitation

tourism

preservation

conservation

Carifesta

We are learning to:

- identify ways Caribbean citizens can show more appreciation for their national and Caribbean identity.

Carifesta

Carifesta is an international and multicultural event that allows artists, musicians and authors to interact with each other and entertain each other. It promotes **cultural awareness** about nations in the Caribbean.

The first Carifesta festival took place in Guyana in 1972 and since then Jamaica, Trinidad and Tobago, Cuba, Barbados, St Kitts and Nevis and Suriname have been among the states to host the festival.

Since this first festival in 1972, Carifesta has been strengthening the **cultural bonds** between the people of the Caribbean.

The festival includes various events, such as:

- musical productions
- plays and concerts
- different types of dances
- exhibitions of visual art, such as paintings, sculpture and photographs
- writers' events – writers launch new books, engage in discussions and give readings of their work
- family and children's events – all are encouraged to visit and participate.

People wear colourful costumes at the Carifesta carnival parade.

> **Did you know...?**
>
> Each Carifesta event is organised around a theme and a symbol. The symbol varies but it often includes: the sun, which symbolises the Caribbean; a wheel, which symbolises positive movements; and a drum, which is a symbol of traditional communication in the Caribbean.

Exercise

1. Why can Carifesta be described as an artistic and cultural 'Olympics'?

2. Complete this definition in your own words: 'Carifesta is an international and multicultural event that…'

3. What would you expect to see and do at Carifesta? Make a list of 10 items or activities.

4. Name two countries that have hosted Carifesta.

5. Work in pairs and find newspaper articles about Carifesta. Find out how the celebrations help to bring people of the region together. Report back to the class with a summary of what you have discovered.

The opening ceremony for the 2015 Carifesta in Haiti.

Aims of Carifesta >>>

"Carifesta embodies Caribbean integration. It is here that the people of the Region come together; co-mingle, creating one community, one people. Further, this event strengthens the bonds between us, displays our creativity and ingenuity and demonstrates to the world the best that this region has to offer." Edwin Carrington, Secretary-General of the Caribbean Community.

The aims of Carifesta are:

- to depict the life of the people of the region – their heroes, morale, myth, traditions, beliefs, creativity, ways of expression
- to show the similarities and the differences between the people of the Caribbean and Latin America
- to create a climate in which art can flourish so that artists feel encouraged to return to their homeland
- to awaken a regional identity in literature
- to stimulate and unite the cultural movement throughout the region.

Benefits to the region >>>

Carifesta brings people from different countries together in an inspirational way, and this helps to promote unity and **tolerance** for others. It also promotes the arts and culture of the Caribbean. This not only helps artists to make a living but it also preserves traditional knowledge and exposes people to new art forms. It gives artists a **forum** where they can interact with other artists and with different audiences.

The festival attracts visitors and this also helps to boost tourism in the country that hosts the festival. Culture, social and economic development are therefore integrated.

Discussion

Work as a class and discuss the benefits of Carifesta. Think about this statement as you begin your discussion:

Culture is the root of development and is central to social and economic development.

These words may help you: tolerance, pride, integration, appreciation, awareness, fun, tourism, unity.

Research

Do your own research and find out more about the history of Carifesta. Then find out where and when the most recent Carifesta took place.

Exercise

6. What are the aims of Carifesta? Suggest an example for each one.

7. 'Carifesta' is an acronym. From which words is its name formed?

8. What do you think a 'regional identity' is, and how does Carifesta promote this?

9. Organise your own Caribbean Cultural Day Programme at school. Brainstorm ideas as a class. Think about what you can do to promote unity, pride, tolerance and appreciation of culture in your community.

Key vocabulary
....

Carifesta

cultural awareness

cultural bonds

tolerance

forum

Caribbean personalities

We are learning to:

- identify and categorise outstanding individuals in politics and economics from the Caribbean region
- explain how their contributions have built Caribbean identity.

There are many **outstanding** individuals who have contributed to the development of the Caribbean identity in the fields of politics, economics, sports, arts, entertainment and science.

Politics

Many leaders have made significant contributions to their country. Read this profile and the case study about other political leaders in the Caribbean.

Michael Manley, Prime Minister of Jamaica, 1959–62.

Profile

Michael Norman Manley (4 July 1893–2 September 1969, born Jamaica)

- National Hero of Jamaica, Jamaican statesman.
- Rhodes Scholar and leading lawyer in Jamaica in the 1920s.
- Advocate of **universal suffrage**, which was granted by the British government to Jamaica in 1944.
- He helped to found the People's National Party (PNP) in elections from 1944 to 1967.
- He served as the colony's Chief Minister from 1955 to 1959, and as Premier from 1959 to 1962.
- He helped to improve agricultural production and put more land to use in the 1950s.
- In 1958, he helped to introduce measures to give more children access to secondary school education.
- In 1960, he helped to introduce a pension scheme for sugar workers.

Research

Research a biography of one individual in the field of politics and economics who made a significant contribution to the Caribbean. You can research the people talked about on these pages or find someone of your own. Make a three-minute PowerPoint presentation of your research to the class.

Exercise

1. What contribution did Michael Manley make to Jamaica?
2. Why do you think Michael Manley was a National Hero of Jamaica?
3. Create a timeline of Mr Manley's achievements. Add it to your portfolio.

Profile

Dr Eric Williams (25 September 1911–29 March 1981, born Trinidad and Tobago)

Dr Eric Williams was educated at Queen's Royal College in Port of Spain. He won a scholarship and went to read History at Oxford University in the UK, where he graduated with a First in 1935. He completed his doctorate a few years later.

On his return to Trinidad, he began to give public lectures on world history. Later, in 1956, he formed the People's National Movement (the PNM). This party won the first elections after Trinidad and Tobago became independent in 1962. He was the first Prime Minster of Trinidad and Tobago and served from 1962 until his death in 1981.

Dr Williams is known as the 'Father of the Nation' in Trinidad and Tobago.

Economics ⟫

Profile

Sir Arthur Lewis (23 January 1915–15 June 1991, born St Lucia)

- Sir Arthur Lewis was well known for his theories on development economics.
- He helped Ghana draw up a Five-Year Development Plan following its independence in 1957.
- He was appointed Vice Chancellor of the University of the West Indies in 1959 and was knighted for his contributions to economics in 1963.
- He was the first president of the Caribbean Development Bank.
- In 1979, he won the Nobel Memorial Prize in Economics.
- Arthur Lewis Community College, St Lucia, was named in his honour.

Discussion

Have a classroom discussion about the contributions made by Michael Manley, Dr Eric Williams and Sir Arthur Lewis to Trinidad and Tobago, Jamaica and St Lucia. How do you think they contributed to Caribbean development and identity?

Sir Arthur Lewis, Nobel Prize winner, 1976.

Key vocabulary

outstanding

universal suffrage

Exercise

4. Why do you think Dr Eric Williams's achievements earned him the title 'Father of the Nation'?

5. Create a timeline of Sir Lewis's achievements. Add it to your portfolio.

6. Use information from the profiles and draw up a table to show the most important information at a glance. You could have headings like this in your table: name, country, role, period(s) of service, other achievements.

Caribbean personalities

We are learning to:

- identify and categorise outstanding individuals in sport and the arts from the Caribbean region
- explain how their contributions have built Caribbean identity.

Sports ▶▶

Cricketers and athletes head up the lists of famous men and women who have made significant contributions, not only to their sports, but also to the cultural, social and economic development of the Caribbean.

Profile

Shelly-Ann Fraser-Pryce (b. 1986, Jamaica, athlete)

- She was the first Caribbean woman to win 100 m gold at the 2008 Olympic Games.
- She was the first woman ever to hold the world titles at 60 m, 100 m, 200 m and 4 × 100 m relay simultaneously.
- She was IAAF World Athlete of the Year in 2013.
- She was named as UNICEF National Goodwill Ambassador for Jamaica in 2010.
- She created the Pocket Rocket Foundation in Jamaica to support high-school athletes from poorer backgrounds.

Shelly-Ann Fraser-Pryce competing in the 200m at the 2012 Olympic Games in London.

Profile

Sir Viv Richards (b. 1952, Antigua, cricketer)

- In 121 Test matches for the West Indies, he scored 8540 runs, including 24 centuries, at an average of 50.23 per innings.
- He only lost 8 test matches out of the 50 he captained.
- He scored over 36 000 runs in first-class cricket.
- He was made a Knight of the Order of the National Hero in his native Antigua and Barbuda in 1991.

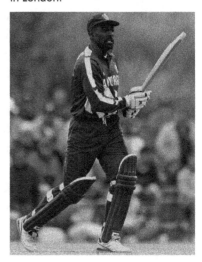

Sir Viv Richards played for the West Indies cricket team and was one of the greatest batsmen of all time.

Exercise

1. What contributions have Shelly-Ann Fraser-Pryce and Sir Viv Richards made to the cultural development of the Caribbean? Write 100 words to explain.
2. How do sportsmen and sportswomen contribute to the development of the Caribbean?
3. Research two other examples of sportsmen or sportswomen who have made a contribution to their countries, and explain how they have done this.

Profile

Sir Derek Walcott (1930–2017, St Lucia, poet and playwright)

- He held professorships at a number of prestigious Universities and Colleges around the world.
- He founded the Trinidad Theatre Workshop in 1959 (it still runs today), which puts on theatre shows, as well as offering educational programmes.
- In 1992, he won the highest honour in literature, the Nobel Prize.
- He wrote over 20 poetry collections, 25 plays and more than a dozen awards.
- He received the Order of Saint Lucia in February 2016.

Profile

Peter Minshall (b. 1941, Guyana, artist, designer and director)

- He grew up in Port of Spain, Trinidad, where he enjoyed the Carnival from an early age.
- After finishing school at the Queen's Royal College in Trinidad, he went to England to study theatre design.
- He designed costumes for the famous Notting Hill Carnival in London, then the 1974 and 1976 Trinidad mas.
- In 1991 and 1995, he collaborated with French musician Jean-Michel Jarre by creating large-scale concert spectacles.
- He designed the opening ceremonies of two Olympic Games – Barcelona in 1992 and Atlanta in 1996.
- In recognition of his career, in 1991 he was awarded an honorary degree by the University of the West Indies.

Discussion

Have a classroom discussion about the contributions made to Caribbean identity and development by sports heroes and people from the arts. How do you think they contributed to Caribbean development and identity?

Derek Walcott was one of the greatest poets and playwrights.

Peter Minshall at home in Trinidad.

Exercise

4. What contribution did Derek Walcott make to the cultural development of the Caribbean? Find a poem of his and read it to the class to support your answer.
5. How has Peter Minshall helped people in the Caribbean to appreciate and enjoy their own culture?
6. Discuss some of the people you have heard about. As a class, compile a list of people who have made outstanding contributions in sports and the arts.
7. Work in groups. Research one of the famous people from the list you have compiled. Find out about the life of the person and their outstanding contributions. Role-play the life of this person, outlining their work. Create a three-minute PowerPoint presentation on your research to the class.

Caribbean personalities

We are learning to:

- identify and categorise outstanding individuals in entertainment and science from the Caribbean region
- explain how their contributions have built Caribbean identity.

The Mighty Sparrow, aka Slinger Francisco.

Entertainment 》

Music is heard everywhere in the Caribbean and there is a wide variety ranging from **calypso** and soca to **reggae**, **merengue**, steel pan and **zouk**.

Singers and musicians have all contributed to cultural development in the Caribbean. They have made the rest of the world more aware of Caribbean life and culture. This in turn has encouraged other artists and musicians in the Caribbean.

Profile

Slinger Francisco (b. 1935, Grenada, a calypso singer and songwriter)

- Also known as the Mighty Sparrow.
- He is known as the 'King of the Calypso World', as he would regularly beat every other competitor in the local calypso singing contests.
- In 1958, he made his first album, *Calypso Carnival*, and has released over 70 albums since, as well as dozens of singles, and performed hundreds of shows all over the world.

Bob Marley (1945–81, Jamaica, singer, songwriter, musician and guitarist)

- With his group the Wailers, he became famous for reggae music in the 1960s, 1970s and 1980s.
- The music became popular internationally and Marley sold more than 75 million copies of his songs.
- In 2004, *Rolling Stone* magazine placed him at number 11 in their list of the 100 Greatest Artists of All Time.
- He is one of the bestselling artists of all time.

Bob Marley, one of the best-selling artists of all time.

Exercise

1. Write your own definitions of calypso and reggae.
2. Why do you think the Mighty Sparrow was known as the 'King of the Calypso World'?
3. True or false? Bob Marley and the Wailers made reggae music popular all over the world.

People who work in science and technology can make enormous changes to human lives. Scientists and researchers are always making new discoveries that can help to treat diseases and save lives.

Profile

Dr Norge Jerome (b. 1930, Grenada, health and nutrition specialist)

- She developed the discipline of nutritional anthropology.
- She studied eating habits of African-Americans and Grenadians.
- She worked for a charity providing solar cookers to refugee camps in Africa.
- The Dr Norge W. Jerome Grenada Teachers' Awards programme is named after her.

Profile

Dr Thomas Lecky (1904–94, Jamaica, pioneering cattle breeder)

- He noticed that the cattle in Jamaica were not suited to the environment, so he spent many years breeding cattle to make them more suitable for the local farmers.
- In 1951, he made his first breakthrough with the Jamaica Hope cattle – a specially bred milk-producing cow. The new breed revolutionised how dairy farming was done in Jamaica and scientists from all over the world went to Jamaica to see how this was done.
- He later developed the Jamaica Red for better beef, and the Jamaica Black, which was more suited for the cooler part of the island. His work inspired animal breeders to follow in his footsteps, but more importantly improved the lives of the cattle farmers in Jamaica.

Research

Research the life of someone from the field of science. Write a brief report, including some biographical detail and their main achievements. Create a three-minute PowerPoint presentation on your research to the class.

Discussion

Why do you think Bob Marley remains famous long after his lifetime? Discuss the difference between cultural heroes such as Marley, and performers who are popular only for a short time.

Key vocabulary

calypso

reggae

merengue

zouk

Exercise

4. Why are developments in medicine and science so important?
5. Why do you think it is important to share such expertise?
6. How did Dr Thomas Lecky improve the lives of farmers in Jamaica?
7. Write a letter to someone of your choice to thank them for their contribution to the development of the Caribbean. Outline in your letter how you feel about being part of the Caribbean and how you would like to contribute to its development.

Global recognition

We are learning to:

- justify how the contribution of these individuals helps to create links with the rest of the world
- value the contributions of outstanding individuals locally and in the Caribbean region.

How individuals have contributed »

We have seen which individuals have contributed to the development of the Caribbean region in the political, economic, sports, arts, entertainment and science fields, but how have they created links with the rest of the world?

The Mighty Sparrow performing in New York, 13 August 2006.

Project

On the internet, research **three** of the outstanding personalities listed and list three or four ways they have helped create links with the rest of the world, as well as in the Caribbean. You should write 100–150 words. For example:

The Mighty Sparrow

As the Mighty Sparrow, Slinger Francisco has entertained audiences across the world for over 40 years as the unrivalled 'King of Calypso'. He has performed in Europe, Asia, Africa, North and South America and across the Caribbean islands.

In 1977, he was awarded the honorary title Chief of the Yorubas in Nigeria. In 1986, New York Mayor Ed Koch declared 18 March as 'The Mighty Sparrow Day'. In 1987, he was awarded an honorary doctorate degree, Doctor of Letters, from the University of the West Indies.

His reputation as the 'King of Calypso' is worldwide. He was an 11-time winner of the Trinidad Calypso Monarch (the first one in 1956, the last in 1992) and he also won the 'King of Kings' competition, in which he defeated other calypso singers from across the world.

Choose from:

Politics: Michael Norman Manley, Dr Eric Williams

Economics: Sir Arthur Lewis

Sports: Shelly-Ann Fraser-Pryce, Sir Viv Richards

The arts: Sir Derek Walcott, Peter Minshall

Entertainment: Bob Marley

Science: Dr Norge Jerome, Dr Thomas Lecky

Activity

Use the internet to research the accomplishments of two outstanding Caribbean personalities and their achievements at international level.

How should we value the **contribution** made by those individuals that we have discussed to what they have done for the Caribbean and beyond?

Their contributions are different because of the different fields that they have been involved in. They have all helped to contribute to improving society, winning medals and trophies for their country, making artistic statements, helping ill people or making contributions to farming.

All of these personalities have also had a positive economic effect on the Caribbean, as well as helping to make people feel good about themselves and their country.

- Dr Eric Williams contributed much of his life to politics and dedicated his life to creating a better society for the people of Trinidad and Tobago.
- Sir Arthur Lewis dedicated his whole life to the study of economics and was able to help countries like Ghana.
- Sportspersons like Shelly-Ann Fraser-Pryce and Sir Viv Richards were dedicated to being the best in their sports and gained worldwide recognition for doing so.
- Peter Minshall knew from a very early age that he wanted to be an artist, which led eventually to his designing the opening ceremonies of the 1992 and 1996 Olympic Games.
- Bob Marley became internationally recognised for his music, and today his records are still influential to new generations of reggae fans.
- Dr Norge Jerome dedicated her career to research into nutrition, which has had a worldwide impact.

Discussion

Discuss as a class which of the personalities we have discussed has contributed the most to the region and why you think this is. Remember, each personality has excelled in different areas, so this might affect your discussion.

Activity

In pairs, create a roleplay where one of you is a TV reporter and the other a famous Caribbean personality. Write a list of questions you would ask them about what they have achieved, and then act it out in front of the class.

Exercise

1. Which personality has contributed globally to a) economics, b) sport, c) entertainment and d) medicine?

2. Choose one of these Caribbean personalities and write 100 words on how they have contributed both to the Caribbean and globally.

3. In groups, research text and photos, and any other relevant illustrations, about any two Caribbean personalities. Create a 'wall of fame' in your classroom.

Key vocabulary

contribution

Questions

See how well you have understood the topics in this unit.

1. Match the key vocabulary word (i–vi) with its definition (a–f).

    i) national identity
    ii) Caribbean identity
    iii) unity
    iv) friendship
    v) cultural diversity
    vi) cultural heritage

    a) a relationship between two or more friends
    b) being joined together or in agreement
    c) mix of cultural backgrounds
    d) a sense of who you are and that you are part of a country
    e) the cultural traditions that we have inherited from past generations
    f) the idea of what it means to belong to the Caribbean region

2. Name three festivals that take place in the Caribbean that celebrate the diverse cultures in the region.

3. Define the acronym CARICOM.

4. Explain how citizens in the Caribbean can help to preserve the natural environment for future generations.

5. Complete this sentence: "The national flower of Guyana is the _____."

6. In what year did the first Carifesta take place?

7. Which word best describes the aims of Carifesta?

    a) weaken
    b) integrate
    c) divide

8. Name one person who has made outstanding contributions to the Caribbean in the field of:

    a) politics
    b) economics
    c) sports
    d) arts
    e) entertainment
    f) science

9. Name the first Prime Minister of Trinidad and Tobago.

10. Name four ways that the environment in the Caribbean is at risk.

11. Name some of the events that take place at Carifesta.

12. What do the symbols of a wheel, the sun and a drum represent for Carifesta?

13. Who was Jamaica's Chief Minister from 1955 to 1959 and Premier from 1959 to 1962?

14. Who founded the Trinidad Theatre Workshop in 1959?

15. Who developed the discipline of nutritional anthropology?

16. Match these famous people to the fields in which they made significant contributions and to the countries they came from.

Column A	Column B	Column C
Michael Manley	entertainment	Antigua
Dr Eric Williams	sport	St Lucia
Sir Arthur Lewis	science	Grenada
Shelly-Ann Fraser-Pryce	science	Guyana
Sir Viv Richards	entertainment	Jamaica
Sir Derek Walcott	politics	Jamaica
Peter Minshall	economics	Trinidad and Tobago
The Mighty Sparrow	politics	Jamaica
Bob Marley	sport	Grenada
Dr Norge Jerome	the arts	Jamaica
Dr Thomas Lecky	the arts	St Lucia

17. Match these famous people (i–v) to their profile (a–e).

   i) Dr Eric Williams
   ii) Sir Arthur Lewis
   iii) Sir Viv Richards
   iv) Bob Marley
   v) Dr Norge Jerome

   a) dedicated her career to research into nutrition
   b) dedicated to being the best in their sports
   c) dedicated his whole life to the study of economics
   d) became internationally recognised for his reggae music
   e) contributed much of his life to creating a better society for the people of Trinidad and Tobago

18. What do you know about reggae music? Write two or three sentences in which you describe the music.

Checking your progress

To make good progress in understanding different aspects of your personal development, check to make sure you understand these ideas.

Identify the characteristics of national identity.

Identify the characteristics of Caribbean identity.

Explain the importance of national and Caribbean identity.

Identify the ways citizens can show appreciation for their national and Caribbean identity.

Explain how patriotism for your country and region can be shown.

Identify the main risks to our environment in the Caribbean.

Name the national emblems of your country.

Research the history of one of the national emblems of your country.

Research the history of Carifesta.

Name people who have made significant contributions to the Caribbean.

Describe how these individuals have contributed to Caribbean identity.

Research the life of someone who has contributed to Caribbean identity.

Unit 3: The physical environment

In this unit you will find out ▶▶▶

Features and landforms
- Major physical landforms: hills, mountains, plains, rivers, coastline, beaches
- Field observation and field sketches

Types of vegetation
- The natural vegetation of the Eastern Caribbean
  - ○ tropical forests, savannah, coastal vegetation
- The economic value of natural vegetation
  - ○ lumber, tourism, arable farming, pastoral farming, fishing, medicinal properties
- Natural vegetation as a habitat for wildlife

The human environment
- Features of the human environment
  - ○ settlements, agriculture and industry, services, recreation, communications, settlement patterns

Population distribution and density
- Distinguish between population distribution and population density
- Choropleth and dot maps
- Population distribution and density in the Eastern Caribbean

The interrelationship between physical landforms or features and human land use
- Differences between physical and man-made features
- Factors influencing land use (relief, drainage, coast, vegetation)
- The development of Bridgetown, Barbados
- Preservation and conservation of the environment

Physical landforms in the Eastern Caribbean

We are learning to:

- describe major physical landforms: mountains, hills and plains
- name and locate major landforms in the Eastern Caribbean.

Mountains 》

Mountains are large features that are usually very steep, over 600 m in height and form a peak at the top. Mountains can be isolated or they may be part of a group called a mountain range.

Isolated mountain peaks such as Mount St Catherine (840 m) in Grenada and Mount Gimie (950 m) in St Lucia are important for the Eastern Caribbean. This is because their height creates a special rainforest-type environment which provides a home to unique plant and animal life.

Guyana is well known for its mountain ranges. The highest peak in Guyana, Mount Roraima (2810 m), is found in the Pacaraima mountain range.

Mount Roraima, Guyana.

Hills 》》

Hills are smaller than mountains and are generally under 600 m in height. They can come in many different shapes but are generally quite rolling.

Barbados and Antigua are considered quite flat but do have hilly sections. In Barbados, the hilly Scotland District in the east rises to the tallest peak, Mount Hillaby (340 m). In Antigua, Mount Obama (402 m) is the tallest peak in the hilly south-western region.

Hills of the Scotland District, Barbados.

Plains 》》》

A **plain** is a large area of flat land.

There are different types of plain depending on where they are found. Some plains are found between mountain ranges or hills. For example, the central plain of Antigua divides the island in two. It separates the south-western volcanic uplands from the north-eastern limestone hills. Other plains are found beside rivers and the coast. When plains are found by the coast, they are called coastal plains. The low coastal plain of Guyana is over 70 km wide in some places. Plains are important because the flat relief makes settlement easy.

> **Did you know...?**
>
> Some islands of the Eastern Caribbean, such as St Kitts and Nevis, are the peaks of large underwater mountain ranges that break the sea's surface.

Physical map of Guyana.

Research the closest hill or mountain to your home.

a) What is its name?

b) How big is it?

c) How was it formed?

d) Which birds and animals live there?

e) What activities do people do there?

Exercise

1. What are the differences between a mountain and a hill?

2. Use the map to answer the following questions.

   a) What is the height of Mount Ayanganna and in which mountain range can it be found?

   b) Which mountain range has the lowest peak?

   c) In which mountain range can a peak of 1128 m be found?

   d) Which mountain range is the largest?

   e) What physical landform divides the Kanuku mountain range in two?

3. Draw an outline map of the country where you live.

   a) Put in a north arrow; label the sea, the capital and the three main towns.

   b) Outline and shade any highlands and plains.

   c) Are the capital and main towns on a highland or plain?

   d) Give one possible reason for your observation in (c) above.

Key vocabulary

mountains

hills

plains

Physical landforms in the Eastern Caribbean

We are learning to:

* describe major physical landforms: rivers, coastlines and beaches
* name and locate major landforms in the Eastern Caribbean.

Rivers

Rivers are major features in some Eastern Caribbean islands. In Dominica, St Lucia and Grenada, high rainfall and volcanic rock have resulted in many rivers. The longest are the Layou River (23.5 km) in Dominica, the Great River (30.6 km) in Grenada and the Roseau River (20.9 km) in St Lucia.

Whatever the length, the characteristics are the same. All rivers start in the hills and mountains. The start of a river is known as the **source**. Rivers flow down hills and mountains and over the flat plains towards the sea, where they end. This is known as the **mouth** of the river.

Layou River, Dominica.

Coastline

A **coast** or **coastline** is an area of land beside the sea. Island nations of the Eastern Caribbean typically have short coastline lengths, for example, Anguilla (61 km), St Vincent (84 km) and Barbados (97 km). These countries often depend on the coast for tourism and coastal management is therefore very important. Coastlines have various features.

Seven Mile Beach, Grand Cayman.

* A **cape (headland)** is a narrow piece of land that extends into the sea. Capes are formed by glaciation or by volcanoes.

* A **bay** is an area where the coastline curves inland. Some of a coastline's best beaches are found in bays. The land beside the coast is not always flat; in fact, a lot of coastlines have tall cliffs beside the sea.

Beach

A **beach** is a part of the coastline where sand or stones build up. Beaches are popular holiday destinations. There are often hotels, guest houses, campsites and parks near sandy beaches, as they attract many tourists.

Sheltered beaches are the most visited due to the calm waters. Beaches on the west and south coasts of Barbados such as Mullins, Dover, Pebbles and Accra are among the island's most famous. Grand Cayman's Seven Mile Beach is located along the western edge of the island's iconic lagoon.

Due to Antigua's winding coastline, there are many bays where up to 365 beaches can be found. Surfing, kayaking, sailing and jet-ski rides are popular at these beaches along with diving, snorkelling, swimming and turtle-watching.

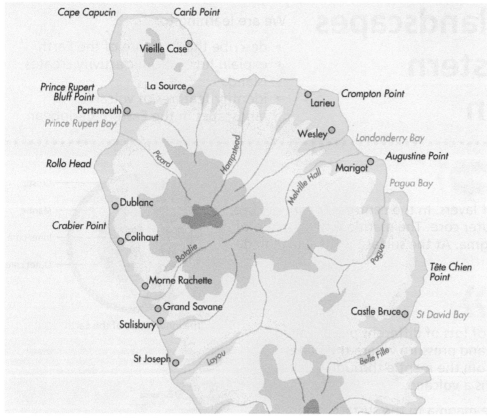

Northern rivers, bays and headlands of Dominica.

Exercise

1. Which is the longest river in Dominica?

2. What is the term used for where a river starts?

3. Explain the difference between a cape and a bay.

4. What economic activity do the beaches in the Eastern Caribbean attract?

5. Use the map to answer the following questions.

   a) List four rivers located on the map.
   b) List two bays where a river mouth is located.
   c) Name the peak of the highland where the most river sources are found.
   d) List three capes on the eastern side of the map.

6. Choose a beach that you have visited. Make a poster inviting tourists to this beach. On your poster describe the natural features (sand, bay) and list some activities that people can do there.

Did you know...?

The island of Dominica gets so much rain that it has a river or stream for every day of the year.

Key vocabulary

river

source

mouth

coast/coastline

cape (headland)

bay

beach

Volcanic landscapes in the Eastern Caribbean

We are learning to:

- describe the structure of the Earth
- explain how volcanic activity creates islands
- identify features of volcanic landscapes in the Eastern Caribbean.

The Earth's structure

Our planet is made of layers. In the centre is the inner core, surrounded by the outer core. The mantle is next, made of liquid rock called magma. At the surface is the crust, made of solid rock.

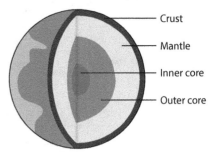

The inner layers of the Earth.

Volcanic islands

The crust is made up of lots of different pieces called **tectonic plates**. Heat and pressure where the plates meet force magma from the mantle through cracks in the crust. This forms a **volcano**.

Volcanoes bring more magma to the surface when they erupt. This magma cools and hardens to form volcanic islands.

Most of the islands of the Eastern Caribbean were formed in this way. In fact, Dominica has nine active volcanoes, St Kitts and Nevis has two, and St Vincent, St Lucia, Grenada, Montserrat, Guadeloupe and Martinique each have one. Antigua's southern portion is volcanic but no active volcanoes remain.

Volcanic landforms

Other volcanic landforms can be found on these islands along with **volcanic cones**. Boiling Lake, Dominica and Grand Etang Lake, Grenada are **crater lakes**, where rainwater has filled volcanic craters. **Hot springs** can be found at Soufrière, St Lucia, where volcanic heat warms underground water. Plymouth, south-western Montserrat, is a **lava field**, formed when lava flows cooled and hardened, leaving a vast plain stretching from inland to the coast.

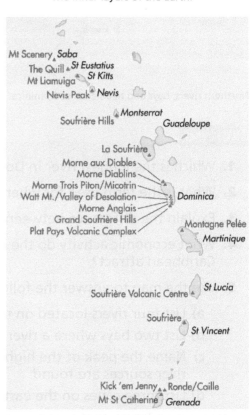

Map of the Leeward Islands' volcanic arc, with active volcanoes shown on each island.

> **Did you know...?**
>
> Grenada's active volcano Kick 'em Jenny is an underwater volcano.

Volcanic landscapes

Volcanic landscapes can be identified based on a few characteristics:

- Caribbean volcanic landscapes usually have high-altitude mountain peaks and ranges. This occurs because the pressure from the Earth that creates the volcanoes also pushes them very high up into the air. The tallest peaks in the Eastern Caribbean are volcanic cones.

- Lush vegetation is also a feature of Caribbean volcanic landscapes. Volcanic ash is full of nutrients, which, when combined with the heavy rainfall that the Caribbean receives, creates excellent soil for plants. Forests, therefore, cover volcanic slopes and locals use them to grow crops.

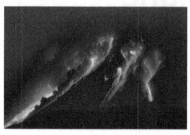

Glowing slopes of Soufrière Hills volcano, Montserrat.

- Rivers are numerous because volcanic rock does not allow water to flow through it. Water must flow across the surface. This creates many river valleys that begin at volcanic peaks and travel to the coast.

- Volcanic rock does not break down easily. When weaker rock breaks down, volcanic rocks are left behind. This creates very uneven, steeply sloping land with many peaks and valleys. This rugged terrain can be found on all volcanic Caribbean islands.

Physical map of St Vincent.

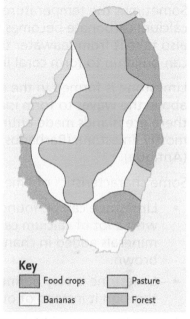

Key

- Food crops
- Bananas
- Pasture
- Forest

Map of land use and agriculture in St Vincent.

Exercise

1. Explain how volcanic islands are formed.
2. Look at the maps of St Vincent.

   a) Name two volcanic peaks.
   b) Name one river. State on which peak its source is located and the direction it is flowing.
   c) Describe the location of another volcanic feature shown.
   d) Explain the distribution of forests on the vegetation map.

Key vocabulary

tectonic plate

volcano

volcanic cone

crater lake

hot spring

lava field

Limestone landscapes in the Caribbean

We are learning to:

- describe the structure and characteristics of limestone
- explain how limestone landscapes are formed
- identify features of limestone landscapes in the Eastern Caribbean.

Limestone 》

Limestone is a type of rock made of many layers of a mineral called calcium carbonate.

Calcium carbonate is usually dissolved in seawater. Sometimes the temperature of the sea changes, and the calcium carbonate becomes solid and builds up. Sea animals also take it from seawater to make their shells. These shells can build up to form coral limestone.

Limestone is formed in the sea and then is slowly pushed up above the waves to form islands. In the Eastern Caribbean there are islands made entirely of limestone (Anguilla), mostly limestone (Barbados), or only half limestone (Antigua).

Some characteristics of limestone are:

- Limestone can be found in many colours. Limestone with a lot of calcium carbonate is whiter, while other minerals added in change the colour to yellow, grey or brown.
- Limestone is very **permeable**. This means water flows through it instead of over it.
- Limestone is very **jointed.** This means many cracks are found within limestone rock.
- Limestone is sturdy. This means it keeps its structure well. This is why limestone cliffs usually have vertical faces and limestone can be used as building blocks.

Limestone can be many colours as seen in this limestone quarry.

Devil's Bridge, Antigua, is a natural limestone landform.

Exercise

1. Name two islands in the Eastern Caribbean that are made of limestone.
2. What mineral is limestone made of?
3. What are two characteristics of limestone?

> **Did you know...?**
>
> Limestone is called sedimentary rock but extreme heat and pressure can change limestone to marble, a metamorphic rock.

Karst is a special name for a landscape created from limestone. Karst is formed when rainwater enters cracks in limestone rock and washes bits of it away. Sometimes the rainwater leaves the limestone underground, creating more karst features. Karst does not have many rivers.

Doline karst has shallow, bowl-shaped holes called dolines, rolling hills, gentle valleys, gullies and many underground features. This is the type of karst found in the Eastern Caribbean.

Cockpit karst has cone-shaped hills with steep sides and deep holes between them called cockpits. This type of karst is found in cockpit country, Jamaica.

Tower/cone karst has more isolated hills with vertical sides and very wide, flat valleys. This type of karst can be found in the Vinales region of Cuba.

Underground karst features at Harrison's Cave, Barbados.

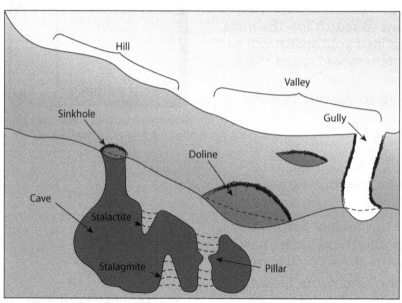
Diagram of surface and underground features of doline karst.

Exercise

4. What are the two ways in which rainwater can create karst features?

5. What is one difference between doline karst hills and cockpit karst hills?

6. What is one difference between doline karst valleys and tower karst valleys?

7. Can you think of a marine environment that is made of limestone?

8. Why do you think karst does not have many rivers?

Key vocabulary

limestone

permeable

jointed

karst

doline

ICT skills

We are learning to:

- use internet resources to find examples of natural landforms in other countries
- cite sources of information using rules that apply
- present using ICT skills.

Internet research 》

You are going to do a research project looking at landforms in the Caribbean. To complete this, you will need to carry out research online. The internet is a great source of information. Whenever you use the internet for research purposes, there are several things to bear in mind.

- Use reliable **search engines**, such as Google, Yahoo and Ask.
- Use exact phrases that you want to search for. The more keywords you use, the more refined your search will be. For example, search for 'mountain range' rather than 'high place'.
- You could use the 'advanced search' feature to make your results even more refined.

Searching for things online has become a part of everyday life.

Citing sources of information 》》

When you **cite** sources (that is, where you found them), the following information should be given:

- The **website address** (or **URL**). This usually starts with http:// You must write it out in full. These can be very long, but it is important you write them down correctly.
- Name of the author – the person who wrote the article or information you are referencing (sometimes their name is 'unknown').
- Title of the article in quotation marks.
- Date of publication online.
- Date when you **retrieved** the information.

> **Did you know...?**
>
> You should cite sources for any research you do, as it shows honesty and integrity for your work.

website address	date information retrieved

https://www.destinationtnt.com/salybia-bay/;
unknown; 'Salybia Bay'; 2017; 14 July 2017

author's name	title	date of publication

Activity

Present using ICT skills

Presentations are usually given using a presentation program; the most commonly used one is Microsoft PowerPoint. Other programs include Prezi and Keynote. These programs are excellent ways of presenting the information that you have found. You are able to customise your presentation to suit your needs.

Follow these steps:

1. Make a list of all the landforms you have studied so far in this unit.

2. Using the internet, find a picture of each landform and some information about them.

3. Create a presentation about these landforms.

Tips to help you »»

Here are some tips for creating a presentation.

- Each slide should have one point or idea. Don't include more than one main idea on each slide.

- Don't give too much written information or use long sentences. Often, a few keywords will be enough.

- Use pictures and diagrams where possible. A slide with a photograph or chart is easier to follow than one with lots of text.

- When you use words, make sure your letters are big enough that people at the back of the room can read them. A good rule is to have no more than five or six words on a line.

- When you do use diagrams and pictures that are not yours, make sure you credit the producer.

Here is an example of a slide with a labelled picture showing two landform features along the coast.

Headland   Stack

Key vocabulary

search engine

cite

universal resource locator (URL)

retrieve

ICT skills

Field observations

We are learning to:

- through field observation, make a well-labelled sketch of a landform in the local area.

Field observation and field sketches >>

Field observation (or **fieldwork**) is the process where you observe people or places (or landform features) in real locations and situations, then collect data about them.

When field observation work is carried out, there are many ways of recording information that you find. One of the most common ways of recording information is by using a **field sketch**.

A field sketch is a simple drawing that is used to highlight specific features or landforms or to show the general landscape. They are very useful techniques and can be used on their own or alongside other field techniques such as photography.

When drawing a field sketch, it is not necessary to show every detail of the landscape or landform, just the key geographical features that are important to your field work.

The photograph below is an example of what you may see if you visit the town of Soufrière, St Lucia, and next to it is a sketch map of what the picture of Petit Piton might look like.

What do you need?

✓ clipboard

✓ pencil

✓ rubber

✓ paper

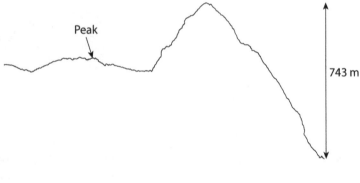

Follow these steps to make a field sketch of a landform in your local area.

- Observe the area around you. Choose a section that you would like to sketch. Your chosen section should have interesting landforms.

- Depending on what you are using your field sketch for, you might need to consider the framing. For example, if you are going to compare your field sketch with a photograph you must make sure that you are using an identical view and that your sketch includes exactly the same landscape/features as the photograph.

- Sketch the outline of the area. Some tips to follow:
  - Identify the major features you would like to sketch.
  - It is helpful to divide the photograph into thirds, showing the foreground, middle ground and background.
  - Start by sketching the things furthest away and work your way forward.

- Label your sketch with a heading, direction and bearing. Label the features on the sketch. It is useful to **annotate** specific features at this point as well.

Doing a field sketch can make you notice things that you would normally miss.

Exercise

For this exercise, you will need a clipboard, a pencil, a rubber and plenty of paper.

- Visit an area of interest near your home. Use your skills in field observation to select a place which has an interesting landform.
- Make a field sketch of the place you have chosen. Refer to the tips above.
- Label the key features of the landscape and annotate any points of interest.

Things to consider

If the weather conditions on the day of your field study are not favourable – for example, if it is very wet – you can take a photo of the scene that you want to sketch and draw the field sketch back home or at school.

Key vocabulary

field observation, or **fieldwork**

field sketch

annotate

The natural vegetation of the Eastern Caribbean

We are learning to:

- describe the natural vegetation of the Eastern Caribbean
- locate areas where these vegetation types are found.

The Eastern Caribbean has diverse natural vegetation including **tropical forests**, **savannah** regions and coastal vegetation. The vegetation on specific islands depends on the local relief, climate and geology, which means that the amount of each type of vegetation and its characteristics also varies on each island.

Tropical forests

Tropical forests occur where there is a warm, wet climate all year. Guyana's forests are true rainforests, where trees and plants grow in layers.

Islands such as St Lucia (77 per cent forested) and Dominica (60 per cent forested) also have rainforests in lowland areas. These islands receive less rainfall but rich volcanic soil allows forests to grow. On these forested islands, highland forest is called montane forest. Montane forests have fewer and shorter trees but a wide variety of other types of plants such as ferns, mosses and lichens.

Plant biodiversity is highest in Dominica, which is home to 1228 **species** of plants and 202 species of land animals, not including insects. About 3.5 per cent of these species are unique to Dominica.

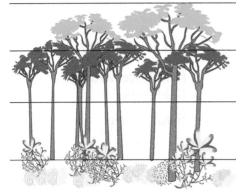

Rainforest structure

Emergent layer is the top layer of the forest, where the tallest trees are found.

Canopy layer is the main layer, with thick dense forest cover.

The understorey is found underneath the canopy and is made up of young trees and shrubs.

Forest floor is mainly covered with fallen leaves.

Activity

Your teacher will show you the video 'Natural Wonders of the Caribbean', which shows the forests of the Caribbean. Watch the video and discuss it in class.

Exercise

1. Using your atlas, study the vegetation map of Dominica and identify at least four areas that have tropical rainforest vegetation.

2. Identify at least three characteristics/ features of the tropical rainforest in Dominica. Using your atlas, study the vegetation map of St Lucia and Grenada.

Savannah >>>

A savannah is an area of grassland. The trees on a savannah are widely spaced out, so they do not form a thick cover, as in forests. There is open space. Because of this open space, the sunlight is able to break through, allowing grasses to grow.

The plants found in savannah regions have to be able to survive in hot climates with little rainfall. Many of the plants and grasses that grow in the savannah have long roots that can reach down to the water table below the surface. This allows them to get water all year round.

The Rupununi Savannah lies in the south-western interior of Guyana. It is 13 000 km², and is divided into northern and southern areas by the Kunuku Mountains.

The Rupununi Savannah has very high biodiversity. It is surrounded by mountains, wetlands and forests. These ecosystems are connected via the Rupununi and this allows special habitats to develop. This means that a wide variety of plants and animals, many of which are unique, are found here.

Coastal vegetation >>>>

Coastal vegetation also needs to be able to survive specific conditions. Plants found in coastal regions have to be able to withstand salty conditions as well as strong winds.

Mangroves are the most common coastal vegetation found in the Eastern Caribbean. Mangroves are trees and shrubs that grow along coastal regions in tropical areas. They can survive in the harshest of environments.

Mangroves generally have to survive in muddy soils, and also in very salty conditions, as they are flooded twice a day. In fact, mangroves survive in water that is 100 times saltier than the water most plants grow in.

Grand Cayman is covered by over 50 per cent mangrove swamp. Most of the mangroves are located in the Central Mangrove Wetland which covers 8500 acres. This area controls water flow, stores nutrients and is a home for young fish. It is important to the entire island's ecosystem.

Activity

Your teacher will organise a field trip to view and classify vegetation types in your local community and environment. Write up to 150 words on what you have observed. Include some sketches.

Activity

Create a photo montage that accurately represents the three vegetation types of the Eastern Caribbean.

Key vocabulary

tropical forest

savannah

species

mangroves

Exercise

3. Identify at least three features of the savannah in Guyana.

4. Explain how plants in the savannah and on the coast are able to survive each climate.

Natural vegetation as a resource

We are learning to:

- appreciate the value of the natural vegetation of the Eastern Caribbean as a resource.

What is a resource? ⟩⟩

A natural resource is something that forms naturally and that we use for other purposes. For example, wood is a natural resource. It grows naturally and we use it to build houses and for fuel. Other resources, such as coal, oil and gas, can be sold to make money for a country.

Economic value of natural vegetation ⟩⟩

Natural vegetation has always been a very useful resource and continues to be today. Thousands of years ago it provided a way of life for humans and today it is still very important, helping the Eastern Caribbean economy.

- **Lumber** (trees) is a big business across the world. In Guyana, forest resources are distributed to international logging companies by the Guyana Forestry Commission. Logs are transported by floating them down-river. There are no roads in the interior forests for vehicles to move logs. Forests on Eastern Caribbean islands are too difficult to access for wide-scale forestry. Forests provide jobs, such as sawmill worker, construction worker and furniture maker.

- Tourism is a great source of income for the Eastern Caribbean. St Kitts and Nevis specialise in 'green tourism'. This includes nature, community and conservation in tourism activity. Popular green tourism sites include Forest Reserve, Atlantic Coast rainforest and Valley of Giants rainforest. There are many jobs in the tourist industry. These include tour guide, hotel or restaurant worker and activity leader.

- **Arable farming** involves growing crops for money. Grenada's tropical fruit exports, such as banana and mango along with spice exports – particularly cocoa and nutmeg – are known worldwide, earning it the name 'The Spice Isle'.

- **Pastoral farming** involves raising grazing livestock for money. The vast Rupununi Savannah grasslands support beef cattle ranching in Guyana.

- Fishing stocks are sustained by mangroves. Mangroves protect young fish from predators and act as nurseries. When large enough, the fish leave for the open sea and coral reefs. This helps maintain offshore fish populations.

Grenadian cocoa and nutmeg.

Eco-tourism in St Kitts and Nevis includes hiking mountain trails.

Research

There are many jobs in the Eastern Caribbean which depend on natural vegetation. Some examples have been given here. Make a list of these and research others. Then produce a graphic organiser showing the industries, job types and where in your country those industries and jobs are.

The table below summarises some of the industries and jobs that natural resources provide in Trinidad and Tobago. Construct a similar table for your country.

Industries/jobs	Resources	Areas
Lumber (sawmill, construction, furniture)	Teak, pine, cedar, mora, crappo, bamboo	Mamoral, Brickfield, Morne Diablo, Cap-De-Ville
Tourism (tour guides, environmentalists, conservationists, rangers, photographers)	Nature parks and reserves, wetlands	Asa Wright Nature Centre, Arena Forest Reserve, Main Ridge Forest Reserve (Tobago), Nariva Swamp, Caroni Swamp
Farming (fishing, agriculturalists, restaurants, caterers and food proprietors)	African perch (tilapia)	Bamboo Grove, Orange Grove

Medicinal properties ⟩⟩⟩

Tropical forests are also home to thousands of species of plants that are used for their **medicinal properties**. Most of the vaccines, drugs and treatments that are used across the world have come from plants found in tropical forests. Quinine (traditionally used to treat malaria) and turbocuarine chlorine (used to treat multiple sclerosis and Parkinson's disease) come from rainforest plants.

Recreation – hiking and bird-watching ⟩⟩

The Eastern Caribbean is home to a wide variety of natural landscapes. Locals and tourists alike enjoy relaxing trips and hikes to these places to observe the beauty of nature.

Graeme Hall mangrove swamp, Barbados, Grand Etang forest, Grenada, Caroni Bird Sanctuary, Trinidad and the Vermont Nature Trail, St Vincent, are beautiful sites to appreciate nature. Can you name any recreational forest, grassland or mangrove sites in your country?

Exercise

1. In your own words, write a report of about 250 words explaining how natural resources can have an economic value. Give examples.

2. Describe how the medicinal qualities of some plants can help us.

Key vocabulary

lumber

arable farming

pastoral farming

medicinal properties

Habitats for wildlife

We are learning to:

- appreciate the value of the natural vegetation of the Eastern Caribbean as a habitat for wildlife and a way of maintaining balance on the Earth.

Natural vegetation as a habitat for wildlife

The tropical forests, savannahs and mangrove regions in the Eastern Caribbean are home to thousands of different species of animals and insects.

Tropical forests

- The warm, wet climate that exists in these forests, as well as the huge variety of plants, make these areas very popular with butterflies.

- Native butterfly species include the Dominican snout butterfly and the St Lucia mestra butterfly.

- Imperial and red-necked parrots are native to Dominican forests, while St Vincent and St Lucia both have one native forest parrot named after the island.

- The mongoose, agouti, opossum, mona monkey and green monkey are some of the animals that can be found in Eastern Caribbean forests.

- Grenada and St Vincent have the highest number of bat species, 15 and 14 respectively.

Savannahs

- The Rupununi Savannah in Guyana is home to over 9000 species, including highly endangered animals and endemic wildlife. 2000 of the these are vertebrates (birds, mammals, fish, reptiles and amphibians).

- The southern Rupununi is home to 457 bird species. These include water fowl like whistling ducks, South America's largest stork species, the jibaru and the harpy eagle, an endangered bird of prey.

- Mammals found in the Rupununi include the giant anteater, giant armadillo and Brazilian tapir. Wild cat species such as the ocelot, jaguar and puma are also found here.

Coasts and mangroves

- Hawksbill and leatherback turtles nest on the islands of the Eastern Caribbean. This is important since these species are endangered.

- Mangroves are often home to many different fish species.

- Snappers, barracuda, grunt and parrotfish are some reef fish species whose young seek shelter in mangroves.

- Migratory bird species use mangroves in the Eastern Caribbean as a stop on their long travels. These include black-bellied plover, upland and solitary sandpipers, greater and lesser yellowlegs and killdeer.

Maintaining a balance >>>

Natural vegetation plays an important role in the world. Tropical rainforests cover 7 per cent of the Earth's land surface and, as we've learned, they provide **habitats** for hundreds of different species of wildlife. However, they also have other very important jobs to do.

Water >>>>

Rainforests play a role in providing water for the Earth. In order to be considered a rainforest, an area must have over 1500 mm of rainfall every year, as well as consistently high temperatures.

The huge amount of rainfall that the rainforests produce each year helps sustain the **hydrological cycle**, otherwise known as the **water cycle.** The water cycle is a continuous process that moves water between the atmosphere, the surface of the Earth and the spaces under the Earth's surface.

The rainfall that is produced within the rainforests provides water to countries all over the world.

Rainforests play an important role in providing water for the Earth.

Atmospheric gases >>

Rainforests are known as 'the lungs of our planet'. This is because the millions of trees in these rainforests absorb carbon dioxide and breathe out oxygen that humans and animals need to survive. By doing this they also help to stabilise the Earth's climate, helping to reduce the effects of climate change.

It is very worrying to learn that many tropical rainforests around the world are being cut down. It is important to protect these valuable resources.

Did you know...?

The Caribbean is considered a biodiversity hotspot. It is believed that 46 per cent of the mammals, 27 per cent of the birds, 93 per cent of the reptiles and 40 per cent of the freshwater fish in the islands are found nowhere else in the world.

Exercise

1. In your own words, explain how our natural habitat maintains the balance of life on Earth. Give examples.

2. Explain why it is important that the rainforests are preserved. Outline the consequences if they are not cared for.

3. Write a poem (two stanzas) explaining the need to save our vegetation. Use the information you have learned in this lesson. Share your poem with your class.

4. Why are rainforests known as 'the lungs of our planet'?

Key vocabulary

habitat

water cycle

hydrological cycle

Natural disasters and the landscape

We are learning to:

- describe natural disasters that affect the Eastern Caribbean
- explain how natural disasters change the landscape
- identify Eastern Caribbean examples of landscapes changed by natural disasters.

Natural disasters

A **natural hazard** is a natural process that can possibly have negative effects. Some of these can be predicted and can be **mitigated**. This means taking steps to reduce negative effects. A **natural disaster** occurs when a natural hazard causes large-scale damage.

A **hurricane** is an intense storm with powerful winds and high rainfall. Hurricanes are placed in categories based on their wind speed, from 1 (slow) to 5 (very fast). Volcanoes shoot gas and ash into the air and pour lava onto the land. Earthquakes shake the land and can be mild or violent; on steep slopes, landslides occur and in river valleys flooding happens.

Usually, the focus is on damage to human life or property, but the natural environment can be affected as well. This means landscape characteristics may change.

A landslide removes hillside forest.

Changes to landmasses

The height and shape of the land may change when earthquakes shift large portions of rock up or down. Long, deep cracks called **faults** may also appear. Lava flows harden to create completely new areas of land, while landslides move rocks from the top to the bottom of slopes. Violent eruptions can even blow the top off a volcanic mountain.

Montserrat's highest peak was Chances Peak (914 m), but since the Soufrière Hills began erupting in 1995, a new volcanic lava peak (1084 m) is now the highest point.

Exercise

1. What is the difference between a natural hazard and a natural disaster?
2. List three types of natural disasters that affect the Eastern Caribbean.

Changes to vegetation ▶▶▶

Category 1 hurricane winds can strip leaves and fruit from trees and twist trunks, while Category 5 hurricanes can uproot trees, flattening lush forests. Landslides remove trees from slopes, and vegetation at the bottom of the slope is buried.

Hurricane Ivan in 2004 caused extreme, irreversible damage to all of Grenada's natural forests. Long-term, specialised environmental protection plans had to be used to help them recover.

Changes to rivers ▶▶

Hurricane rains make rivers wider and deeper, and make them flow faster. This means river water can wash away large amounts of soil, leaving rocky terrain behind and lowering the land's overall height. Lava flows and landslides can block a river's path and change its course.

The Sandy River was temporarily blocked by the 1998 Portland landslide in north-eastern Jamaica, causing flooding.

A lava flow from Soufrière Hills, Montserrat, has changed the shape of the coast

Changes to coasts ▶▶▶

Hurricane winds cause strong waves which beat the coast for many hours. This washes sand away, pushing the shoreline back, creating rocky beaches and changing the shape of the coastline. Debris swept downstream by a flooded river is washed into the sea, muddying the shore and coastal waters.

Where lava flows reach coasts, they harden to form a new, rock coastline with a different shape. Moule à Chique in southern St Lucia is a cape that was formed by hardened lava flows and ash.

Research

1. Choose two different types of natural disaster that have affected your country (one historic and one recent) and prepare a PowerPoint presentation showing:

   a) the basic details of the disasters (when, where)
   b) how they affected human property and life
   c) how they affected the natural environment
   d) how your country recovered from the disasters
   e) how these types of disasters can be mitigated

2. For each of the following areas, describe how one named disaster can change its characteristics:

   a) land   b) forest   c) river   d) coast

Key vocabulary

natural hazard

mitigate

natural disaster

hurricane

fault

The human environment

We are learning to:

- identify and locate examples of human land uses on a map of the Caribbean.

Features of the human environment

The **human environment** refers to an area where humans live and work. The human environment contains the following:

- **Settlements:** these are places where people settle down and live, including cities, towns, villages, hamlets, boroughs and counties.
- **Agriculture:** forms of agriculture include sugar cane, rice, cocoa, coffee, coconuts, market gardening and dairy farming.
- **Industry:** industrial estates and large factories.

Basseterre, St Kitts is an example of a human environment.

Settlements

Thousands of years ago all that people looked for in a settlement was food, water and shelter. Settlements became larger if they were able to offer more. For example, some settlements were good defensive sites because they were situated somewhere safe, such as on a hill.

- The smallest type of settlement is a **hamlet**. A hamlet is just a small number of houses. All settlements start off as hamlets.
- A **village** is bigger than a hamlet, with a population of several hundred to several thousand people. Hamlets and villages are found in rural areas.
- **Towns** are larger than villages and are generally built-up areas that have large populations.
- **Cities** are the largest type of settlement and have the highest number of buildings and people living there. Many cities have rivers running through them. For example, the Demerara River runs through Georgetown, Guyana.
- **Capital cities** are where the government of that country is located. They don't have to be the largest city in the country. Belmopan is Belize's third largest city, but it is the capital city because this is where the government buildings are.

Activity

Do you live in a village, town or city? What other villages, towns and cities, and other settlements, are close to where you live? Trace a map of your country and add these places to the map.

Exercise

1. What three elements make up the human environment? Give examples.
2. Explain the differences between a village, town and city.

Agriculture

Farming is an important human land use. There are two main types of farming:

- **Livestock farming** is the rearing of animals such as sheep, cattle, pigs and hens.
- **Arable farming** is the growing of crops, such as sugar, coffee, cocoa, rice, bananas and paw paw.

Agriculture is becoming less important in the Eastern Caribbean. In St Vincent and the Grenadines, 22 per cent of the population is employed in agriculture, while in Barbados the figure is less than 3 per cent. Agriculture is 4 per cent of the overall income earned by countries of the OECS (Organization of Eastern Caribbean States).

A rum distillery in Barbados.

Industry

Land is also used for industry. There are three main types of industry:

- **Primary industries** are those that involve extracting natural resources. Guyana makes most of its income from mining gold, diamonds and aluminium ore.
- **Secondary industries**, otherwise known as manufacturing industries, are those that are involved with making things. St Kitts and Nevis makes over 6.5 per cent of its income from manufacturing. Electronics and boating equipment are the main manufacturing exports.
- **Tertiary industries** are service industries that involve selling products. Research, banking, tourism and retail are examples of tertiary industries.

Primary industry is limited on Eastern Caribbean islands since mining and quarrying often harm the natural environment.

Manufacturing may focus on the use of local produce like fruits, vegetables and spices to make jams, sauces and seasonings. Countries may also import raw materials for manufacture. At Campden Park **industrial estate** in St Vincent, raw grain is imported and milled to make flour. Flour makes up 10 per cent of St Vincent's exports.

> **Did you know...?**
>
> The majority of Eastern Caribbean industry is tertiary. Tourism in Grand Cayman earns over 50 per cent of the country's income while the island's offshore banking sector is the 6th largest in the world.

Key vocabulary

human environment

settlement

hamlet

village

town

city

capital city

livestock farming

industrial estate

Exercise

3. Describe the differences between livestock and arable farming.

4. Explain the differences between primary, secondary and tertiary industries.

5. Draw a graphic organiser to show how primary, secondary and tertiary industries are organised.

The human environment

We are learning to:

- identify and locate examples of human land use on a map.

Services 》

Services are public utilities and amenities that are provided for settlements where people live. The number of services that are found in an area depends on the size of the settlement. Services can be divided into low-, middle- and high-order services.

- Low-order services are those that are used often, most likely on a daily basis, such as schools, post offices, churches and markets.
- Middle-order services are used less frequently, and include hairdressers, banks and pharmacies.
- High-order services are those that are not used very often – for example, a hospital or a police station, or very expensive shops.

Recreation 》》

Recreational facilities are services or places where people go to enjoy themselves or visit as tourist destinations. Most settlements have some form of recreational facility, even if it is just a park. However, the main ones are found in large towns and cities.

- Museums such as the St Lucia Folk Research Centre and Grenada National Museum are examples of recreational facilities. These are very popular with tourists, so they are located in cities, as this is probably where tourists will stay.
- Major sporting venues are most commonly located in the largest settlements. Cricket grounds such as Kensington Oval in Barbados and Warner Park Sporting Complex in St Kitts are known worldwide.
- Victoria Park, Antigua, and Queen's Park, Barbados, are two examples of large parks found in urban areas.

Grenada National Museum.

Activity

Use an atlas, or find some photographs of Antigua that have been taken from a plane. Identify the different uses of land that you can see in the pictures.

Project

On a map of St Lucia:

a) find the capital city and two towns

b) locate two examples of human land use in agriculture, industry, services, recreation and communication

Exercise

1. Explain the differences between low-, middle- and high- order services, and give examples.

2. Why do you think we need recreational facilities?

Communications >>>>

In geography, the term **communications** refers to transport facilities, such as roads, railways, ports and airports. If a country is well connected, it is said to have good communications. Cities have far better transport facilities than villages, because they have more people who need them.

Roads

Some Eastern Caribbean countries have extensive road networks that cross the country, connecting places quite well.

In Antigua, many roads connect the capital, St John's, to the entire country. Eastern roads include the Sir Sydney Walling Highway and Pares Village Road, which enter the parishes of St Peter and St Philip. All Saints Road and Buckley's Main Road go to the southern parish of St Paul. Valley Road and Old Road circle south-west into St Mary parish. Friar's Hill Road runs north and Sir George Walter Highway runs north-east into St George parish.

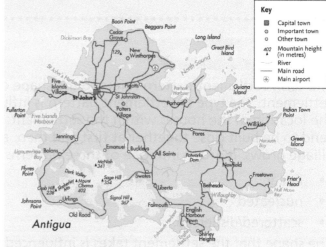

Communications map of Antigua.

Other islands have limited major roads that run along the coast to avoid central, rugged, forested areas. From the capital city, Basseterre, St Kitts' road network is entirely coastal. This avoids the central Northwest and Southeast mountain ranges.

Ports and airports

Ports allow ships for trade and tourism to dock. Many cruise trips travel through the Eastern Caribbean, docking for one day at each island port.

Airports may be built for large airplanes and international flights, for example Grantley Adams International Airport, Barbados. George F. L. Charles Airport, St Lucia, is built for smaller airplanes and inter-island flights.

Exercise

3. Look at the maps and answer the following questions:

    a) Leaving Freetown using the main road to get to Christian Hill, Antigua, name two places you would pass on the way.

    b) Where in Antigua is the airport located?

    c) Using the main road from Swetes to Old Road, which hills will you pass?

    d) Which towns must you go through when travelling from Shirley Heights to All Saints?

Key vocabulary

services

recreational facilities

communications

Settlement patterns in the Eastern Caribbean

We are learning to:

- name and describe different settlement patterns in the Eastern Caribbean.

Settlement patterns ⟩⟩

The term **settlement pattern** refers to the shape of the settlement. The type of settlement pattern is influenced by the location of the houses within the settlement. Houses tend to be built close together at first and then, as the village grows, it grows into one of three patterns:

- linear
- nucleated
- scattered/dispersed.

The shape that the settlement takes is influenced by the surrounding land.

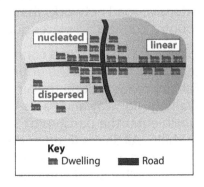

Linear settlement pattern ⟩⟩⟩

Linear settlement patterns are settlements where houses and buildings are built in lines.

This might be along roads, rivers or along the coastline. If a settlement is built along a river, it shows that the river was the main reason for the settlement to be built there.

If a settlement is built along a road, the road predates the settlement, so people have chosen to build there because this area most likely has good communications.

In the Eastern Caribbean most linear settlement occurs along roads. This is because these roads usually connect major towns, so building along them allows easy access to transport to and from these towns. Development of tourism also promotes linear coastal settlement. Building side by side along a stretch of coastal road allows hotels access to beach-front property.

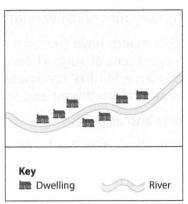

Examples of linear settlements – the first shows a settlement built around two roads, the second by a river.

Exercise

1. Explain, in your own words, the term settlement pattern.
2. Why do think a linear settlement pattern has that name?

Nucleated settlement pattern >>>

Nucleated settlement patterns are those where the houses and buildings are grouped closely together.

The houses and buildings are generally clustered around a central point, such as a church, village green or town square. All sizes of settlements may follow a nucleated pattern.

In the Eastern Caribbean, nucleated settlements traditionally formed around areas of fertile land. Most towns and villages in the Eastern Caribbean are on flat coastal land and tend to be nucleated, especially those where sheltered bays allow harbours for overseas trade to develop.

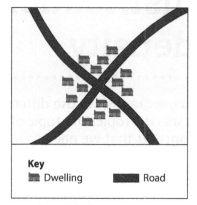

Key
🏠 Dwelling   ▬ Road

A nucleated settlement.

Scattered/dispersed settlement pattern >>

The words scattered and dispersed both mean 'spread apart'.

In **scattered** and **dispersed** settlements, the houses and buildings are spread far apart over a large area. They are generally just individual buildings, so they do not form a specific settlement.

Scattered/dispersed settlements are found in the interior mountainous and forested regions of islands such as St Lucia and St Vincent.

It is difficult to build on hilly land, so large settlements tend not to be built here.

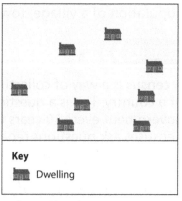

Key
🏠 Dwelling

A dispersed settlement.

Exercise

3. Why do you think nuclear and scattered patterns are called what they are?

4. In a nuclear pattern, what are the buildings typically grouped around?

5. What type of settlement pattern do you have where you live?

6. Talk to an older person (such as one of your grandparents) about the community where he or she grew up. What form of settlement was it? Ask the person why he or she thinks that particular form of settlement was established.

Key vocabulary

settlement pattern

linear settlement

nucleated settlement

scattered/dispersed settlement

Population distribution and density

We are learning to:

• distinguish between population distribution and population density.

In geography, we use different terminology when studying a specific topic. The topic of population has many new concepts that we need to understand.

Population

The word **population** refers to the total number of people living in a specific geographic area at a particular point in time. When we talk about population, we might refer to the population of a village, town, city, country or the world.

Census

A **census** is a way of collecting the population information of a country. This is a questionnaire that is given out by the government every 10 years to every household in the country. Censuses ask questions regarding how many people live in the house, the age of every household member and each person's occupation. The government uses the information to find the population of the country.

Population density

The term **population density** refers to the average number of people living in one square kilometre. Population density is calculated by dividing the number of people in an area by the size of the area.

Areas can be sparsely, moderately or densely populated. A high population density means that there are a lot of people living per square kilometre, while a low population density means there are few people living per square kilometre.

Did you know...?

The population of the 15 CARICOM members in July 2016 was estimated as follows:

Antigua and Barbuda 93 581

The Bahamas 327 316

Barbados 291 495

Belize 353 858

Dominica 111 219

Grenada 73 757

Guyana 735 909

Haiti 10 485 800

Jamaica 2 970 340

Montserrat 5 267

St Kitts and Nevis 52 329

St Lucia 164 464

St Vincent and the Grenadines 102 350

Suriname 585 824

Trinidad and Tobago 1 365 000

Exercise

1. In your own words, explain the difference between population density and population distribution.

2. What is a census? How often does one take place?

3. What is the difference between a sparsely, moderately or densely populated area?

4. How is population density calculated?

We work out the population density so that we can understand how well populated an area is. This allows us to compare one area with another.

Population distribution

Population distribution refers to how the population is spread out. Population distribution is described as dense or sparse.

We know the world has a population of approximately 7 billion people. However, these people are not evenly spread out across the world. Some counties, such as China and India, have approximately 1 billion people each. Other countries have much fewer people.

Mumbai is the most populous city in India. In 2017, its population was estimated to be 22 million.

Urban and rural

Urban areas are built-up areas such as towns and cities, which have many shops and services. They tend to have a lot of people living there, with moderate and high population densities.

Rural areas are villages and hamlets with not many services. These settlements have few people living there and therefore have low population densities.

Project

Carry out a project to learn about the population of the country that you live in. Follow these steps:

1. Choose a country to study.

2. Make a glossary of words related to population. These are the aspects of population that you are going to research.

3. Do some online research. Find out about the population of your country. Learn about:

   • the total population
   • the population density
   • the population distribution.

4. Write two paragraphs about the population in your country.

Key vocabulary

population

census

population density

population distribution

urban areas

rural areas

A dispersed settlement: choropleth and dot maps

We are learning to:

- define terms and concepts related to population distribution and density
- interpret choropleth maps and dot maps.

Choropleth maps 》

A **choropleth map** is a type of map that shows the population density of an area or country. Each country is coloured according to population density, and the darker the colour, the denser the population. A choropleth map can be a very effective way of comparing areas and countries.

The disadvantages of using this type of map are:

- It can be difficult to interpret, as it might be hard to distinguish between similar shades.
- They give the false impression that abrupt changes occur at the boundaries of shaded areas, where quite often the change is more gradual.
- They are often unsuitable for showing total values, such as the total population of a country.

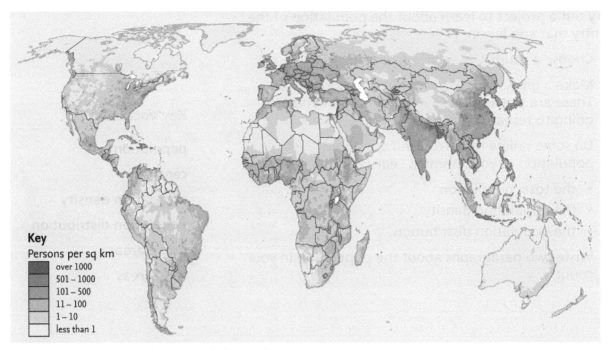

Key
Persons per sq km

	over 1000
	501 – 1000
	101 – 500
	11 – 100
	1 – 10
	less than 1

Choropleth world map showing the population density.

Dot maps ▶▶▶

A **dot map** is a type of map that shows population distribution and population density. A dot symbol represents a certain number of people. Usually 1 dot = 10 000 people.

There are many advantages of using dot maps. They can be used to compare population patterns within a country or between countries. They are easy to construct and interpret by counting the number of dots.

The main drawback of using dot maps is that they can be quite time-consuming to construct.

When making a dot map, there are a couple of things that need to be considered. First, you must think about the size of the dot and what value the dot will have. Using many small dots to represent smaller values is more effective than using fewer larger dots.

Activity

In the previous lesson you carried out a project about population distribution in the country where you live. From the data collected in that project, make a dot map to show the population distribution in your region.

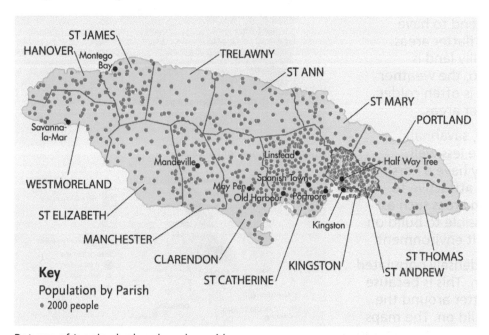

Dot map of Jamaica, broken down by parish.

Key
Population by Parish
● 2000 people

Exercise

1. Explain what choropleth and dot maps show.

2. Make a table showing the advantages and disadvantages of using choropleth dot maps.

3. Look at the map and answer the questions:

   a) Where in Jamaica is there the greatest and least population density and distribution?

   b) Why do you think those areas have the greatest population density and distribution?

Key vocabulary

choropleth map

dot map

Population distribution in the Eastern Caribbean

We are learning to:

• analyse reasons for the population distribution in the Eastern Caribbean: physical features, agriculture, fresh water, climate, soils, communications.

The Caribbean's population distribution is dependent on a number of different factors.

Physical features 》

Physical features are hills, mountains, rivers, lakes and other features of the landscape. Areas that are mountainous and hilly tend to have lower populations than flatter areas. This is mainly because hilly land is difficult to build on. Also, the weather in mountainous regions is often colder and wetter than in flatter areas.

In Trinidad, for example, savannah regions such as Aripo are less well populated, because they have a harsh environment that is not attractive to people. Similarly, swamp areas such as Nariva are almost impossible to build on and have a more difficult environment.

Coastal areas are more densely populated in the Eastern Caribbean. This is because the land tends to be flatter around the coast and is easier to build on. The maps show how the populations in St Lucia and Barbados are spread out.

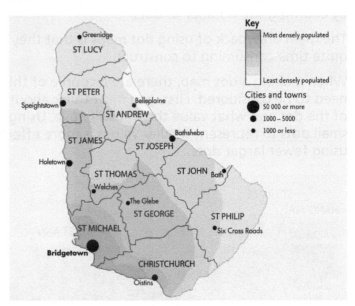

Population density map of Barbados.

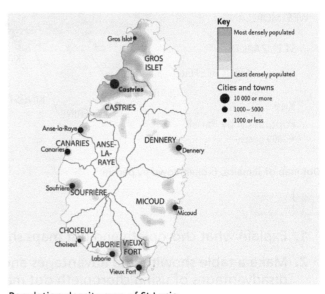

Population density map of St Lucia.

Exercise

1. Compare the population density maps of Barbados and St Lucia. Look back in the unit and explain any similarities and differences in the population distributions of these countries.

Agriculture and soil >>>

Populations tend to be higher in areas where there is good, fertile farmland. The St George Valley in Barbados has good farmland and therefore has a moderate population. Most farming activity tends to take place in the western half of the country, and for this reason it has the highest number of people living there. Areas that have thin soils, such as mountainous and hilly regions, are not suitable agricultural land, so people tend not to locate there.

Fresh water >>>

Traditionally, people wanted to live near to a river, where they could access the fresh water to drink, wash and fish. However, today this is less important. Historically, most settlements were beside rivers, but accessing fresh water is no longer a problem. Today, there are few areas that are uninhabitable because they do not have access to fresh water.

A farmer tends his crops.

Climate >>

Climate is one of the biggest factors that affects population distribution. People often want to live in areas where there is a 'nice' climate – that is, one that is not too hot, not too cold, not too wet or not too dry. On Eastern Caribbean islands, most people live on the western side, because the climate is better there. There is less rainfall compared to the east.

Communications >>>

Some islands have limited road networks due to mountainous terrain. In these islands most roads are coastal, for example, in Grenada. Flat islands are covered by extensive road networks across the central areas, for example, in Barbados and Anguilla. People want to live near to areas that are well connected to cities and towns, so that they are able to access services and amenities more easily.

Exercise

2. Draw a mind map to help explain some the factors which affect population distribution in the Eastern Caribbean.

3. Why do you think so few people live in central and western Guyana, while the east coast is densely populated?

4. How do you think the physical features of St Vincent affect where people decide to live?

5. What physical features do you think contributed to the development of where you live?

Key vocabulary
....

physical features

Population distribution and density in the Caribbean

We are learning to:

- calculate the population densities of Caribbean countries
- account for the population distribution and densities of Caribbean countries.

Calculating population density

Population density is calculated by dividing the population by the size of the area.

$$\text{Population density} = \frac{\text{Population}}{\text{Area}}$$

St Vincent has a population of 110 200 and an area of 389 square km. Therefore, to work out the population density:

$$\text{Population density of St Vincent} = \frac{110\,200}{389}$$

$$= 283 \text{ (people per square km)}$$

The table below shows the population, area and population density of other Caribbean countries.

Barbados has a population density of 638.

Reasons for the differences in population densities

There are many reasons why some Caribbean countries are more densely populated than others. If we look at two Caribbean countries in more depth, the reasons should become clear.

According to the table below, Barbados has the highest population density of the listed Caribbean countries, with 638 per square km. Guyana is last, with only 4.

Country	Density	Country	Density
Antigua and Barbuda	195	Guyana	4
The Bahamas	25	Haiti	409
Barbados	638	Jamaica	248
Cuba	102	St Kitts and Nevis	192
Dominica	96	St Lucia	270
Dominican Republic	220	St Vincent and the Grenadines	259
Grenada	300	Trinidad and Tobago	264

There are several reasons why Barbados has a high population density:

- It has an appealing climate. It has a tropical monsoon climate, which means it has two seasons, one of which is wet. It doesn't experience too many natural disasters, such as hurricanes.

- A good climate means productive agriculture. Tobacco, cotton, ginger and sugar cane have been grown on Barbados and exported across the world.

- Barbados has large cities such as Bridgetown and Oistins. The country is very small and is very well connected.

- Barbados is a rich country. It is ranked as the 53rd richest country in the world, and its people enjoy a moderate **standard of living**, with good services and amenities. This has attracted a lot of migration over the years. Barbados continues to receive many immigrants today from countries such as Syria and Lebanon.

- Historically, Barbados has had a problem with its high birth rate, which means lots of babies were born. This has led to an unusually high population for such a small country.

Guyana, on the other hand, has the lowest population density of all the Caribbean islands. There are several reasons for this:

- More than 80 per cent of the country is covered in tropical forest, which is protected by the government. There are a number of indigenous groups that live inside the tropical forests, but these numbers are low.

- Only 2 per cent of the land is used for agriculture. This is partly because most of the land is forested, but also because the climate is not very suitable for productive farming.

- Guyana is a relatively poor country and the people living in the settlements there have a relatively low standard of living, particularly those living in rural areas. Not all households are equipped with clean, running water, and **sanitation** is very poor.

Guyana has a population density of 4.

1. In your own words, explain why Barbados has a higher population density than Guyana. Use a graphic organiser to help you.

2. Look at the table. Put the countries in order according to their population density, from the highest to the lowest. Where is St Vincent?

Key vocabulary

standard of living

sanitation

Physical and man-made features

We are learning to:

- differentiate between physical and man-made features
- describe man's impact on the environment.

Differences between physical and man-made features

Physical features are any naturally forming features on the Earth's surface, such as mountains, lakes, rivers, valleys, beaches, canyons, caves and cliffs.

Man-made features are those that have been created entirely by humans, such as skyscrapers, monuments, cathedrals, highways, bridges, ports, canals and dams.

Parliament Building, Bridgetown, Barbados is an example of a man-made feature.

Activity

Decide whether each feature below is physical or man-made. Draw a line to connect each feature to the correct box.

Physical

Chancery Lane Swamp

St John's Cathedral

Soufrière Hills

Wallblake House

Darkview Falls

Kim Collins Highway

Fort George

Gros Piton

Boiling Lake

Man-made

Exercise

1. In your own words, explain the terms physical features and man-made features. Give examples of each.

2. List four physical features in the country where you live.

3. List four man-made features in the country where you live.

4. Draw a map of the country where you live. Show the four physical features and the four man-made features that you identified in questions 2 and 3.

Activity

Draw a graphic organiser showing the different types of physical features and man-made features in the Eastern Caribbean.

Man's impact on the environment >>>

There are many ways that man has interfered with natural processes. Some of these have been to the benefit of man and others have been detrimental.

Destruction of tropical rainforests >>>

One of the clearest examples of man's negative impact on the environment is the destruction of tropical forests. In 1950, tropical forests covered approximately 15 per cent of the Earth's surface. Today this has been reduced to about 6 per cent. In the Caribbean, a lot of forests have been cut down to make space for agriculture. Many governments have used laws to protect forests. In St Lucia, the government has reduced the amount of forest lost annually from 500 hectares to less than 100 hectares. In fact, across the Caribbean, **reforestation** is now happening.

The destruction of tropical forests can have detrimental effects on our planet.

The cutting down of rainforests is called **deforestation,** which is having detrimental effects on our planet:

- Climate change. Trees breathe in carbon dioxide, which warms our planet. Fewer trees leads to more carbon dioxide, so temperatures increase.
- Loss of species. 70 per cent of the world's species live in forests. The loss of their habitats leads to extinction.
- More deserts. Deserts form as forests are cut down.
- Loss of medicines. Some traditional medicines are made from forest plants.
- Increased flooding. Forests absorb water like a sponge. When the trees are gone, the risk of flooding increases, and communities are not protected.
- Poor farmland. Forests make the soil richer. Without forests, the soil is not as healthy. The result might be food shortages.

Is this deforestation sustainable? Man cannot continue to cut down rainforests at this same pace. As many as 320 square km of forest are lost every day, and in 100 years' time rainforests could be completely destroyed.

Discussion

With your class, think of some positive ways that people have changed the environment. Then think of some negative ways. Make lists.

Exercise

5. How much of the Earth's surface was covered in rainforest in 1950 and in 2017?
6. By how many hectares has St Lucia reduced its annual deforestation?
7. Explain the term deforestation.
8. Write about 150 words discussing some of the reasons why the rainforests are being cut down.

Key vocabulary
....

man-made features

reforestation

deforestation

Factors influencing land use

We are learning to:

- describe the main factors influencing land use
- analyse connections (benefits and disadvantages) between physical landforms and human land use.

Relief »

There are many factors that influence the use of land, including relief, drainage, coast and vegetation. **Relief** refers to the height and shape of the land. This is perhaps the most important factor affecting land use.

- It is very difficult and expensive to build in mountainous and hilly areas. It is easier to build houses and roads on flat land; therefore the largest settlements are found in lowland areas. Examples are Basseterre, St Kitts; Kingstown, St Vincent; and Soufrière, St Lucia. All are built in lowland areas.
- Farming is very difficult in mountainous and hilly areas. Arable farming is almost impossible, because soils are very thin and infertile, so crops don't grow well.
- Temperatures are much cooler in mountainous regions. For every 300 m in height, there is a temperature drop of between 1 and 3 degrees Celsius. Crops don't grow well in these conditions.

Grand Etang National Park in central Grenada is an example of the relief of land.

Drainage »»

Drainage is the process by which water is carried away from an area. If drainage is poor, water remains in the ground.

- Some areas of land, such as mangrove swamps, can be completely flooded twice a day. It is not possible to use this land for any form of building.
- People do not build in areas with poor drainage, as they do not want their houses or businesses to be damaged by flooding. Since the land is soggy, any buildings would be very unstable.
- Farming cannot take place here either, because crops do not grow in soils that are very moist.

Exercise

1. In your own words, explain the terms relief and drainage.
2. Why would buildings not be built in mountains and in swamps?

Activity

Local developers are going to build a new water park near a forested area close to your community. Role-play a town meeting to discuss the proposal. Divide the class into two, where one group is in favour of the development and the other is against it. Use the internet to research some of the points you would like to raise.

Coastal regions can have plenty of land use opportunities or very few, depending on the coastline.

- Low-lying coastlines have far more opportunities to build or farm than the higher ones. Quite often, people build settlements around the **perimeter** (the edge) of an island, or along the coastline, because the land is flat and therefore suitable to build on.

- Grenada, St Vincent and Dominica rise sharply into rugged hills and mountains. This means that most settlements and roads are built along the narrow, lowland coastline.

- Coastal areas that are high and have many cliffs are subjected to many natural processes that will limit land use activity. Coastal cliffs are attacked by waves constantly and land can regularly fall into the sea. For this reason, these areas are very unstable and it would be unsafe to use the land here for houses or roads.

Coastal cliffs are attacked by waves constantly and over time land can fall into the sea.

Vegetation >>

The amount of natural vegetation in an area will also affect land use.

- Areas covered in thick, dense forest are not suitable for building on, unless the forest is cleared first.

- Deforestation leads to other problems, such as increased levels of carbon dioxide, loss of habitats for animals and an increased risk of flooding.

- It is only possible to farm in these areas on a small scale. Indigenous people use rainforests to farm land on a very small scale.

Exercise

3. Why is it sometimes easier to build around the edge of an island?

4. Why would it be unsafe to have buildings near coastal cliffs?

5. How would the amount of natural vegetation affect land use?

Key vocabulary
....
relief

drainage

perimeter

The development of Bridgetown

We are learning to:

- examine factors that influenced the development of Bridgetown, Barbados.

Bridgetown is the capital of Barbados. It is the largest and most densely populated area in the country. Bridgetown is the most important town for the economy of Barbados as it is the centre of government, trade and commerce.

Origins of Bridgetown

Bridgetown is located on the western coast of Barbados. European colonisers of the island recognised its value as a natural harbour in a time where maritime trade was important.

As more settlers arrived and trade in enslaved people increased in the 17th century, the city became the island's main settlement and port. Bridgetown's main activities included warehousing sugar, molasses and rum; and importing and exporting goods.

The Mutual Building, Bridgetown, Barbados, is an example of historic architectural heritage.

Modern Bridgetown

The sugar trade is no longer the island's main industry. The focus of the city has changed from the Careenage (old port) to the Central Business District (CBD). The CBD is dominated by commercial buildings such as banks, offices, shops and markets. The port was moved from central Bridgetown to northern Greater Bridgetown. This move served the main tourism industry since there was space to construct a modern cruise ship terminal.

People left their residences in the city centre to escape the bustle of the city and high land prices, since commercial and administrative land use began to spread to these areas. Agricultural land close to the city was then developed into **suburban** residential areas such as Hastings and Britton's Hill. Road networks also connected the city to the whole island and public transport became reliable and private transport more common. People now **commute** to work.

Manufacturing has also moved to the central area. Here, activities include food processing, warehousing and the production of clothing, plastics and handicrafts.

Communications Highways 1 to 7 all run directly into Bridgetown, linking the city to the entire island, including the Grantley Adams International Airport. Three bus terminals

Did you know...?

Historic Bridgetown and its Garrison was designated a UNESCO World Heritage site in 2011.

Activity

Using an atlas, draw a map outlining the boundaries of the main town in your country. Put in the Central Business District, important public buildings, main roads, any ports or harbours and the locations of three recreation sites.

service the island from Bridgetown, including the Princess Alice Terminal and Fairchild Street Terminal.

Bridgetown's architecture is a mix of old and new. Some buildings have fully modern styles like the Royal Bank of Canada and the Frank Walcott Building. Buildings such as the Mutual Building and St Mary's Church keep their historic 17th–19th-century architecture. This mix gives the city a fresh, modern feel without losing its rich heritage.

Recreational areas in Bridgetown include the Careenage boardwalk, Independence Square, Queen's Park and the Garrison for leisure walks, while Brownes Beach and Pebbles Beach to the south provide water sports, sunbathing, turtle-watching and diving. At the Careenage docks, pleasure craft such as the MC *Buccaneer* and the *Jolly Roger* provide tours around the island. Frank Collymore Hall is the island's premiere performance art venue while the Grande Salle is an iconic visual arts exhibition gallery.

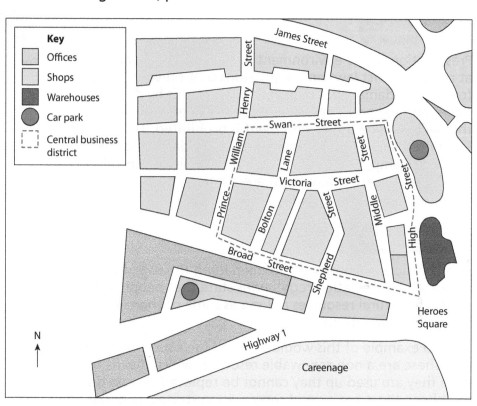

Exercise

1. Consider the diagram of Bridgetown's central business district. Name four streets that are part of Bridgetown's Central Business District.

2. Explain why residents have moved out of central Bridgetown.

3. How does Bridgetown maintain both modern and historic character?

4. Which recreation activities are available in Bridgetown?

Key vocabulary

suburban

commute

Preservation and conservation of the environment

We are learning to:

- differentiate between preservation and conservation of the environment
- justify the need for the sustainable use of physical resources to protect the environment.

We often refer to preservation, conservation and sustainability when we talk about the environment. The natural environment needs to be protected so that future generations can enjoy its benefits as much as we do today.

Coral on a St Lucian reef.

Preservation

Preservation of the environment means protecting areas at risk with strict laws and regulations that prevent them from being damaged. Countries might do this by declaring them national parks or nature reserves, where any activity that will damage the environment is prohibited. The Soufrière Marine Management Area, St Lucia; the Salina Reserve swamp, Grand Cayman; and Dominica's Central Forest Reserve are examples of areas heavily protected by legislation.

Conservation

Conservation is concerned with managing the use of natural resources. Conservation regulations state that people can use these natural resources as long as some of them are left for future generations.

A good example of this would be fossil fuels such as oil and gas. These are a non-renewable resource, which means that once they are used up they cannot be replaced. Across the Caribbean there are several conservation strategies designed around the use of the tropical forests.

Sustainability

Sustainability is concerned with the use of natural resources in such a way that their quantities are maintained. If sustainability is practised, the resource will be available for future generations.

It is often possible to replace renewable resources, such as trees, as they are used. For example, if a forest is deforested, more trees can be planted in its place.

Activity

In groups, discuss the difference between preservation, conservation and sustainability. Give examples of each one and share your ideas with the other groups.

Case study

Using and protecting our natural resources

Our planet has many resources that humans have enjoyed for thousands of years. There are amazing landscapes that should be protected, wildlife and plant species that need to be protected and natural resources that must be maintained.

You are going to choose an area in your country and examine the positive and negative effects of the way the land is used. You will decide whether the land is being used well, and give recommendations on what else could be done. Then you will share your ideas in a presentation to the class.

Planting new trees helps combat the effects of deforestation.

Follow these steps:

1. Choose a place in your country that is rich in natural resources.

2. Decide whether the resources are renewable (they can be replaced) or non-renewable (they can never be replaced).

3. Do some research to find out how the land is being used. For example:
   - Are the resources being used? If so, what for?
   - Are the resources being preserved by the government? If so, how? What laws exist to protect the area?
   - Are there any conservation strategies in the area? If so, what are they?
   - If the resources in the area are renewable, are they being used with sustainability in mind?

4. Conduct field observations, interviews and surveys to help with your project.

5. Decide whether or not you think the use of the land you have chosen is acceptable. Why?

6. Create a PowerPoint presentation to share information on your chosen place.

Your presentation must include the following:
- location of study
- the way in which the land is used
- positive and negative effects of land use
- evidence of primary and secondary sources of information – for example, library and internet sources, articles from newspapers, magazines, journals
- proper citation of sources.

Key vocabulary
....
sustainable/sustainability

Questions

See how well you have understood the topics in this unit.

1. Match the key vocabulary word with its definition.

    i) natural resource

    ii) physical features

    iii) man-made features

    a) naturally forming features such as mountains, rivers, lakes, cliffs and caves

    b) features created by humans, such as buildings, roads, ports and airports

    c) something that forms naturally and that we use for other purposes

2. Mark the following features on this map of Guyana:

    a) Pacaraima Mountains   **d)** Acarai Mountains   **g)** Cuyuni River

    b) Kunuku Mountains   **e)** Rupununi Savannah   **h)** Mazaruni River

    c) Kamoa Mountains   **f)** Essequibo River

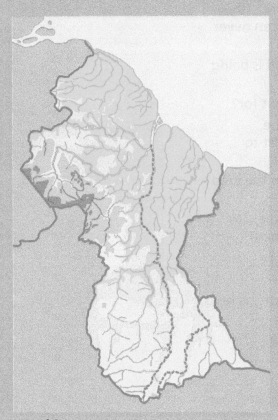

Map of Guyana.

3. Fill in the missing information needed when citing sources.

https://www.destinationtnt.com/salybia-bay/;
unknown; 'Salybia Bay'; 2017; 14 July 2017

4. **a)** List three volcanic landforms that can be found in the Eastern Caribbean.

    b) Explain why a volcanic landscape may have high altitude and many rivers.

5. For each natural disaster below, state two ways it may alter the landscape:

    a) volcanic eruption   **b)** hurricane   **c)** landslide

6. Describe how vegetation is used to make money in the Eastern Caribbean.

7. Write definitions for each of these terms:

    a) settlement   **c)** village   **e)** city

    b) hamlet   **d)** town   **f)** capital city

8. Identify these settlement types.

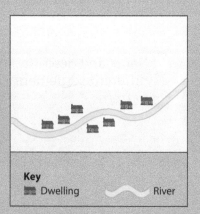

Key
Dwelling   River

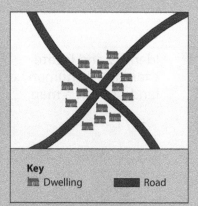

Key
Dwelling   Road

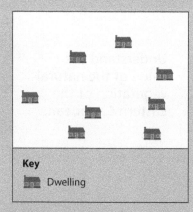

Key
Dwelling

9. Explain the differences between a choropleth map and a dot map.

10. List three volcanic landforms that can be found in the Eastern Caribbean.

11. Explain why a volcanic landscape may have high altitude and many rivers.

Checking your progress

To make good progress in understanding different aspects of the physical environment, check to make sure you understand these ideas.

Name and locate major landforms in the Eastern Caribbean.

Describe major physical landforms: mountains, hills and plains, rivers, coastlines and beaches.

Describe features of volcanic and limestone landscapes in the Eastern Caribbean.

Make a presentation using ICT skills.

Make a field sketch of a landform in your local area.

Describe the natural vegetation of the Eastern Caribbean.

Understand the value of the natural vegetation of the Eastern Caribbean.

Identify and locate examples of human land-uses on a map.

Name and describe different settlement patterns.

Distinguish between population distribution and population density.

Analyse reasons for the population distribution in the Eastern Caribbean.

Describe man's impact on the environment and the role of preservation and conservation of the environment.

End-of-term questions

See how well you have understood the ideas in Unit 1.

1. In your own words, explain the difference between an employer and an employee.

2. Match the major groups (i–x) with the job classification in each group (a–j).

i) group 1	**a)** skilled agricultural, forestry and fishery workers
ii) group 2	**b)** armed forces
iii) group 3	**c)** plant and machine operators and assemblers
iv) group 4	**d)** professionals
v) group 5	**e)** elementary occupations
vi) group 6	**f)** clerical support workers
vii) group 7	**g)** sales and services workers
viii) group 8	**h)** craft and related trades workers
ix) group 9	**i)** technicians and associate professionals
x) group 10	**j)** managers

3. Explain the importance of the following category of worker to the economic development of the Eastern Caribbean:

   a) primary sector

   b) secondary sector

   c) tertiary sector

   d) quaternary sector

4. Explain the difference between a need and a want.

5. In your own words, explain the benefits of savings and what might prevent someone from saving. Write 100 words.

6. Write a short essay of 150 words on the importance of planning a budget.

See how well you have understood the ideas in Unit 2.

7. Why is it important for the countries of the Caribbean region to retain their identity? Write a short paragraph to explain.

8. Read 2.3 and 2.4. Write a short essay on the different ways that Caribbean citizens can show appreciation for their national and Caribbean identity.

9. Explain the role that patriotism plays in respecting our national and Caribbean identity.

10. Explain how the following personalities have contributed to building Caribbean identity:

    a) Michael Manley

    b) Sir Viv Richards

    c) Sir Derek Walcott

    d) Dr Eric Williams

    e) Bob Marley

    f) Dr Norge Jerome

11. Write a short essay, explaining the role of CARICOM and Carifesta in establishing cooperation and integration in the Caribbean region.

12. Read 2.5, 2.6 and 2.7, and create a timeline showing the contributions made to the Caribbean by the personalities discussed.

Questions 13–18 >>>

See how well you have understood the ideas in Unit 3.

13. Read 3.1 and 3.2. Write a report of 250–350 words detailing the major physical landforms that can be found in the Caribbean. Include examples for each landform and add photographs to your report.

14. Identify the three different types of natural vegetation that can be found in the Caribbean.

15. Name four ways in which the natural vegetation of the Caribbean contributes to the economy.

16. The following categories of the human environment can be found in the Caribbean. Give examples from your country of:

    a) settlements

    b) agriculture

    c) industry

    d) services

    e) recreation

17. Give reasons for the distribution of the population of your country.

18. Explain the difference between physical features and man-made features. Give three examples in your country for each.

Unit 4: *Personal development*

In this unit you will find out »»

Groups in society

- Explain the term group
- Identify the different types of groups people belong to:
  - social (family and friends)
  - school
  - religious groups
  - sports
  - charity and community
  - cultural
- The functions of groups
- The characteristics of groups
- Different types of groups and their characteristics
  - primary and secondary groups
  - formal and informal groups
- The differences between groups
- The benefits of being a member of a group
- Roles and responsibilities in groups and group cohesion
- Ways groups can overcome issues that arise

Leadership

- Define the terms leader, leadership, power and authority
- The qualities of a good leader
- Different types of leaders and leadership styles
  - democratic
  - authoritarian
  - laissez-faire
- The different types of leaders and their characteristics

The role of a leader

- The role of leaders in a group
- The qualities of a good leader

Groups in society

We are learning to:
- define the term group
- identify and examine the different groups to which people belong.

Groups

We all belong to **groups**. A **social group** is made up of two or more people who work together to achieve a common purpose or goal. For example, you can be a part of a family, a club or class at school, a church group or a sports club.

Groups allow us to:

- work towards a common aim or goal/objective
- share common interests and needs
- create a sense of **unity**
- create a sense of identity and **belonging**
- do activities together or **interact** together often
- have common rules of behaviour, sanctions or rewards.

Groups that do not have these characteristics are not classed as social groups, because they are temporary or do not fulfil all or any of the above characteristics; for example, a crowd at a sporting event.

One of the first groups you are part of is the family group, as you are born into that group. Later you will become part of a wider community group, and then as you go through life you will become part of a number of groups.

Family and community groups are the first types of group that you will be part of.

Examples of groups

People can belong to many different groups. Groups can be classified in different categories. For example:

- **primary groups** – small groups which people interact with often; for example, your family

Exercise

1. Write your own definition of 'social group'.
2. Give two examples of a social group.
3. What do groups allow us to do?
4. Is a crowd of people at a sporting event classed as a group? Give a reason for your answer.
5. Name the first social group that you became a member of.

Discussion

In groups, brainstorm the definition of 'group' and think of as many different types of group as you can.

- **secondary groups** – usually larger groups which meet less often; for example, your class at school
- **formal groups** – groups which have a structure, membership requirements, and rules and regulations; for example, a church group
- **informal groups** – more casual groups than a formal group, which see people come together with a common interest; for example, a sports club.

Each group type has goals or objectives that are unique to that group. Some objectives are clearly defined and can be carried out over a long period of time, while other goals can be specific to a particular group's needs.

Here are some examples:

Group type	Example	Goal/objective of the group
Social (family and friends)	Family, close friends, school friends, neighbourhood friends, your class at school	To provide physical and emotional needs Families also have customs and traditions which bind them together
School	In-class or in-school clubs	To learn new skills in a subject over a school year
Religious	Church, mosque, temple	To share a common faith
Sports	Tennis club, soccer club, hockey club, swimming club, football team, cricket team, netball team	In your cricket team, to improve your all-round skills
Charity and community	Lions, Rotary, youth outreach clubs	To help members of the community
Cultural	Drama group, debating club, Toastmasters, choir, orchestra or band	To put on a stage show

Exercise

6. Name four different categories of groups.

7. Look at the table. Choose two group types – for example, sports and cultural – and choose one example of a group in that 'type' you are a member of. Describe the goal(s) of the group.

groups

social group

unity

belonging

interact

primary groups

secondary groups

formal group

informal group

4.1

The functions of groups

We are learning to:

• explain the functions of groups.

Functions of groups ❯❯

A **function** refers to how something works or operates, the job something does. Groups have many different functions. The mind map summarises the functions of a group.

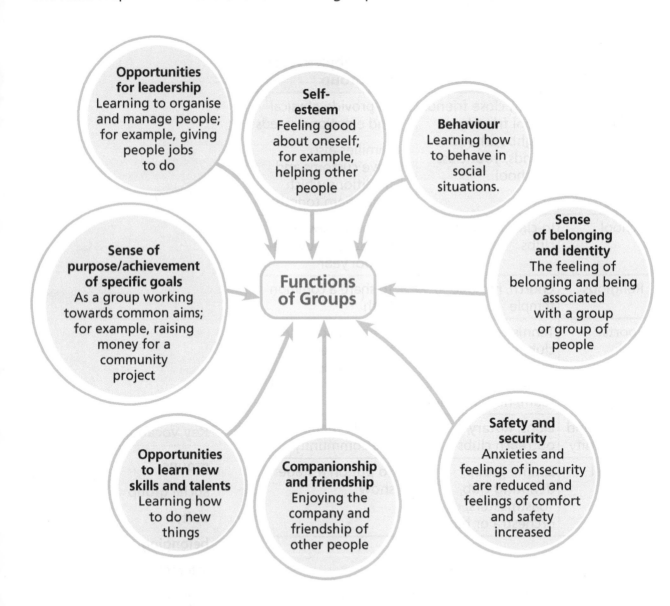

Opportunities for leadership
Learning to organise and manage people; for example, giving people jobs to do

Self-esteem
Feeling good about oneself; for example, helping other people

Behaviour
Learning how to behave in social situations.

Sense of belonging and identity
The feeling of belonging and being associated with a group or group of people

Sense of purpose/achievement of specific goals
As a group working towards common aims; for example, raising money for a community project

Functions of Groups

Opportunities to learn new skills and talents
Learning how to do new things

Companionship and friendship
Enjoying the company and friendship of other people

Safety and security
Anxieties and feelings of insecurity are reduced and feelings of comfort and safety increased

Read what these students say they get from belonging to groups.

My debating club has improved my communication and leadership skills.

In my church youth group, we all cooperate to help our community. I've also made some great friends.

With my choir I get to display my singing talent. I love singing!

My friendship circle is so important to me. I can confide in my friends and trust them.

My photography club is helping me reach my goal of becoming a photographer and journalist.

Exercise

1. Identify and explain in 250 words the functions of a group.

2. For one group that you are member of, create a mind map which shows its functions.

3. Complete this quiz by matching each group function to the statement that fits best.

   i) A sense of belonging

   ii) A sense of identity

   iii) Companionship

   iv) A sense of purpose/achievement of goals

   v) Developing leadership ability

   vi) Opportunities to develop and learn new skills and to show talents

   vii) Safety and security

   a) We have made some amazing changes in our community.

   b) I feel safe and happy among my friends.

   c) We are all different, but we are learning how to do something new.

   d) I am learning how to organise and lead a group.

   e) I enjoy spending time together with the people in my group.

   f) I feel at home here – everyone understands me and I fit in.

   g) This is who I am!

4. Choose and write about any of the above functions your group serves for you. Write about 250 words.

5. Look at the speech bubbles. Write a short sentence for each one, explaining why you think that group is helping the student.

Project

Think about a group you belong to. Use a concept map to emphasise the functions of that group. Use the example on page 110 to help you.

Discussion

Discuss the ways groups can effectively carry out their functions.

Key vocabulary

function

The characteristics of groups

We are learning to:

- describe the characteristics of groups.

Characteristics of groups ⟫

We categorise groups in different ways, according to several characteristics. The mind map summarises the characteristics of a group.

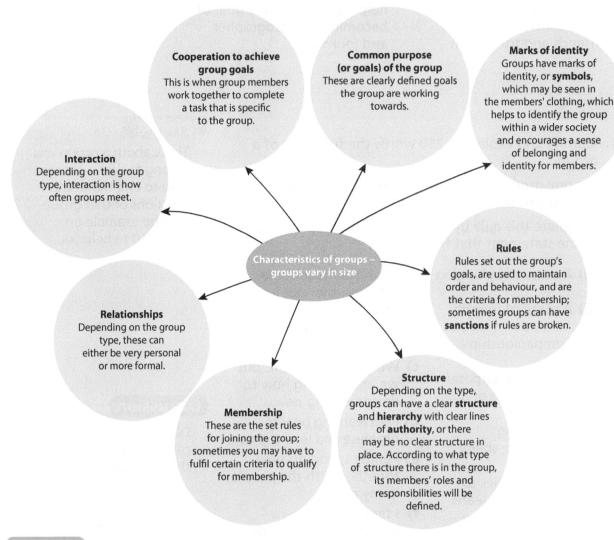

Cooperation to achieve group goals
This is when group members work together to complete a task that is specific to the group.

Common purpose (or goals) of the group
These are clearly defined goals the group are working towards.

Marks of identity
Groups have marks of identity, or **symbols**, which may be seen in the members' clothing, which helps to identify the group within a wider society and encourages a sense of belonging and identity for members.

Interaction
Depending on the group type, interaction is how often groups meet.

Characteristics of groups – groups vary in size

Rules
Rules set out the group's goals, are used to maintain order and behaviour, and are the criteria for membership; sometimes groups can have **sanctions** if rules are broken.

Relationships
Depending on the group type, these can either be very personal or more formal.

Membership
These are the set rules for joining the group; sometimes you may have to fulfil certain criteria to qualify for membership.

Structure
Depending on the type, groups can have a clear **structure** and **hierarchy** with clear lines of **authority**, or there may be no clear structure in place. According to what type of structure there is in the group, its members' roles and responsibilities will be defined.

Exercise

1. Explain in your own words the main characteristics of a group.

2. Think about any of the groups that you belong to. Do your groups show any of these characteristics? If so, which ones?

Marks of identity ▶▶▶

Marks of identity are used by groups to give their group an identity or sense of belonging. Examples include:

- a school uses a letterhead, a uniform and a badge to distinguish its members from other groups
- a sports team uses a symbol or badge on their kit
- a Scout or Girl Guide group uses a logo as part of the group's identity
- a youth club may have a logo to identify themselves
- a church group may use a symbol from their faith
- a political party may use a symbol associated with their politics
- a trade union uses a logo with a message that reflects the objectives of the group.

Project

In groups, discuss a group you would like to form. It could be a sports club, a reading club – anything you like. In 400 words, write down four characteristics that you would like the group to have.

Size of groups ▶▶▶

Groups come in different sizes. They can vary from just two to many hundreds. The size of a group can also help to determine how well the group stays together.

- A **dyad** is a group of two. It is the smallest group. If one person doesn't cooperate, the group falls apart.
- A **triad** is a group of three. If there is conflict between two members, the third member may help the others reach a solution. If the members cannot agree, and one leaves, the group may continue to exist as a dyad.
- Larger groups have more than three members. In very large groups, the members may not even know each other. For example, some large companies have hundreds or thousands of members. The citizens of a large country such as China make up a group of more than a billion members.

Cub Scouts, Brownies and Girl Guides all wear uniforms to identify their group.

Exercise

3. Is it a dyad, a triad or a larger group?

   a) a school class **c)** a church youth group

   b) two girls in class **d)** three children from the same neighbourhood

4. Give an example of a dyad, a triad and a larger group that you belong to.

5. In groups, brainstorm ideas about characteristics of groups and see if you can think of at least two examples of each one. Put your ideas into a graphic organiser, like the one on page 112, to help formulate your ideas.

Key vocabulary

symbol

sanctions

structure

hierarchy

authority

dyad

triad

Different types of groups

We are learning to:

- identify different types of groups and their characteristics.

Primary groups »

The characteristics of a primary group include:

- They are small in size.
- The relationships are very personal and intimate.
- Contact often takes place, and is face-to-face.
- Because they are a small size, each member often interacts with all the others.
- They create a sense of belonging and loyalty.
- The bond between members is based on emotions.
- Members are accepted because of who they are and what they are like.

Primary relationships are often those first experienced in life and cannot be replaced. Examples are family and close friends, who provide each other with love, care and support.

A sports club is an example of a secondary group.

Secondary groups »»

The characteristics of a secondary group include:

- They are a larger size than a primary group.
- The relationships are less personal.
- Contact is less frequent, impersonal and more formal.
- Members only interact with some of the other members, but not all.
- Members may only be accepted if they contribute something to the group, like complete a task.

People join these groups based on shared interests and activities. Examples are sports groups and political organisations.

Exercise

1. Define primary and secondary groups.

2. Explain the difference between primary and secondary groups. Give an example of each.

3. Secondary groups are your family and friends. True or false?

Groups can be classified as formal or informal depending on their organisation, structure and characteristics. A formal group is often formed to fulfil a task or activity, while an informal group is made up of people with shared interests and likes.

A formal group has the following features:

- written rules – what the members must follow, and what happens if they do not follow the rules
- a clear division of work and power – who does what, and who takes responsibility and makes decisions
- a hierarchy or structure, which explains different levels of authority
- membership requirements – what to do to join and a procedure for replacing members
- fixed meeting times – when and where it meets
- organised activities – what the group does.

Examples are churches, schools, companies and service organisations.

An informal group has the following features:

- it is small to medium-sized
- it has goals but these are not usually written down
- activities can change quickly
- members usually know each other or have a personal connection to one another
- there is no strict structure; leadership may come from age, status, experience or who has been in the group the longest.

Examples are our families and friendship circles.

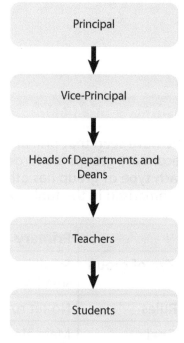

Principal

↓

Vice-Principal

↓

Heads of Departments and Deans

↓

Teachers

↓

Students

Example of hierarchy in formal groups.

Exercise

4. List groups that you belong to. Mark each group with 'P' for primary or 'S' for secondary. Are there more primary or secondary groups?

5. Write your own definitions of a formal and informal group and give one example of each.

6. What are the main differences between formal and informal groups?

7. Why do you think informal groups are usually small to medium-sized? (Think about what is needed for a larger group.)

Differences between groups

We are learning to:

- explain the differences between primary and secondary groups
- explain the differences between formal and informal groups.

Primary and secondary groups 》

We have seen that primary groups are small and close, while secondary groups are larger and are not as close or intimate. Each type of group has other differences and these are summarised in the table below.

	Primary	Secondary
Size of group	Small in size and confined to a small area	Large – can contain thousands of members
Rules	No set rules	Can have more formal rules
Goal	Main aim is to fulfil all the needs of its members; provides emotional benefits such as love, care, support and security	Aim is to satisfy the specific needs of its members; helps its members to complete tasks and goals
Activities	Emotional depth; activities are often spontaneous	Superficial relationships
Degree of interaction	Intimate, face-to-face, informal	Less intimate, not face-to-face, informal
Membership requirements	Share close, personal, intimate and long-lasting relationships	Temporary and voluntary
Structure/ hierarchy	Position in the group is according to birth, age or sex	Position in the group is by role
Examples	Family, the neighbourhood, close friends	Political parties, voluntary organisations, trade union, sport, cultural groups

Exercise

1. What are the main differences between primary and secondary groups?

2. Give an example of a primary and a secondary group.

3. Think of a group that you belong to. Is it a primary or secondary group? Why do you think this is?

4. Explain in your own words the goals of both a primary and a secondary group.

Formal and informal groups 〉〉〉

We have seen on page 109 that a formal group is often formed to fulfil a task or activity, while an informal group can be formed within the formal group and is made up of people with shared interests and likes.

	Formal	Informal
Size of group	Determined by the aims of the group, but are usually large	Tend to be small
Rules	Written rules with sanctions	There are no written rules
Goal	Clearly defined and lasting; can last for several years	Can change as activities change in the group; can have a short time span
Activities	Has organised activities, fixed meeting times	Activities occur spontaneously
Interaction	Interaction may be formal and limited	Is unstructured and open
Membership requirements	Must satisfy certain guidelines	No fixed criteria; members can join and leave very quickly
Structure/ hierarchy	Clearly defined hierarchical structure, with status, roles and clear lines of authority	No clear structure, with an unofficial leader
Leadership emergence	Leaders are **appointed or elected**	Leaders may come from age, status, experience or who has been in the group the longest.
Examples	Sports club, school, political party, trade union, scouts	Friendship groups in church, school, playing in the street

Exercise

5. What are the main differences between formal and informal groups?

6. Write approximately 250 words that explain the differences between two named groups in formal and informal or secondary and primary groups.

7. Which type of group shows the following characteristics?

   a) The meetings can be at fixed times.

   b) It has no clear structure.

   c) It can last for several years.

   d) It has written rules.

Key vocabulary

appoint

elect

Benefits of groups

We are learning to:

- explore the benefits of being a member of a group
- explain roles and responsibilities in groups and group cohesion.

Benefits of group membership

Each group is different. Members participate in groups for a wide variety of reasons. Let's look at benefits that groups offer their members and what happens when members no longer experience these benefits. Belonging to a group can bring a number of benefits to someone:

- gaining a sense of their own **independence**
- a sense of belonging is a strong part of being part of the group
- groups allow their members opportunities to display their talents or to learn new skills
- taking **responsibility** for their role within the group
- cooperating with other members of the group and working together as a team
- making well-informed decisions
- learning to resolve problems and differences
- helping create a sense of identity and understanding who you are and what you believe in
- accepting authority and being loyal to the group
- giving opportunities for leadership
- dealing with different personalities and being tolerant of others' views and ideas.

Exercise

1. Read the statements below. Match each statement to one of the factors above.

   a) "At my youth group, I feel like I am part of something."

   b) "My church group keeps me strong in my faith. That's part of who I am."

   c) "At my art club, I get to display my special talent for drawing."

   d) "My choir group has a lot of rehearsals. But we're all committed to attending every rehearsal. No one wants to let the others down."

Activity

You are the PRO (Public Relations Officer) of a community basketball group. Write an article for the school newspaper to highlight the benefits of being a member of the group.

It is important for a group to work well together to achieve their goals.

Roles and responsibilities ▶▶▶

In Book 1, we discussed the **roles** and responsibilities each member of a family plays and what happens when those roles and responsibilities are not fulfilled: the family cannot carry out its functions.

This applies to any other groups, no matter their size, whether they are formal or informal, primary or secondary.

Each person in a group has their own role and responsibility, and if everyone does not do their part it cannot function properly. For example, if you play on a sports team, and you don't turn up at the match, the team cannot play.

When any group members do not carry out their specific role or responsibility, it will become difficult for that group to achieve its goals.

Members will also start to lose their sense of belonging to the group and the group may break up.

Group cohesion is the group's ability to stick or stay together and last.

There are a number of factors which make good group cohesion:

- good communication and cooperation
- the same goals and interests
- commitment from the members
- a sense of belonging to the group
- a good strong identity for the group
- effective leadership
- plenty of opportunities to use new skills
- working together as a team.

School is an example of a formal group.

Discussion

As a class, discuss the benefits of belonging to a group.

Exercise

2. Think of a group you belong to. List three benefits of being in that group.

3. Write a letter inviting other students to join a basketball group. Outline the benefits of joining the group.

4. In your own words, define the terms role and responsibility.

5. Name three factors that contribute to group cohesion.

Key vocabulary

independence

responsibility

role

group cohesion

Overcoming group issues

We are learning to:

- examine ways groups can overcome issues that arise.

Issues within groups 》

Sometimes issues can happen within a group. There can be many reasons for this:

- People are individuals and sometimes they just disagree with each other or are not happy with other members' behaviour.
- Dissatisfaction with the leader – are the leaders capable of guiding the group? Are there opportunities for developing new leadership skills? Sometimes a leader can be too **controlling** and will not empower members to do the tasks that they should be doing.
- Lack of cooperation – do members cooperate well? If members do not cooperate, the group's aims will not be met.
- Members may be in **competition** with each other. For example, they both may want the same position of leader in the group.

We have seen how, if everyone fulfils their roles and responsibilities, the group will stay together. Those same factors which make a group cohesive can also create problems in a group:

- bad communication and lack of cooperation
- different goals and interests
- lack of commitment from members
- no sense of belonging
- lack of identity
- ineffective leadership
- lack of opportunities to use new skills
- not working together as a team, but as individuals.

People have to work together to achieve results.

Exercise

1. Give three reasons why you think issues can sometimes arise within groups.
2. Why do members of a group need to cooperate and work well together?
3. Choose three factors which should make a group cohesive but which can pull it apart. Suggest how these could be overcome.

Activity

A local group is having problems with lack of cooperation between its members to achieve its goals. In groups, discuss strategies to deal with this.

Ways to overcome issues

When issues begin within groups, they need to be dealt with quickly, so that they do not begin to affect the overall running of the group and put the aims of the group at risk. Resolving issues can involve:

- **Compromise** – this is finding a way between two conflicting members, opinions or ideas. Each side has to make a concession, meaning that they find common ground that they can agree on to *solve the problem* and reach their common goal.
- Talk to the leader of the group about the problem and ask them to resolve it. If the problem in the group is the leader themselves, then this needs to be discussed as a group with the leader.
- Cooperate more closely together and work together as a team to achieve the group's goals.

Compromising is often a balance of giving and taking.

Case study

We couldn't keep our charity group together

What kind of group did you start? A charity club.

What was it called? The Helpers.

Where was it based? At our school.

How many people were interested? Lots of students seemed interested, but only 12 came to the first meeting. Then it got smaller each time.

What were the problems? We couldn't agree how to start. Some people wanted to work with children and others wanted to work with elderly people. There were sub-groups that didn't agree with the rest of the group. The leader of the group made decisions the rest of the group did not agree with.

Questions

1. What factors caused the charity group to fail?

2. What should they have done differently?

3. What would you have done to make the charity successful?

4. Think of a problem you have experienced in a group you belong to. Create a comic strip of the issue and how it was resolved.

Key vocabulary

controlling

competition

compromise

Leadership

We are learning to:

- define the terms leader, leadership, power and authority
- state the qualities of a good leader.

What is a leader? >>

A **leader** is someone who leads or guides a particular group, and who is in overall charge of that group. A leader is someone the rest of the group follows.

Leadership is shown when the leader (or leaders) influence the group to achieve a common objective. Leadership has a direct impact on the way in which a group functions. It is important to have effective leadership that encourages cohesion within groups. When we talk about **leadership qualities,** we mean those personal qualities that make someone good at leading others.

Leadership qualities >>>

Good leaders must have good leadership qualities. A good leader should be able to:

- *communicate well* with the members
- be able to *deal with people*
- *set goals* for the group and *put members' needs* first
- *allocate resources* to achieve the group's goals
- *motivate and persuade* other members to achieve the group's goals
- be **honest**, *reliable* and *fair*
- be **responsible**
- *command respect* of the members and *be **respectful*** towards them
- be *open to and apply good ideas* from members
- be *influential* on how people think and act.

Exercise

1. Explain in your own words the terms leader and leadership.
2. Write a list of the qualities that you believe people need in order to become leaders.
3. Decide on the three most important qualities in a leader. Use the word cloud to help you.

Discussion

In groups, discuss the difference between power and authority.

honest trustworthy persuasive reliable disciplined having integrity selfless fair hardworking responsible respectful kind calm good communicator tolerant

Activity

Describe qualities a good leader should have. Write about 150 words.

Key vocabulary

leader

leadership

leadership qualities

honest

responsible

respectful

A good leader needs to have **power** in their group to make the group function. Power is the ability of one person or group to exercise influence and control over others.

Authority is the right to exercise power over others. There are three types of authority that we accept in free society:

- **Charismatic authority** – A charismatic leader has a strong personality and a special ability to inspire others. Groups follow this kind of leader because they want to, not only because a law or tradition tells them to.

- **Traditional authority** – Traditional leaders get their power from customs or traditions. Often, they are connected to the religious tradition of a country or group. Kings and queens are examples of traditional leaders.

- **Rational-legal authority** – In many groups, organisations and countries, people elect leaders into power by **voting**. They are voted into power, and when they resign, or when they no longer receive any votes, their authority ends.

Case study

Great leaders

Nelson Mandela is famous for helping to unite South Africa to end apartheid. He was a great advocate for peace and forgiveness, even though jailed for 27 years while doing this. Despite this, Mandela was able to gain the respect and trust of all his followers, and other world leaders, which helped South Africa to heal the wounds of apartheid.

Sir Grantley Adams was one of the great leaders of Barbados. He made a huge contribution to the nation, setting it on a path to independence. He worked hard to end the dominance of the plantation owners in the country, known as the 'plantocracy'. He is considered a national hero of Barbados, and the country's airport is named after him.

Questions

1. What type of leader do you think Nelson Mandela was?

2. What qualities as a leader did Sir Grantley Adams have?

3. Write your own definitions of the terms power and authority.

4. Explain in your own words the three types of authority in society.

Project

Find out more information about one of the leaders on this page. Consider the following:

- When were they born?

- Where did they come from?

- What was their most famous achievement?

- What qualities do you think they had?

- Why do you think they were successful leaders?

Nelson Mandela was imprisoned for 27 years in his fight to end apartheid in South Africa.

Key vocabulary

power

charismatic authority

traditional authority

rational-legal authority

voting

Types of leaders and their styles

We are learning to:

- identify different types of leaders and leadership styles
- differentiate between the different types of leaders and their characteristics.

Leadership types 〉

Leaders make decisions in different ways. There are three key leadership styles or types: democratic, authoritarian and laissez-faire.

Democratic leaders:

- discuss issues as a group and accept those decisions
- encourage and value opinions and feedback from members
- accept suggestions from the members.

Decisions can be slow to make, but they are democratic.

Authoritarian leaders:

- make all the decisions on their own and tell the group what to do
- do not give the members the opportunity to give their opinions or feedback
- do not accept suggestions from members.

Decisions may be quick and easy to reach, but not all members will always agree with them.

Laissez-faire leaders:

- let the group make its own decisions, in its own way
- do not enforce rules, and fail to discipline members.

This can be effective if the members are skilled, educated and do not need much direction, but may fail in the long term if members do not complete tasks or achieve their goals.

Ralph Gonsalves is the current Prime Minister of St Vincent and the Grenadines.

Exercise

1. Identify which leader would:

    a) make decisions the group would not like

    b) let the group run on its own

    c) share opinions and ideas with everyone in the group

2. Write your own definitions of the three types of leadership. Add them to your portfolio.

Research

Choose one of the types of leadership discussed, and research and find examples of the one you have chosen. For example, it could be a local group or a world leader. Write a short piece about the leadership type you have chosen.

The table below summarises the differences between the three leadership types.

Democratic	Authoritarian	Laissez-faire
discusses issues as a group	makes all the decisions on their own	no discussion
values opinions and feedback	no opportunity to give opinions or feedback	no discussion
accepts suggestions from members	does not accept suggestion from members	no discussion

Case study

Leadership types

A. Joanne is the chair of her local youth club. She has not attended a meeting for six months and has not organised a committee meeting in that time. The club is in urgent need of resources, but without a meeting nothing can happen.

B. Michael runs a book club. They meet every Tuesday night at a place and time he decides, and each week they read a book he has decided on.

C. Rianna runs a group in her community health centre which helps women who are pregnant with their first child. She asks the group what they would like to know and organises sessions around this.

D. George runs a local neighbourhood watch group and has heard there have been some problems in the area recently. He has arranged a meeting with the group to decide what they should do to help protect the neighbourhood.

Questions

1. Identify the leadership type in each of the scenarios in the case study.

2. Decide which case study these sentences describe:

   a) While discussions continue, a situation may get worse or the group may fail.

   b) Everyone can share their opinion and ideas.

   c) The leader may make decisions the group does not like.

3. Which type of leadership do you think is best suited to running a country? Why?

4. Look at the table above. In your opinion, which is the least effective leadership type. Why?

Key vocabulary
....

democratic leader

authoritarian leader

laissez-faire leader

The role of a leader

We are learning to:

- examine the role of leaders in groups
- defend the qualities of a good leader.

Role of leaders in a group

We have already looked at the qualities that a leader of a group should have (page 122), that they should be able to use their power and authority effectively (page 123), as well as the types of leader (page 124) and the differences between leadership types (page 125). But what is the role of a leader?

A leader has many roles to fulfil in a group. These help them to:

- achieve their goals or aims and allow members to be happy and comfortable
- represent the group they lead, both within the community and with other local groups, and to be a role model
- stay **focused**, give direction and provide guidance on achieving their goals
- **mediate** on issues which arise in the group
- keep a sense of order and structure within a group.

Each of these roles can be applied in our everyday groups – such as our youth group – but they can also apply to leaders who work in the community, at council level, government level or world leaders.

lead achieve goals represent community focused give direction give guidance mediate support issues keep order structure aims happy

Activity

Students work in groups to role-play a dramatic piece which highlights one role of a leader.

Exercise

1. Draw a mind map to illustrate what you understand by the role of a leader in a group. Use the word cloud to help you.

2. Add to the mind map the qualities a leader should have for each of these roles. See page 122 for ideas about qualities.

3. True or false? A leader's role is to:

   a) let a group get on with things in their own way

   b) mediate between members who disagree

   c) help the group achieve their goals

   d) help the group choose a different goal each week

Project

Roleplay a situation in which two students imagine that they are campaigning to be a leader of a formal group. Get them to reflect on the qualities they possess to be leader or wish to develop to become a leader.

Case study

Defending leaders

Being a leader is a difficult job. We have already seen that group cohesion is important for keeping a group together, but sometimes a group, and in particular the leader, can face unexpected problems or challenges.

Often it is not the leader who has caused the problem or difficulties, but they get criticised by the other group members anyway. Sometimes it is easier to blame the group leader, because they are in the position of leadership and authority, rather than to accept that the problems may have been caused by the group members.

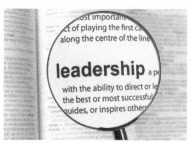

Leadership is the ability to give direction.

Matthew has been running a youth club group in his town for three years. The club has a committee which has six members, including Matthew.

All this time, Matthew has been managing the finance, finding venues and resources, and running the sessions. Some of the committee members are not doing their roles in the way they should be, but because Matthew enjoys the sessions with the children he has not said anything. All the children respect Matthew as their leader, and like him because he listens to them and lets them act out their ideas. The children's parents are happy with Matthew as the leader.

Two of the committee members want Matthew to be replaced as leader because they do not think he is running the club correctly. The children and parents have heard about this and are sad that Matthew may have to go. They are campaigning to let him continue as leader.

Research

Using books or the internet, research one famous leader and outline their achievements and role as a leader. Make a short presentation to the class.

Questions

1. What role does Matthew have at the youth club?

2. Do you think the group shows good group cohesion? Why/why not?

3. Do you think Matthew is doing a good job, or should he be replaced as the leader of the group? Why?

4. If you were Matthew, what would you do?

5. Why do you think it is difficult being a leader?

6. Your youth group is about to choose a new leader. Outline the three qualities you want this leader to have.

Key vocabulary
....

focused

mediate

127

Questions

See how well you have understood the topics in this unit.

1. Match the key vocabulary word with its definition.

   i) groups

   ii) informal group

   iii) formal group

   iv) leader

   v) leadership

   a) a group that has written rules, a clear division of work and power, and procedures for replacing members

   b) a group is made up of two or more people who do things together to achieve their common goals

   c) when a leader (or leaders) influences a group to achieve a common objective

   d) a group that does not have written rules or objectives or a strict hierarchical structure

   e) an individual who influences the behaviour or actions of another person, or who directs and guides a group towards decisions

2. Complete this table with the group type: school, social (family and friends), sports, cultural, religious, charity and community

Example	Group type
Family, close friends, school friends, neighbourhood friends, your class at school	
In-class or in-school clubs	
Church, mosque, temple	
Tennis club, soccer club, hockey club, swimming club, football team, cricket team, netball team	
Lions, Rotary, youth outreach clubs	
Drama group, debating club, Toastmasters, choir, orchestra or band	

3. Name four functions of a group.

4. Complete this sentence about the characteristic of a group: "Groups have _____ which may be seen in the members' clothing, which helps to identify the group within a wider society."

5. True or false?

    a) A characteristic of a primary group is its large size.

    b) A characteristic of a secondary group is that it meets less often.

    c) A characteristic of a formal group is that it has written rules to follow.

    d) An example of an informal group is your family.

6. Name four benefits of belonging to a group.

7. Give three examples of a problem that you can get in a group.

8. Explain why compromising is one way to solve group problems.

9. Which of these qualities should the leader of a group have?

    a) communicate well

    b) not able to deal with people

    c) be unreliable

    d) set goals for the group

    e) show respect

10. Match these terms with their definition:

    i) charismatic authority

    ii) traditional authority

    iii) rational-legal authority

    a) a form of leadership in which people come to a position of power through traditions or customs, because it has always been that way

    b) a form of leadership in which people come to positions of power through a fair system of rules and laws

    c) power that comes from one's exceptional personality or character, or powers of persuasion

11. Name three roles that a leader has in a group.

12. This word cloud shows some of the qualities a good leader should have. Take three of these words and write a sentence for each one describing the quality a leader should show.

honest trustworthy reliable persuasive having disciplined selfless fair integrity hardworking responsible respectful kind calm good communicator tolerant

Checking your progress

To make good progress in understanding different aspects of your personal development, check to make sure you understand these ideas.

Explain the term group.

Identify the different groups to which people belong.

Name the different categories of groups.

Explain the functions of groups.

Describe the characteristics of groups.

Explain the differences between groups.

Name the benefits of belonging to a group.

Examine how groups can overcome issues within groups.

Identify factors which help keep groups together.

Identify the qualities of a good leader.

Identify different types of leaders and leadership styles.

Examine the role of leaders in groups.

Unit 5: How we govern ourselves

In this unit you will find out

Introduction to government

- Explain the terms government, constitution, democracy, referendum, secession and anarchy
- Explain the main characteristics of a democracy
- Why we have a government
- What would happen if we had no government
- The structure of central government in the Eastern Caribbean
  - ○ the legislature
  - ○ the executive
  - ○ the judiciary
- The structure of local government in the Eastern Caribbean
- The functions of central and local government
- The systems of government in the Eastern Caribbean
  - ○ Crown Colony
  - ○ constitutional monarchy
  - ○ republicanism
- The electoral system
- History of governance in Grenada

Humanitarian law – promoting respect for humanity

- The Rule of Law
- What is humanity?
- How international and local agencies promote respect for humanity
  - ○ United Nations
  - ○ Amnesty International
  - ○ Variety, the Children's Charity, Barbados
- How we can show respect for others

Functions of government

We are learning to:

- define the relevant terms: government, constitution, democracy, referendum, secession and anarchy
- list the functions of a government.

Government ▷▷

A **government** is a group of people who manage the affairs or goals of a country, as well as regulating the activities of its society. In most countries today, governments are elected by the **citizens** of a country. The main functions of government include:

- making and enforcing laws to help maintain order
- providing economic policies that that will allow businesses to create jobs and provide services
- providing public services like education, health care, road building, and utilities such as electricity and water
- protecting its citizens with police and armed forces
- working with other countries to promote trade and international cooperation.

Democracies are countries in which all eligible citizens have an equal say or participation in the decisions that affect their lives.

Democracy ▷▷▷

Democracy is a form of government in which all **eligible** citizens have an equal say or participation in the decisions that affect their lives. Most Caribbean countries are democracies.

- Democracy is based on the **principles** of fairness, justice, respect and honour.
- Everyone should be treated equally and fairly, and with respect.
- There should be respect for the law, for human rights and for civil liberties.
- There should be free and fair elections to choose people who will govern.
- The people who are elected to serve should do so with honour and be held accountable for what they do.

Research

Work in pairs and do some research on recent referendums held in different countries. What question did the voters have to consider? What was the outcome of the referendum?

Exercise

1. Research and write your own definition of government and democracy. Add them to your portfolio.

2. What are the main functions of government? Think of an example from your country for each one.

Constitution >>>

The **constitution** is a written document that sets out the laws by which a country is governed. It outlines:

- how government is structured
- the powers of government
- the rights and responsibilities of its citizens
- how governments are chosen
- the role of the civil service.

Referendum >>

A **referendum** is an opportunity for eligible people to vote on a particular issue. Referendums play an important role in modern democracies, because they allow people to have a say in how they are ruled.

Secession and anarchy >>>

When a country or group separates from a larger group to which it belongs, this is known as **secession**. An example includes the withdrawal of Southern states from the federal union in 1860/61 at the start of the American Civil War.

Anarchy is when **law and order** break down in a country and is often characterised by an absence of government, political disorder, and confusion and lawlessness.

Discussion

The countries of the Caribbean have formed many groups to promote regional integration. Discuss what advantages or disadvantages integration could have for the region. Is your country part of the OECS or CARICOM? Discuss whether you think your country should secede from these groups.

Exercise

3. On which principles is democracy based?

4. Research and write your own definitions of constitution, referendum, secession and anarchy. Add them to your portfolio.

5. Complete this quiz by matching each term to the statement that fits best.

   i) government   a) the principles and laws by which a country is governed

   ii) democracy   b) when a country or group separates from a larger group or country

   iii) constitution   c) a system of government

   iv) referendum   d) the power and authority to rule a country

   v) secession   e) when law and order break down

   vi) anarchy   f) when people vote on an issue

Key vocabulary

government
citizen
democracy
eligible
principles
constitution
referendum
secession
anarchy
law and order

How democracies work

We are learning to:

- outline the main characteristics of a democracy
- explain non-confrontational ways to bring changes in government.

Characteristics of a democracy

The characteristics of a democracy include:

- that elections are fair and are open to all citizens of voting age
- the establishment of basic human rights and the protection of those human rights
- tolerance, cooperation and compromise; for example, citizens have the right to free speech and can form political parties unopposed
- the right to challenge a government's decisions.

Voters lining up in Trinidad to elect their government representatives.

An important characteristic of a democracy is **majority rule and minority right**. When decisions are made based on the majority of the population's wishes, this could easily lead to the oppression of those who did not agree or vote along with the majority. Minority rights keep this from happening by taking an individual's rights and needs into account along with the majority rule.

Direct and representative democracy

Democratic governments exist around the world and fall into the categories of **direct** and **representative democracies**.

- Direct democratic governments allow citizens of legal voting age to establish rules and laws, and permit citizens to directly participate in making public policy.
- Representative democracies use elected officials for rule-making, so it is more feasible for smaller communities.

Exercise

1. Explain in your own words the characteristics of a democracy.
2. Explain in your own words the two categories of democracy.

Discussion

In groups, use the internet to research either the conflicts in Syria or those in Venezuela. What type of democracy do they have in those countries? Why do you think it is the citizens who are suffering?

Characteristics of a representative democracy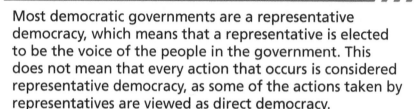

Most democratic governments are a representative democracy, which means that a representative is elected to be the voice of the people in the government. This does not mean that every action that occurs is considered representative democracy, as some of the actions taken by representatives are viewed as direct democracy.

The representative or governing body may put forward a mandate or referendum on a law, which can stem from meetings held by representatives in the area they represent or groups from the area requesting the changes. This can also apply to a nominee calling for votes to be re-counted in an election. These are all direct actions that do not proceed to be voted on by the people, although they can be requests or suggestions from them.

A representative democracy allows freedom of speech, the press and religion, allows personal liberties, and is a peaceful, non-violent way of running the country.

Non-confrontational ways to bring changes in government

Non-confrontational means dealing with situations in a calm, **diplomatic** manner that is not aggressive or threatening. In a political sense, this means bringing about changes by peaceful means, through:

- peaceful protests, marches or strikes
- writing protest letters
- forming pressure groups against the government
- having free and fair elections
- non-violent civil rights movements.

Exercise

3. Does your country have a direct or representative democracy?
4. Explain the characteristics of a representative democracy.
5. In what ways can changes in government be made by using non-confrontational means?
6. Draw mind maps showing features of a democracy.
7. Working in groups, brainstorm examples of the characteristics of a representative democracy in a Caribbean country of your choice.

Key vocabulary

majority rule and minority right

direct democracy

representative democracy

non-confrontational

diplomatic

The reasons for government

We are learning to:

- examine the reasons for having a government
- examine the consequences for citizens and a country if there is no government.

Why do we need a government? »

All **modern states** have governments, although they are not always the same. The governments cost a lot of money to run, so we need to ask ourselves, why do we need a government?

We need a government for the following reasons:

- Convenience – Humans are gregarious (social) beings. As such, it is more convenient and practical for a group of people to make rules and laws than for each member of the entire country to become involved.

- Qualification of leaders – All the people in a country cannot spend all their time making rules; instead, this authority is given to their leaders who are most qualified to do so.

- A group accomplishes more than an individual – As most governments comprise a group of persons, they are more able to get things done, because a group can accomplish jobs that are too big for one individual to do.

- Law and order – In order for a country or society to move forward, and for the citizens to have freedom to live without fear for their lives and property, there must be law and order. Selecting a government and giving it powers to make and maintain laws helps to ensure order in a country. Without a government, there would be chaos, confusion and anarchy in society.

Police officers help to protect the community.

Did you know...?

Governments help to make laws, enforce order, create economic policies; provide services like health, education, police, fire services, armed forces, transport infrastructure, water, electricity, rubbish and sewage collection, national security, leadership at home and abroad; and work towards the goals that the country would like to achieve.

Exercise

1. Write a paragraph of 300 words outlining why a country needs a government.

2. Why do you think it is easier to run a country as a group than as individuals?

3. What helps to ensure law and order in a country?

4. Create a mind map of all the services that a government provides.

Case study

What would happen with no government?

Can you imagine what it would be like if the government in your country was unable to provide:

- Laws – Who would protect you? It would be difficult to resolve conflicts in a peaceful way and people would be able to do as they pleased. Imagine if people were allowed to set up private armies and take any land that they wanted for themselves.
- Law enforcement – What would happen if there were no police? Who would look after the citizens?
- Economic policies – What would happen if there were no policies encouraging trade? How would the economy work? How would overseas deals be negotiated? Would there be any banks? Where would we keep our money?
- Basic services – Where would you get water? How you would you cook if you had no gas or electricity? How would you be able to watch television and surf the internet?
- Education – Where would you get your teaching from? What would happen if there were no rules at your school? What would happen if there were no school governors or local authority?
- Health care – What would happen if there were no hospitals, community care, doctors, maternity wards, chemists?
- Road regulations – What would happen if there were no traffic rules to ensure that people use roads in a sensible way? The roads would be chaotic. What would happen if there was an accident?
- Refuse collection – Imagine if people were allowed to throw their rubbish anywhere and no one collected and disposed of it.
- National security – What would happen if we no longer had the army and coastguards? Who would protect the country?

Questions

1. Work in groups and brainstorm this question: If there were no government, what would be the consequences for your country?
2. Create a mind map to record your ideas.
3. Choose the five most important reasons for having a government and present these to the rest of the class.

Discuss your ideas as a class and draw up an agreed list of reasons for having a government.

Research

Work in groups and find out what basic services the government provides in your area. Make a list of these services.

Bin bags waiting for collection and disposal – who would take care of these if no one collected them?

Key vocabulary

modern states

Structure of central government

We are learning to:

• describe the structure of central government in the Caribbean.

Composition of government »

Caribbean governments are divided into three branches – the **Legislature,** the **Executive** and the **Judiciary.** These three branches cooperate and interact but they also help to ensure fairness in the government. The three branches of the government operate according to the constitution of the country.

The Legislature »»

The Legislature is also known as the **Parliament**. The Legislature makes laws, approves national budgets, amends the constitution and monitors the executive actions of government. In some countries it is made up of two houses: the Upper House **(Senate)** and the Lower House **(House of Representatives)**. This is called a **bicameral system**.

The Senate is made up of appointed members usually selected by the Head of State. **Senators** are usually independent, which means they are not part of a particular party. However, they have knowledge and expertise that can be useful nationally. The **Representatives** are elected by the people and are part of particular political parties. Barbados and St Lucia have bicameral systems.

In some countries such as Dominica and St Vincent and the Grenadines there is only one house in the Legislature. This is called a **unicameral system**.

The Head of State »»»

In some countries the head of state is the **Governor-General**. In these countries the role is ceremonial as the Prime Minister usually has full authority. The Governor-General is the representative of the Queen. In other countries the **President** is the head of state, who does not sit in Parliament, but who has the power to call Parliament to a sitting, to extend the sitting of Parliament and to dissolve or end Parliament. The President exercises power in consultation with the Prime Minister and the leader of the Opposition.

Parliament Buildings in Bridgetown, Barbados.

Members of an **Electoral College** elect the President in a secret ballot. This Electoral College is made up of members of the Senate and the House of Representatives.

Exercise

1. Name the three branches of government in the Caribbean.
2. Write your own definitions of the Legislature, the Executive and the Judiciary. Add them to your portfolio.

Did you know...?

The idea of having three branches of government dates back to the time of the ancient Greeks.

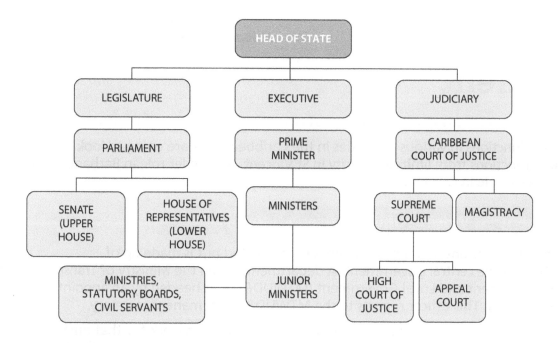

The Executive

The Executive is made up of Members of the **Cabinet**. The Cabinet consists of the **Prime Minister**, or head of government, and the other junior ministers and civil servants.

The Cabinet controls the government and provides direction and leadership. However, the Cabinet is responsible to Parliament and cannot carry out actions that are not approved by Parliament.

The Judiciary

The Judiciary is the branch of government that ensures that the laws are interpreted and applied fairly. These functions are the responsibility of the court system, which maintains law and order. It decides whether a person accused of breaking the law is innocent or guilty.

The following table summarises the three branches of government and the role of each branch.

Exercise

3. Which branch of government makes the policies that guide the actions of the government?
4. The Minister of Finance is part of the Cabinet. Research and name other ministers in the Cabinet. Discuss your findings as a class.
5. Work in groups and make a short presentation to the class on the structure of the government in your country. Use a diagram to illustrate your presentation.

Key vocabulary

Legislature

Executive

Judiciary

Parliament

Senate

House of Representatives

bicameral system

Senators

Representatives

unicameral system

Governor-General

President

Electoral College

Cabinet

Prime Minister

Structure of local government

We are learning to:

- describe the structure of local government in St Vincent and the Grenadines, Barbados and Guyana.

Local government functions in various capacities in the Caribbean. We are going to look at local government functions from limited capacity in St Vincent, to a wider role in Barbados and finally to a large-scale role in Guyana.

Local government: St Vincent and the Grenadines

Local government in St Vincent and the Grenadines is not elected but is made up of administrative arms of the central government. A department within the Ministry of Transport, Works, Urban Development and Local Government (MTWUD&LG), is headed by an appointed **local government officer**. This officer reports to the MTWUD&LG permanent secretary.

Each of the country's districts has a local government authority and a clerk for that authority who reports to the officer. Ultimately, through the local authority clerks, local government officer, and **Member of Parliament** for an area, consultations with citizens are held through village **councils** and town boards. Local authorities provide sanitation, road and infrastructure maintenance, community markets and collection of property tax on the behalf of central government.

Local government: Barbados

In Barbados, local government sits within the Department of Constituency Empowerment (DCE) within the Ministry of Social Care, Constituency Empowerment and Community Development. The **30 constituencies** (electoral districts) of the island are each represented by a **constituency council**.

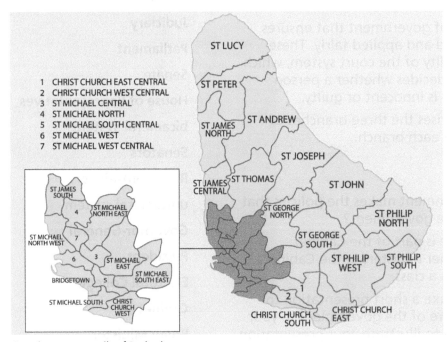

1   CHRIST CHURCH EAST CENTRAL
2   CHRIST CHURCH WEST CENTRAL
3   ST MICHAEL CENTRAL
4   ST MICHAEL NORTH
5   ST MICHAEL SOUTH CENTRAL
6   ST MICHAEL WEST
7   ST MICHAEL WEST CENTRAL

ST LUCY
ST PETER
ST ANDREW
ST JAMES NORTH
ST JOSEPH
ST JAMES CENTRAL
ST THOMAS
ST JOHN
ST GEORGE NORTH
ST PHILIP NORTH
ST GEORGE SOUTH
ST PHILIP WEST
ST PHILIP SOUTH
CHRIST CHURCH SOUTH
CHRIST CHURCH EAST

ST JAMES SOUTH
ST MICHAEL NORTH EAST
ST MICHAEL NORTH WEST
ST MICHAEL EAST
BRIDGETOWN
ST MICHAEL SOUTH EAST
ST MICHAEL SOUTH
CHRIST CHURCH WEST

Constituency councils of Barbados

Councillors are appointed after being vetted and recommended by senior civil servants. The constituency council is made up of 15 members from the community with relevant experience and links to special interest groups.

The council's roles include providing information to assist the government in allocating resources to address the needs and concerns of constituents, coordinating on larger projects and carrying out smaller community projects of their own.

Local Government: Guyana ⟫⟫

Local government in Guyana is a well-organised part of the country's governing structure. The **Municipal** and District Councils Act 1988 and the Local Government Act 1988 are laws that govern how local government functions. The Ministry of Local Government and Regional Development looks after this part of government. It links the local organisations to the central government and makes sure the local organisations are functioning according to the constitution. The local organisations are:

Regional Development councils (10 in total): provide education, health and agricultural support. They are headed by a Regional **Chairperson** who sets up advisory committees along with the main finance, works and social development committees.

Neighbourhood Democratic councils (65 in total): deal with waste collection, sanitation, roads, dams and markets. There are two essential committees: finance and works.

Municipalities (6 in total): deal with drainage, irrigation, waste collection and infrastructure maintenance. A **mayor** is in charge, and establishes the essential finance, works and social development committees and advisory **committees**.

Amerindian Village councils (75 in total): enable the indigenous people to manage their own affairs.

Regional development councils of Guyana

Key vocabulary

local government

local government officer

Member of Parliament

council

constituency

constituency council

councillors

municipal

chairperson

mayor

committees

Functions of government

We are learning to:

- identify and explain the functions of central and local government
- demonstrate awareness that service and caring are integral to the functions of good governance.

The functions of central and local government ⟫

Central government helps to make laws, enforce order, create economic policies, provide services like health and education, national security, and leadership at home and abroad.

Local government provides the basic services that we need for small geographic areas, such as a city, town, county or state. Local government receives grants from central government to provide services.

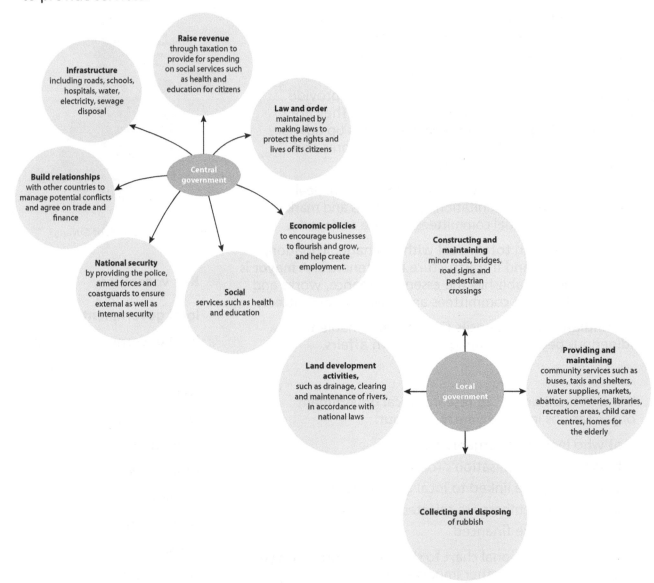

The **governance** of a country relates to the way that a country is governed, how public affairs are conducted and how public resources are managed by those in power and authority.

Good governance depends on a number of factors:

- its citizens taking part in deciding how the country is run through voting and knowledge of the political system of the country
- making sure the judicial system remains independent and fair
- assuring government is run in an open fashion and is seen to be above the abuse of power and authority
- seeing that the government of a country is held **accountable** and their decision making is checked for corruption or wrongdoing
- making sure the needs of the citizens are met by government – if they fail to do so, they will be voted out at the next election
- ensuring that citizens should be given access to information by government under freedom of information laws as to how resources and money are allocated and how decisions are made
- seeing that the government makes good use of its natural, human and financial resources for the benefit of the country
- making sure the functions of government are carried out efficiently
- ensuring that a country's constitution recognises that its citizens have basic human rights.

Project

Find letters in the local newspaper which comment on the central or local government's performance. Decide if they are happy with their performance or unhappy with it. Then, write a letter to the editor of the newspaper either praising or criticising the government's performance.

Exercise

1. In your own words outline the functions of central and local government.

2. Give three examples of services that are provided by **a)** central and **b)** local government in your country.

3. Who finances the services provided by local government?

4. In your own words describe what is good governance. Write about 50 words.

5. Why do you think governments should be held to account?

6. Research things that central or local governments do that are not part of their normal activities; for example, giving assistance to victims of natural disasters.

Key vocabulary

governance
accountable

Systems of government

We are learning to:

- describe the systems of government: Crown Colony and Constitutional Monarchy.

Crown Colony ⟫

Crown Colony Government was a system of government by which British colonies were ruled. It consisted of:

- a **Governor**: representing the Crown (monarch), he was the only one able to pass laws. The Governor had full power over all three branches of government: the Executive, Legislative and Judiciary.
- a **Council**: these were prominent members of society. They were chosen by the Governor to advise him, but they were unable to pass laws.

Ultimate power was kept by the monarch (Crown) in Britain and therefore a law passed by the Governor could be overturned by the Crown if the ruling monarch didn't agree with it.

Guyana was ruled under this system from 1796 to 1966, then became a **republic** in 1970.

St Lucia was a French Crown Colony from 1674 and switched hands between the French and the British until 1814 when it was declared a British Crown Colony under the Treaty of Paris. St Lucia became independent in 1979 and currently has a constitutional monarchy form of government.

```
┌─────────────────┐
│      CROWN      │
└─────────────────┘
         │
         ▼
┌─────────────────┐
│    GOVERNOR     │
└─────────────────┘
         │
         ▼
┌─────────────────┐
│ APPOINTED HOUSE │
└─────────────────┘
```

The organisation of government in a Crown Colony.

Constitutional monarchy ⟫⟫

There are some countries in the Caribbean that are constitutional or parliamentary monarchies. For example, Jamaica is a **constitutional monarchy** because it has a parliament and a monarch as the head of state. A **monarchy** is a system where a state can be headed by a monarch or sovereign. This is usually for as long as the monarch lives.

King George III was the King of England when Guyana was placed under British Crown Colony rule in 1796.

Exercise

1. Write a paragraph giving your own definition of a Crown Colony.
2. Between which years was Guyana ruled as a Crown Colony?
3. What system of government did St Lucia adopt in 1814?
4. In your own words, define the term monarchy.

In a **constitutional monarchy**, a **colony** has become independent from the colonial power. The Governor who was appointed by the colonial power is replaced by a Governor-General, who is now the head of state.

Although the Governor-General is head of state, they represent the monarch symbolically. They do not have any real power, having only limited constitutional powers.

The Prime Minister is in charge of the government and the Governor-General acts on the advice of the Prime Minister.

The Prime Minister holds the real power, as the government is responsible for the country's internal and external affairs.

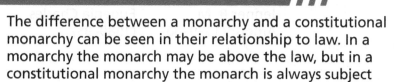

Difference between a monarchy and a constitutional monarchy

The difference between a monarchy and a constitutional monarchy can be seen in their relationship to law. In a monarchy the monarch may be above the law, but in a constitutional monarchy the monarch is always subject to law.

The countries in the Caribbean that are currently constitutional monarchies are: Antigua and Barbuda, Bahamas, Grenada, Jamaica, St Kitts and Nevis, St Lucia and St Vincent and the Grenadines. The United Kingdom is also a constitutional monarchy.

> **Did you know...?**
>
> The first British Governor of Barbados was Henry Powell (1627–28). Barbados became a republic on 30 November 2021.

Exercise

5. Write a paragraph outlining your understanding of constitutional monarchy.

6. True or false?

    a) In a constitutional monarchy, the Governor-General holds all the power.

    b) Guyana is a republic.

    c) A Crown Colony government has a Governor who holds executive, legislative and judicial power.

7. Research the various types of government that have existed in your country. Create a timeline of this and add short notes about the importance of these dates.

Key vocabulary

Crown Colony

Governor

republic

parliamentary monarchy

monarchy

constitutional monarchy

colony

Republicanism

We are learning to:

- describe the systems of government: Republicanism and British Overseas Territories.

Republicanism »

A republic is a country where the monarch has been replaced by a President as head of state. There are two types of republic:

- A presidential republic, where the head of state is also the head of government. The executive president has full constitutional powers. An example of this type of republic is Guyana.
- A parliamentary republic, where the head of state holds a ceremonial function and the Prime Minister is the head of government. As a result, the Prime Minister has executive authority. Trinidad and Tobago and the Commonwealth of Dominica practise such a system, and have limited constitutional powers.

Dominica became a republic on 3 November 1978. This event is celebrated through:

- Heritage Day: where each year a different village is celebrated and community members are awarded
- Creole Day: a day celebrated through wearing colourful national dress to celebrate unity and love of country
- Market Day: a celebration of local fruit, vegetables, flowers and products.

Presidents	Prime Ministers
Sir Louis Cools-Lartigue (1978–79)	Patrick John (1978–79)
Fred Degazon (1979–80)	Oliver Seraphin (1979–80)
Jenner B. M. Amour (1979–80)	Eugenia Charles (1980–95)
Aurelius Marie (1980–83)	Edison James (1995–2000)
Sir Clarence Seignoret (1983–93)	Rosie Douglas (2000)
Crispin Sorhaindo (1993–98)	Pierre Charles (2000–04)
Vernon Shaw (1998–2003)	Osborne Riviere (2004–04)
Nicholas Liverpool (2003–12)	Roosevelt Skerrit (2004–present)
Eliud Williams (2012–13)	
Charles Savarin (2013–present)	

The first **head of state (President)** of Dominica was Sir Louis Cools-Lartigue (acting). The first Prime Minister was Patrick John. The table shows a list of the Presidents and Prime Ministers of Dominica and the dates of their terms of office since it became a republic.

Exercise

1. Write a paragraph giving your own definition of republicanism.

2. How is independence celebrated in Dominica?

3. Draw a timeline to show the Presidents and Prime Ministers of Dominica from 1978 to the present.

Parliament Building, Dominica.

A British Overseas Territory is a former colony of the British Empire which has not been granted independence, or has chosen to remain a territory of Britain. In the Caribbean a number of British Overseas Territories exist: Anguilla, Bermuda, the British Virgin Islands, the Cayman Islands, Montserrat and Turks and Caicos.

These countries were formerly referred to as British Dependent Territories but are now known as British Overseas Territories following the British Overseas Territory Act of 2002. As a result of this Act, citizens of these countries by birth have access to full British citizenship and those who became citizens of these territories by marriage or through migration can apply for British citizenship.

The governmental structure for Caribbean British Overseas Territories is seen below:

- Queen Elizabeth II: head of state
- Governor: the Crown's representative in the territory handling foreign affairs and ceremonial roles. Has a much more active role in the affairs of the country than the Governor-General in a constitutional monarchy
- **Premier/Chief Minister**: elected democratically, usually because they are the leader of the winning political party in an election
- Cabinet: individuals appointed by the Premier to assist in handling the day-to-day running of the country. These people are called **Ministers** and the department they work within is called a **Ministry**.
- Legislature: functions in the same way as the legislature of constitutional monarchies
- Judiciary: usually there is a local legal system based on English common law.

Chief Ministers	Governors
Ronald Webster (1976–77, 1980–84)	1982–83: Charles Henry Godden
Emile Gumbs (1977–80, 1984–94)	1983–87: Alastair Turner Baillie
Hubert Hughes (1994–2000, 2010–15)	1987–89: Geoffrey Owen Whittaker
Osbourne Fleming (2000–10)	1989–92: Brian G. J. Canty
Victor Banks (2015–present)	1992–95: Alan W. Shave
	1995–96: Alan Hoole
	1996–2000: Robert Harris
	2000–04: Peter Johnstone
	2004–06: Alan Huckle
	2006–09: Andrew George
	2009–13: Alistair Harrison
	2013–17: Christina Scott
	2017–20: Tim Foy
	2021–present: Dileeni Daniel-Selvaratnam

Discussion

Why do you think the Prime Minister needs a Cabinet to assist in leading a country?

Exercise

4. Draw a diagram to show your understanding of the structure of the republican system in Dominica.

5. What is a British Overseas Territory?

6. List two things that the British Overseas Territories Act 2002 introduced.

7. How is the Premier/Chief Minister of a British Overseas Territory chosen?

Key vocabulary
....

head of state

President

Premier

Chief Minister

Ministers

Ministry

The electoral system

We are learning to:
* explain the electoral system.

Electoral systems

Elections are held at regular intervals that vary by country to choose people who will serve in national and local government. People are chosen according to an electoral process, which is described in the constitution of the state.

These are stages of the electoral process:

* Prime Minister announces the date for the election.
* Political parties nominate their candidates.
* Political parties draw up their manifestos and begin their election campaigns.
* Members of the **electorate** (voters/electors) check they are registered to vote.
* The electorate vote for the candidates of their choice on election day.
* Votes are counted and candidates with the highest number of votes in each constituency become members of the Legislature/Parliament.
* The leader of the party with the highest number of elected members of the House becomes the Prime Minister.
* Other members of the House form the Opposition.

An **elector** is a person who has the right to vote in an **election**. The electorate is all the people in the country who are eligible and registered to vote in an election.

A **candidate** in an election is a person who seeks to be nominated or elected to a position in the national or local government. If the candidate gets enough **votes** and is elected, they represent the people who have voted.

Research

Research the election results in your country for the last three elections to find out which political parties are most likely to win the vote in a particular area and which areas are more likely to change political party. Can you think of any reasons why a particular party may have strong support in certain areas?

Exercise

1. What is the difference between a candidate and an elector?
2. Describe the electorate of your country in one sentence.
3. Draw an organiser to show the stages of the electoral process.

Women display their red index fingers after casting their votes to elect a political party into government on election day.

First-past-the-post system ⟩⟩⟩

In many countries the **first-past-the-post system (FPPS)** is part of the electoral system. In FPPS:

- The country is divided up into constituencies. Each political party will nominate someone for each constituency.
- The candidate who gets the most votes is the winner.
- In some systems candidates have to win a majority of the votes, in other words, more than 50 per cent of the votes.
- The party that wins the most constituencies wins the general election and will form the new government.
- The Prime Minister or President is chosen from the winning party.
- The leader of the opposition is chosen from the party who has the second-highest number of seats.

Proportional representation ⟩⟩⟩⟩

In some countries candidates are elected through a system of **proportional representation**. In this system voters vote for a political party. Each party draws up a list of candidates for an election.

The number of candidates who are elected depends on the number of votes cast for the party. The chosen candidates are therefore not elected directly by voters in a constituency.

A man fills a billboard with preliminary results at a party headquarters during general elections.

Case study

Election time

Read the following results from an imaginary parliamentary election and answer the questions below:

Results	
Candidate A (Blue Party)	14 780 votes
Candidate B (Green Party)	17 890 votes
Candidate C (Red Party)	11 301 votes

Total number of votes cast: 43 971 votes.

Questions

1. Which political party won this seat in Parliament?
2. Did any candidate win a majority of the votes?
3. Which system was used to declare the winner of this election?
4. Create a graph to show the results of this election.
5. In your own words, explain both the first-past-the-post system and proportional representation. Do internet research to find the advantages and disadvantages of each system.

Key vocabulary

electorate

elector

election

candidate

votes

first-past-the-post system (FPPS)

proportional representation

Case study: History of Grenada's government

We are learning to:

- identify and explain the changes in government structure in Grenada.

Early people and colonial power

Grenada, like many islands of the Eastern Caribbean, has a very colourful past when it comes to its government. The first inhabitants are thought to have been a tribe known as the Arawak. Next, by the time of colonial exploration of the Caribbean, the Kalinago (or Carib) indigenous people inhabited the island.

The first attempts to settle the island were met with violence, but eventually in 1637 the French were able to settle after building a fortified settlement and engaging in negotiations with the local Carib chief to divide the land. Fighting between the French and indigenous people ended in French victory in 1654, after which point the entire island was controlled by the French. Up to 1664, private Frenchmen claimed ownership of the island. King Louis XIV then acquired the island and it became a French colony.

Almost one hundred years would pass before the British took control of Grenada during the Seven Years War in 1762, with the Treaty of Paris recognising British rule of the island in 1763. The French recaptured the island in 1779, and finally the island was returned to the British in 1783 with the Treaty of Versailles. At this time, the head of government was the Governor, under an old representative system of government.

Stamp from the Soviet Union bearing the image of Maurice Bishop.

One government for the British islands

In order to better manage their West Indian colonies, the British established Barbados as the main island for government purposes. This meant that the Governor of Grenada was now called the **Lieutenant-Governor** and was subordinate to the Governor of Barbados. In 1833, the islands controlled by the British were governed as the British Windward Islands Administration and the Lieutenant-Governor continued in his role. However, after Barbados left the group the role of **Governor-in-Chief** of the group moved to St George's, Grenada's capital, and Grenada became the seat of colonial government for the British Windward Islands until 1958, when the group was dissolved and replaced with the Federation of the West Indies.

Fort George, St George's, Grenada, was originally built by the French and named Fort Royal.

Crown Colony government >>>

In 1877 a British Crown Colony government replaced the old representative system. Under the old system there was a Governor, representing the monarch, a council of advisors and an assembly. The three passed laws as a group and usually the assembly, made up of plantation owners, made laws to benefit themselves and keep the masses under their control. Sometimes these laws even ignored the will of the monarch. Under the Crown Colony government, the assembly was removed; only the Governor and his council remained, and only the Governor could pass laws. This restored some power to the Crown.

In 1925 the constitution was modified to allow Grenadians to vote for five of the fifteen council members. The vote was restricted to wealthy landowners. In 1950 this elected number increased to eight members and all adults were allowed to vote. The Grenada United Labour Party, led by Sir Eric Gairy, won six of these eight seats. In 1960 another step away from Crown Colony government was taken when the post of Chief Minister was added to the constitution. Herbert Blaize of the Grenada National Party became Chief Minister, as he was the leader of the majority party in power. After the Federation of the West Indies failed in 1962, Grenada became an **'associated state'** of the British Empire as part of the 1967 Associated Statehood Act. The Chief Minister became the Premier, and the country gained full control of its own affairs.

Independence and communism >>

Grenada became independent in 1974 and a constitutional monarchy was introduced, with Sir Eric Gairy as the first Prime Minister. Political unrest resulted in an armed coup in 1979, led by Maurice Bishop. The constitution was suspended and the **communist** People's Revolutionary Government was established, with Bishop as its leader. In 1983 internal struggles led to the execution of Bishop and the establishment of a military government. Six days after the death of Bishop, the United States of America invaded Grenada, overthrew the government and restored democratic elections.

Research

Research and write a report describing the changes in government in your country, and the events that influenced those changes. Try to analyse the information you collect:

a) Did changes happen slowly and in small steps or very suddenly?

b) Who were the important people involved?

c) Compare and contrast what you discover with what happened in Grenada.

Exercise

1. Draw a timeline showing who governed Grenada up to the year 1783.

2. Which two groups was Grenada's government a part of while it was under British Crown Colony government?

3. What are two differences between the old representative system and Crown Colony government?

4. Why did the US invade Grenada in 1983?

Key vocabulary

Lieutenant-Governor

Governor-in-Chief

associated state

communist

The Rule of Law

We are learning to:

- define and explain the terms Rule of Law and humanity
- describe how the Rule of Law protects the rights of others and promotes respect for humanity.

What is the Rule of Law?

The **Rule of Law** is the simple principle that no one is above the law. This applies to all people and institutions of a particular country. A democratic country should have a Rule of Law – if it does not have one, then that country is not being run in a democratic way. The Rule of Law suggests that:

- no one can be punished or made to suffer unless a breach of law is proved in an ordinary court
- no one is above the law and everyone is equal before the law regardless of social, economic or political status
- the Rule of Law includes the results of judicial decisions determining the rights of private persons.

The Rule of Law helps to protect the rights of a country's citizens and promotes respect for humanity.

World Human Rights Day is on 10 December each year. It commemorates the day in 1948 when the United Nations adopted the Universal Declaration of Human Rights.

What is humanity?

Humanity is the characteristic or quality of being kind, thoughtful and sympathetic towards others. Democracy is a core value of many countries and organisations around the world, including the United Nations, of which Trinidad and Tobago is part. A key part of a democratic country is the respect for human rights and freedom for its citizens.

A definition of human rights is that they are "rights inherent to all human beings, whatever our nationality, place of residence, sex, national or ethnic origin, colour, religion, language, or any other status. We are all equally entitled to our human rights without discrimination."

Exercise

1. In your own words define the terms Rule of Law and humanity.
2. List the groups of people who are entitled to human rights without discrimination against them.

Discussion

In groups, discuss the definition of 'human rights'. Why do you think that there is a World Human Rights Day each year?

Most countries have a written constitution which outlines its citizens' rights. You can find out about all your rights as a citizen by reading your country's constitution.

Case study

The Constitution of St Lucia

Read this extract from the Constitution of St Lucia.

Whereas the People of Saint Lucia

a) affirm their faith in the supremacy of the Almighty God;

b) believe that all persons have been endowed equally by God with inalienable rights and dignity;

c) recognise that the enjoyment of these rights depends upon certain fundamental freedoms namely, freedom of the person, of thought, of expression, of communication, of conscience and of association;

d) maintain that these freedoms can only be safeguarded by the rule of law;

e) realise that human dignity requires respect for spiritual values; for private family life and property; and the enjoyment of an adequate standard of economic and social well-being dependent upon the resources of the State;

f) consider that individually, each person has duties towards every other and to the community and is under obligation to observe and promote the rights, freedoms and values recognised in this constitution;

g) desire that this Constitution shall reflect and make provision for ensuring and protecting these rights, freedoms and values.

Exercise

1. Draw a mind map that summarises the principles of the Constitution of St Lucia above.

2. Which of these rights and freedoms do you think are the most important in your lives? Try to rank these rights and freedoms in order of importance.

Key vocabulary

Rule of Law

humanity

Promoting respect for humanity

We are learning to:

- describe how international and local agencies promote respect for humanity.

Several organisations around the world have been set up to help people. Organisations like the United Nations and Amnesty International are a few international examples.

United Nations

The **United Nations** (UN) was founded in 1945, shortly after the end of World War II, to help and maintain international peace and security. The UN has since actively encouraged international cooperation. It does this by working to prevent conflict and helping parties in conflict to make peace, have peacekeepers and get conflicting parties together. Since then, its aims have extended to:

- protect **human rights** worldwide
- deliver humanitarian help when it is needed; for example, to help those displaced by famine, war or natural disaster by supplying food, water and shelter
- promote sustainable development, to help provide prosperity and economic development, promote greater wellbeing and protection of the environment
- uphold international law, by work carried out by courts, tribunals and treaties, and to impose sanctions when there is a threat to international security and peace.

There are currently 193 countries that are members of the UN, including Trinidad and Tobago, who joined in 1962.

Amnesty International

Amnesty International was founded in 1960 and is an organisation that campaigns for **justice** wherever in the world it has been denied or abused.

- They defend people's right to freedom, truth and **dignity**, and also protect people from injustice.
- They also investigate and expose abuse, and encourage all people, governments, political organisations and businesses to remember that individuals have human rights, which should be supported.

The United Nations symbol.

Activity

Write an essay entitled 'Why I would like to be employed with the United Nations'.

'We are about Donatella, our Syria researcher who has repeatedly braved the dangers in the country to collect evidence of war crimes – driven by her commitment to gather independent information and bring those responsible to justice.' (Amnesty International)

Case study

Variety, the Children's Charity

Variety, the Childrens' Charity of Barbados, was registered in November 1984. The charity raises funds for sick, disadvantaged and disabled children in Barbados and the Eastern Caribbean.

December 2015:

> Variety, the Children's Charity of Barbados and Beacon Insurance is one example of a charity and a business coming together to bring cheer to 250 children this Christmas.
>
> Donnah Russell, Executive Director of Variety, the Children's Charity of Barbados, noted that the charity's annual Christmas party was hosted by Beacon Insurance this year. She thanked Beacon for their generous support at a time when it was most needed and welcomed them on board the Variety family.
>
> The party is a part of Variety's Future Kids programming, which seeks to give children the gift of social experiences and play. For many of them, watching the feature film *Peanuts*, compliments of Olympus Theatres, was their first time at the movies.
>
> During the film the children were treated to popcorn, drinks and snacks, including the Christmas traditional ham cutter. The day's activities also included disco dancing and a visit from Santa, who handed out treats. As the children left the cinema they were presented with a loot bag from Beacon Insurance.
>
> https://www.varietybarbados.org/beacon-shines-light-at-christmas-for-variety-kids/

Questions

1. What are the aims of Variety, the Children's Charity?
2. Why was Variety set up?
3. Describe what Variety did for local children at Christmas in 2015.
4. Use the internet to research more information about Variety, Barbados.
5. Research the functions of all the agencies discussed and add them to your portfolio.
6. Why do agencies like these need to be set up?

Project

Work in groups. You have been asked to set up an organisation to help people in your country.

a) Decide who you would like to help.

b) Decide what your aims are.

c) Give your organisation a name.

d) Give your organisation a logo.

Variety, the Children's Charity of Barbados.

Key vocabulary

United Nations

human rights

Amnesty International

justice

dignity

Promoting respect for humanity

We are learning to:

- explain how an individual can show respect for others.

We discussed in Form 1 that having **respect** for something or someone can mean admiring them. We respect the achievements of a great sportsperson, for example.

But respect also has a more important side to it. Respect means recognising the **rights** and feelings of other people and not wanting to harm them. We respect other members of our families, our religious leaders and other people. By respecting other people in our community and country, we help to create a great country.

Respect should be shown to everyone in the world.

How can we show respect for other people's feelings?

There are many ways we show respect to other people, whether it is at home, school or in the community:

- Respect other people's opinions, ideas and beliefs.
- Don't insult people or make fun of them.
- Listen to others when they speak (and don't interrupt).
- Be considerate of people's likes and dislikes.
- Don't talk about people behind their backs.
- Be sensitive to other people's feelings.
- Don't pressure anyone to do something they don't want to.
- Be as helpful as you can be in a situation.
- Congratulate someone for something well done.
- Remember to say 'Please' and 'Thank you'.
- Cooperate and work together.
- Treat others as you would want them to treat you.

Exercise

1. Write your own definition of respect. Add it to your portfolio.
2. With your partner, brainstorm five ways you can show respect at school and at home.
3. How many of the ways to show respect have you done today? See how many you do this week.

Activity

Write slogans for ways to show respect for other people's feelings and differences. Your teacher will display these in the class.

Case study

Respect

A At home

Joanne and Michael have been married for 15 years and live in their home with their three children – Lisa, Ava and the eldest, Richard, who is 13. Recently, Richard has been staying out late, has not been doing his homework and has started to miss days at school. Michael noticed that a small amount of money had gone missing.

His parents are worried about what is happening. When they tried to talk to Richard about his behaviour, he got very angry and started to shout at this parents, told them it was none of their business and ran out of the house.

B Community

George and Floyd were good friends and had always done things together. When they started the second year of secondary school, they met a group of boys in the neighbourhood and would meet up with them after school. Sometimes they would pitch marbles in the street or play football.

After a while, George and Floyd started to get bored, but there was nowhere else to go. However, they heard that a youth club may be starting in the community, but didn't know when or where.

One night after school they met the group of boys in the neighbourhood and, while they were playing football, the ball got kicked through an old hall's window. One of the boys broke in to get the ball, but while they were inside the boys messed up the hall and left it in an awful state.

The next day George's mum told him she had found out where the new youth club was meeting. After school, George and Floyd went to the club, but when they got there they realised it was the same hall the group of boys had messed up. They were terribly ashamed, but didn't say anything.

Questions

1. What do you think the moral of these stories is?
2. How do you think Richard should have behaved to his parents?
3. Why did George and Floyd feel ashamed?
4. Choose five words from the word cloud that you feel best describe respect.

admiration compliment courtesy generous look up to please regard appreciate sincere dignity honour polite cooperate value considerate help esteem kind popular listen thank you

Key vocabulary

respect

rights

Questions

See how well you have understood the topics in this unit.

1. Match the key vocabulary word with its definition.

   i) government
   ii) constitution
   iii) democracy
   iv) secession
   v) anarchy

   a) the principles and laws by which a country is governed
   b) when a country, or a group, separates from a larger group
   c) a group of people, usually elected, who have the power and authority to manage the affairs of a country
   d) a system of government in which a country's citizens choose their rulers by voting for them in elections
   e) when the absence of a government causes a breakdown of law and order in a society

2. Which of these is a characteristic of a democracy?

   a) unable to question government decisions
   b) the rights of a country's citizens to choose their own government representatives at regular periods
   c) that elections are closed to the public

3. Name two reasons why we need a government. Write 50 words.

4. Name five services that we would not have if we had no government.

5. Name the three branches of government in the Caribbean.

6. Identify whether the following are functions of central or local government:

   a) providing services such as buses, taxis and shelters, water supplies and markets
   b) infrastructure including roads, schools, hospitals, water, electricity, sewage disposal
   c) constructing and maintaining minor roads
   d) collecting and disposing of rubbish
   e) law and order is maintained
   f) social services such as health and education

7. Name the two regional governmental groups that Grenada was part of during colonial rule.

8. Complete this sentence: The _____ is the simple principle that no one is above the law.

9. What is involved in the independence celebrations in Dominica on:

   a) Heritage Day

   b) Market Day

   c) Creole Day

10. Match the Prime Ministers of Dominica (i–vii) to their years (a–g) in office.

    i) Rosie Douglas

    ii) Roosevelt Skerrit

    iii) Oliver Seraphin

    iv) Patrick John

    v) Osborne Riviere

    vi) Edison James

    vii) Eugenia Charles

    a) (2004–04)

    b) (2004–present)

    c) (1978–79)

    d) (2000–04)

    e) (2000)

    f) (1995–2000)

    g) (1979–80)

11. What is a British Overseas Territory? List the British Overseas Territories in the Caribbean.

12. Complete the map to show the 10 regions of Guyana.

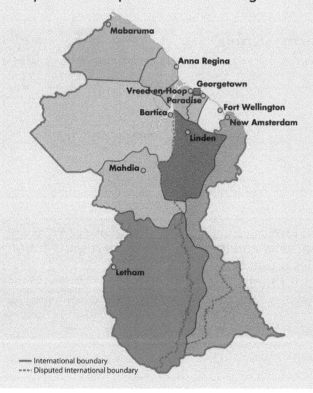

— International boundary

---- Disputed international boundary

Checking your progress

To make good progress in understanding how we govern ourselves, check to make sure you understand these ideas.

Name the main characteristics of a democracy.

Explain why we have a government.

Explain what would happen if we had no government.

Explain the structure of central government in the Caribbean.

Explain the structure of local government in St Vincent and the Grenadines, Barbados and Guyana.

Explain the functions of central and local government.

Describe systems of government in the Caribbean.

Explain the electoral system.

Explain the history of governance in Grenada.

Explain what is meant by the Rule of Law and humanity.

Explain how international and local agencies promote respect for humanity.

Explain how we can show respect for others.

Unit 6: My community

In this unit you will find out

My community
- The path to colonialism, life as a Crown Colony
- The transatlantic slave trade, emancipation
- Immigration and indentureship
- Diversification and unification within the Leeward Islands

Sources of historical data
- Primary sources

Historical sites and landmarks
- Historical sites and landmarks in the region
- The origins and significance of historical sites and landmarks
- Evaluation of multiple sources of information

Social composition of the region
- Historical factors that have contributed to the social development of the region
- The impact of historical events such as
  - enslavement, indentureship, inter-island migration
- The social development of various communities:
  - gender, race, class
- The value of diversity in various communities

Economic development of the region
- Historical factors that have contributed to the economic development of the region
- Development of industries, such as sugar, rice, cocoa, oil
- Comparison of the economic development of various communities
  - life in the village and the city

The path to colonialism

We are learning to:

- define and apply various concepts: colonialism and Crown Colony.

Colonialism

Colonialism occurs when a powerful country, such as Britain, directly controls less-powerful countries, such as the islands of the Caribbean, and uses those countries' resources to increase its own power and wealth.

The path to colonialism

The islands of the Caribbean changed hands among different European powers, including Britain, France and Holland.

For example, St Lucia and Grenada changed hands back and forth between the British and the French.

The French established plantations with the use of enslaved African people on both islands. The British took control of Grenada through the Treaty of Versailles in 1783 and of St Lucia through the Treaty of Paris in 1814.

After the British gained control of the islands they began to **exploit** their natural resources. Raw materials, such as sugar, were exported back to Britain to be refined, and the islands became more reliant on imported goods.

To maximise the opportunity for wealth, the British, like the French, brought in large numbers of enslaved African people to work on the plantations. The Africans were subjected to terrible conditions on their journey. Many died making the crossing from Africa.

Cane cutters on a sugar cane plantation, Barbados.

Project

Throughout this unit you will create a timeline of events. Add short notes about the importance of the dates.

Did you know...?

Before Trinidad and Tobago became a unified state, Tobago was colonised by the European colonial powers of France, Holland and Britain 22 times in total.

Exercise

1. In your own words, define the term colonialism.

2. List the different European countries that colonised the islands of the Caribbean.

3. How did the British exploit the islands of the Caribbean for commercial gain?

Life as a Crown Colony 〉〉〉

All the British colonies in the Caribbean were given the status of Crown Colony with the exception of Barbados. The ruling system of a Crown Colony was made up of:

- a Governor, who ruled the island and represented the British Crown in London
- a Legislative Council, chosen by the Governor to help him run the island.

Before Crown Colony rule the colonies were ruled by a representative system of government. This allowed for wealthy **planters** to be elected by virtue of their ownership of property to an Assembly, which administrated the affairs of the colony under the authority of a Governor.

With the coming of Crown Colony government the Assemblies were dissolved and wealthy planters were nominated by the Governor to serve on the Legislative Council.

Neither the representative system nor the Crown Colony system of government were truly representative of all the people in the colonies. They only represented the wealthy planters.

With the end of enslavement and immigration, Black and Indian people demanded a voice in the running of the government. They expressed their discontent through strikes, riots and the formation of trade unions and political parties.

John Pope Hennessy, Governor-in-Chief of the Windward Islands, 1873–77.

Exercise

4. In your own words, explain the term Crown Colony.

5. Who made up the Assembly under the representative system of government?

6. Do you think colonialism was good or bad for the islands? Write 100–150 words.

7. Start your timeline by adding any key information you have studied.

Key vocabulary

colonialism

exploit

slaves, enslaved people

planters

The transatlantic trade of enslaved people

We are learning to:

- define and apply various concepts: transatlantic trade of enslaved people and emancipation.

Africans come to the Caribbean

The **transatlantic trade of enslaved people**, originally known as **the transatlantic slave trade**, was the transportation of people from Africa to the American continent to be sold as enslaved people in the 17th to 19th centuries. An estimated 10 million people were forcibly removed from Africa, enslaved, and taken to provide labour on sugar, cocoa, coffee and cotton plantations.

Life on the plantation was harsh. Enslaved people worked for ten hours per day, for six days of the week. Some worked in the field, planting, cutting and harvesting sugar cane. Others worked as domestics in the planters' houses, cooking, cleaning, washing and taking care of the planters' children. Others worked as blacksmiths, masons or factory workers.

The enslaved person was the property of his or her master. Enslaved people had absolutely no rights or freedom. They had no physical, economic, political, social or religious freedom.

The enslaved African people came from Central and West Africa, in particular the Hausa, Yoruba, Congolese, Igbo and Malinké communities.

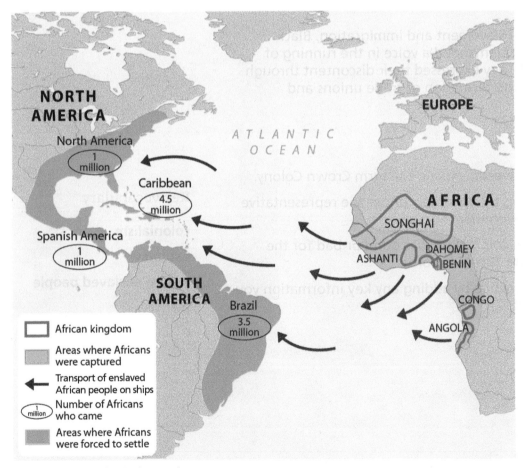

Map of the transatlantic slave trade.

Emancipation »»

Emancipation is the removal of restraint or restrictions on an individual or a group of people. The trade of enslaved people was a very profitable business for nearly 300 years. Enslaved people all over the world were treated with great cruelty. They were forced to do hard manual labour and live under terrible conditions. So why did this end? There were humanitarian, intellectual and economic reasons for this.

- Strong moral convictions led people to believe that slavery was an **inhumane** practice.
- People were also becoming more aware of humanitarian ideas like liberty and equality, and the concept that everyone should have these rights, not just a few privileged people.
- Economists argued that enslaved people's labour was inefficient, and that the cost of having enslaved people was more expensive than paying for hired help.
- Economists wanted **free trade** policies, which meant buying from the cheapest supplier. Sugar from the plantations where enslaved people were forced to work was more expensive than sugar from other countries, where labourers were paid for the work they did.
- Plantation owners had begun to face competition from the sugar beet industry in European countries.

In Britain, a Member of Parliament called William Wilberforce heard about the terrible conditions under which enslaved people were brought to the West Indies. He introduced a bill in the British Parliament to stop the practice of slavery in the British Empire. He died soon after the law was passed.

On 1 August 1834, the Emancipation Bill came into effect. This **abolished** slavery in the British Empire, including the British colonies in the Caribbean. Today, most former British colonies in the Caribbean celebrate Emancipation Day on 1 August or the first Monday in August.

William Wilberforce is remembered for his campaigns to stop the trade in enslaved people.

Discussion

Discuss this question in groups: 'If you had been a plantation owner, would you have supported or opposed the abolition of slavery? Why/why not?'

Exercise

1. Explain in your own words what led to the emancipation of enslaved people.
2. How did the ideas of liberty and equality affect people's attitude to enslavement?
3. Imagine you are an enslaved person working on a sugar plantation in the Caribbean. In 150 words write about your experiences.

Key vocabulary

transatlantic trade of enslaved people

emancipation

inhumane

free trade

abolish

Immigration and indentureship

We are learning to:

- define and apply various concepts: immigration, indentureship, belief systems.

Indentureship ⟩⟩

When slavery was abolished in 1838, most of the enslaved people left the plantations to set up their own small farms and industries. This meant that there were not enough people to work on the plantations and this affected the economy of the islands.

The plantation owners approached the British government to set up an **immigration** system to help with the labour shortage. This became known as **indentureship**. The **immigrants** came on a voluntary basis, unlike the earlier enslaved people, who were forced. Indenture was a system where persons gave their labour willingly and were bound by a contract to work for an employer for a fixed term, usually on the plantations. Upon completion of the contract, they were free to go.

Europeans came from Scotland, Portugal, Malta and Germany to the Caribbean. They were often destitute or homeless and came to start a new life. Immigrants from China also came to the Caribbean and settled mainly in Jamaica, Trinidad and Guyana.

Most of the immigrants at this time came from India. Between 1845 and 1917 about 416 000 East Indians came to the Caribbean under the indentured labour system. The indentured system came to an end in 1917.

Some Indian immigrants decided to stay and make the Caribbean their permanent home after they had completed their indenture. They brought their families to the islands, bought land and started their own businesses. For example, today the descendants of these labourers make up 35 to 40 per cent of the population of Trinidad and Tobago.

1839: First European immigrants arrive

⟱

1845: First Indian labourers arrive in Trinidad aboard the ship *Fatel Razack*

⟱

1852: Chinese immigrants arrive in Jamaica

⟱

1917: System of indentured labour comes to an end

Did you know...?

One scheme allowed male Indians who had lived in Trinidad for 10 years to get 10 acres of Crown land instead of a free return to India.

Exercise

1. In your own words, define **a)** immigration and **b)** indentureship.

2. Write a short explanation of the differences between slavery and indentureship.

3. Explain briefly why indentured labourers came from India to the Caribbean.

Research

Work in pairs. Find out more about an Indian or Chinese family that came to work in the Caribbean. Complete this for homework.

There are many factors that contributed to the end of the system of indenture. For example:

- Nationalism in India. India was a British colony at this time and a **nationalist** movement was taking root. Leaders like Mahatma Gandhi and Gopal Krishna Gokhale questioned the system of indenture.

- Humanitarian ideas. In 1911, the Government of India issued a statement about the indenture system. It said that "more and more [people] were coming to believe that the system is objectionable and should be discontinued".

- Unhappiness about working and living conditions. Workers were unhappy with their low wages and the lack of jobs, and some blamed the indenture system for this. The Indian immigrants were also finding work on the plantations less and less attractive. Although governments put systems in place to protect the immigrant workers, they were not very effective.

- The living conditions of the immigrants were poor, they were not able to move around freely, and many workers were mistreated and punished severely for minor offences. Eventually this led to clashes with the authorities.

- The Indian immigrants started to leave the big plantations to become small independent sugar farmers. For example, by 1902, more than half the sugar produced in Trinidad was produced by these independent farmers.

- Disruptions caused by World War I. From 1914 until 1918, the world was at war. This caused disruptions in shipping, which meant that workers could not travel safely between India and the Caribbean.

Newly arrived Indians in Trinidad, circa 1897.

> **Did you know...?**
>
> Indian Arrival Day is celebrated on 30 May every year in Trinidad and Tobago – the first country to start this holiday.

Exercise

4. Explain in your own words the factors that contributed to the end of the indentured labour system.

5. Work in pairs. Make a poster that shows the cultural influence of these Indian immigrants on the islands of the Caribbean. Think about food, music, names and businesses.

6. Take key dates from the information you have studied and add them to your timeline.

Key vocabulary

immigration

indentured/indentureship

immigrant

nationalist

Peasant farming

We are learning to:

* define and apply various concepts: peasantry and migration.

Farming after emancipation – peasant farming 》

In the aftermath of emancipation, there was a mass **migration** of formerly enslaved people within the Caribbean. This was caused by:

* movement after indentureship periods had expired
* peasantry farming causing internal migration of formerly enslaved people and past indentured immigrants.

Peasant farmers acquired post-emancipation land through:

* being allowed to stay on estate land
* saving money, or pooling resources to buy land
* renting small areas of land
* squatting on land owned by the Crown.

Drying cocoa beans, Douglaston Estate, St John, Grenada.

This was the beginning of **peasant farming** in the Caribbean, which is basic small-scale farming for subsistence, with any surplus being sold in local and regional markets. Produce from peasant farmers in Grenada and St Vincent was sold at markets in Trinidad.

Peasant farmers were able to cultivate crops or buy equipment with little or no initial expense. The formerly enslaved people left the plantations to form independent peasant communities and free villages.

A wood engraving of a cocoa plantation in Grenada, 1856.

The new peasant farmers mostly reared livestock, grew vegetables and cultivated various crops. Examples include:

* yams, cassava, corn, coconuts and peas
* sugar, cocoa, bananas, arrowroot, nutmeg and coffee
* poultry and other livestock.

As the peasant farmers produced more livestock and food, they were able to sell their extra produce at the local markets.

Exercise

1. Define peasant farming. How did peasant farmers acquire their land? Give three examples.
2. Make a list of crops grown in the Caribbean after emancipation. Find out more about one of the crops on the list. What does it look like? How is it grown?

The role of women in peasant farming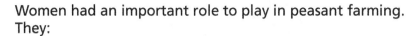

Women had an important role to play in peasant farming. They:

- worked alongside the men doing the farming
- looked after the animals
- carried and sold goods at market
- earned additional money for the household by taking on sewing or washing duties
- raised the children and kept the house.

Case study

Peasant farming in Grenada

In his book *Grenada: Island of Conflict*, author George Brizan recorded these observations about peasant farming in Grenada:

After 1838 the peasantry grew in numbers from decade to decade. The dearest wish of the freedman was to have his own independent plot; this signified to him in a very real way his transition from slavery to freedom. Ownership of land, no matter how little, became the most important criterion of freedom to the Grenadian. With the growth of the peasantry, village after village sprang up, for example La Tante, Belle Vue, Chantimelle, Munich, Springs and Grand Anse.

Exercise

3. What roles did women have in peasant farming?

4. Do you think life was easier as a peasant farmer than working on a plantation or under the indenture system? Give reasons for your decision. Write 100–150 words.

Research

In groups, imagine you are a peasant farmer. Research a day in the life of a 19th-century peasant farmer. Write out their daily routine, which crops they would grow and the animals they would keep.

Key vocabulary

migration

peasant farming

Diversification and unification

We are learning to:

• define and apply various concepts: diversification and unification.

Changes in agricultural activities

After emancipation, agriculture began to diversify. Further diversification also took place when the indentured labour system was ended. Diversity was an important step in the development of agriculture in the Caribbean, which for a long time had been a **monoculture** based on sugar production.

Agricultural **diversification** meant that a wider range of crops was grown across the country:

• the growing of ground provisions such as yam, cassava, dasheen
• the rearing of livestock
• the growing of vegetables such as corn and peas
• the cultivation of fruits such as cocoa, bananas, citrus fruits and nutmeg.

There were several advantages to diversification:

• More and more people were able to feed and support themselves by growing their own food and raising livestock (peasant farming).
• People developed skills and experience as they started to farm new crops. This gave farmers the ability to respond to changes in the market. For example, the demand for cocoa expanded as the finished product became more popular with the European public due to big brands like Cadbury's chocolate.
• There was less reliance on sugar farming – so, when sugar prices collapsed or demand for sugar dropped, farmers were able to make a living from producing other crops.
• Crops were grown throughout the year, so people had food, work and income all through the year.

Women carrying cocoa pods.

Research

Research the following benefits of agricultural diversification:

a) the links between agriculture and other industries

b) how it can create employment

c) how exporting goods can earn money for the country

d) how it can cut a country's food bill

Write 150–200 words.

Unification in the Leeward Islands ▶▶▶

Unification is the process where two countries, or more, join together. Unification among the islands of the Leewards was a common trend. Examples include St Kitts, Nevis and Anguilla; Antigua and Barbuda; and the British Virgin Islands. These unions were all formed by the British government as a means of making the islands more economically viable.

St Kitts, Nevis and Anguilla were unified in 1967. In 1971 Anguilla opted to leave the union and return to being a British overseas territory. In 1988 Nevis held a referendum to separate from St Kitts, but the majority of the voters chose to remained unified.

Antigua and Barbuda gained their independence from Britain in 1981 as a united state.

The union of the British Virgin Islands includes the islands of Tortola, Virgin Gorda, Anegada and 50 other smaller islands. They form part of the British Overseas Territories. The others include the Cayman Islands, Turks and Caicos Islands, Montserrat and Anguilla. The citizens of these states are considered full British citizens.

The Lumber and Store Hotel, Nelson's Dockyard, English Harbour, Antigua

Exercise

1. Explain what agricultural diversification means.

2. How does diversification help with employment?

3. If you owned a small farm and you wanted to provide your family with food and a secure income throughout the year, what would you try to do? Why?

4. Explain in your own words the term unification.

5. Note key dates from the information you have studied and add them to your timeline.

6. You have been asked to research an historical event that has happened in your country. What primary sources do you think you will need? List them and then do some research. Write 100–150 words.

Key vocabulary

monoculture

diversification

unification

Historical data sources

We are learning to:

- define and apply various concepts: primary and secondary sources
- identify examples of primary sources
- analyse primary sources of data
- use and appreciate the variety of sources used to collect data
- work collaboratively.

Primary sources »

A **primary source** is a document or physical object that was written or created at the time that provides direct or first-hand evidence about an event, object, person or work of art.

Primary sources are usually found in museums and libraries, for example, the Barbados National Archives.

Examples of primary sources include:

- photographs, diaries, letters
- autobiographies, biographies
- birth and death certificates
- places, such as historical buildings or cemeteries
- speech, and audio and video recordings.

Other examples can include drawings, posters, literature, art, music, artefacts (coins, clothing, tools, furniture, fossils), newspaper articles, emails, the internet or government documents (reports, bills, proclamations, hearings, etc.), research data and reports.

If you want to find out what life was like under indentureship, you should study these sources.

This map showing the West Indies is an example of a secondary source.

Did you know...?

A **secondary source** is a book or document that was created by someone who did not experience first-hand or participate in the events or conditions being researched. Examples of secondary sources include:

- textbooks, bibliographies and biographical works
- reference books such as dictionaries, encyclopedias and atlases
- articles from journals, magazines and newspapers
- books published after the events have occurred
- history books.

Exercise

1. Write your own definition of a primary source.

2. How many examples of a primary source do you have in your school?

3. Working in groups, create a brochure giving information about a historical event that has happened in your country. Use primary and secondary sources to collect information and draw up a timeline of the event. Present your work to the rest of the class.

There can be a wide range of primary sources to draw from. One of many sources of historical information is the Barbados National Archives.

Case study

Sir Ralph Abercromby.

Barbados National Archives

The Barbados National Archives houses a treasure trove of manuscripts, letters, reports, charts, photographs, maps, deeds and wills that date back to the early days of the island's settlement in the 1600s.

The materials in the archive are available for use by the public. The archive is a means of conserving and preserving the island's history and heritage.

Records can be viewed if you book in advance, and there is no charge to view them. Examples of some of the things you could see include:

- Notes on the West Indies during the expedition under the command of the late General Sir Ralph Abercromby, including observations on the island of Barbados, written by George Pinckard in 1806.
- The newspaper *The Liberal* (1837–60). This newspaper highlighted the plight of the oppressed.

Questions

1. In your own words, explain how the National Archives help to preserve the heritage of Barbados.

2. Is the newspaper *The Liberal* a primary or secondary source? Why?

The National Archives of Trinidad and Tobago.

Research

Most countries have National Archives or a Department of Archives. Do your own research to find out:

- Where are your country's National Archives?
- What can you find out about the building which hosts the National Archives (see the National Archives of Trinidad and Tobago pictured above)?
- Can you freely visit your National Archives?

Key vocabulary

primary source

secondary source

Historical sites

We are learning to:

- identify and describe historical sites and landmarks in the community
- investigate the origins and significance of historical sites and landmarks.

Historical sites and landmarks

Historical sites and **landmarks** are places where aspects of our political, military, cultural or social history are preserved. There are laws to protect historical sites and landmarks because of their special heritage value.

They may be buildings, landscapes or places with interesting structures or relics. Some countries have buildings that have been standing for thousands of years, such as the Pyramids of ancient Egypt or the ruins from ancient Rome or Greece.

Examples of the different types of historical sites and landmarks in the Caribbean include:

- Buildings – Nelson's Dockyard in Antigua was constructed in the late 17th and 18th centuries. It was named after Horatio Nelson, who served there from 1784 to 1787.
- Monuments – the Emancipation statue in Barbados symbolises the breaking of the chains of slavery.
- Churches – The Church of St Andrews Parish, Barbados, was first built of wood in 1630. It was destroyed by a hurricane in 1831 and rebuilt with stone in 1846.
- Schools – St Joseph's Convent, St George's, Grenada, was founded in 1876 by the Sisters of Cluny. Famous Caribbean women attended the school including Dame Eugenia Charles of Dominica.
- Parks – St Vincent and the Grenadines Botanical Gardens on St Vincent are the oldest in the western hemisphere. The collection was started in 1765.
- Houses – Romney Manor, St Kitts, was the original home of Kalinago Chief Tegreman. In the 1620s it was the home of Sam Jefferson, who is believed to be the great-great-great grandfather of United States President Thomas Jefferson.
- Cemeteries.

Brimstone Hill Fortress, St Kitts.

Romney Manor, St Kitts.

Exercise

1. In your own words define what a historical site is.
2. Which island has the oldest botanical gardens in the western hemisphere?

Case study

Brimstone Hill Fortress

Brimstone Hill Fortress in St Kitts is an excellent example of a well-preserved military fortress. The fortress was constructed between the 1690s and 1790s. It was designed by British engineers and built by enslaved African people. The entire site covers approximately one mile. It is designated a UNESCO world heritage site.

Research

Brimstone Hill Fortress has been designated as a UNESCO world heritage site.

Do your own research using primary and secondary sources and find out:

- What does a world heritage site mean?
- How does a site qualify to be a world heritage site?
- Are there other world heritage sites in the Caribbean?

Produce a brochure to highlight the origins and significance of other world heritage sites in the Caribbean.

Include any interesting stories or historical details about them, along with detailed pictures or drawings.

Exercise

3. Create a timeline of the historical sites and landmarks discussed.

4. In groups, brainstorm the location of a historical site or landmark in your area, then write:

   a) what it was originally used for and what it is used for now

   b) why you think it forms an important part of our heritage

Project

You are going to prepare a presentation about a historical site in the Caribbean to present to your class.

Each group will research and create a presentation about one of these sites: Nelson's Dockyard, Church of St Andrew's Parish, St Joseph's Convent, St Vincent and the Grenadines Botanical Gardens or Romney Manor.

Research where it is, when it was established, what it was used for and six facts about its history. Collect photographs, draw pictures or create a poster. Then, as a group, create your presentation on your computer and present it to the class.

Key vocabulary

historical site

landmark

Comparing data sources

We are learning to:

- compare and evaluate multiple sources of information
- synthesise and draw conclusions from different sources
- value and display respect for historical sites and buildings
- work collaboratively.

Compare and evaluate multiple sources of information

It is important for researchers and students to be able to compare, contrast and evaluate information from different sources. Quite often, the full story of a particular topic does not begin to come together until you have seen or read different accounts, and you begin to draw conclusions about that topic.

Cannons at Fort Shirley, Dominica.

We have seen that there are many different sources of primary and secondary information that we can draw from.

We can also learn from the **oral tradition** of a culture. This is where knowledge and experiences of the past are passed down through the generations using spoken word, by performance poetry, storytelling or poetry recital.

Respect for historical sites

It is important to be a good citizen and show respect and look after our historical sites and heritage for future generations to use. We do this by:

- protecting and preserving the historical sites
- keeping their environments clean
- having laws to protect the sites from being destroyed
- educating the public about the heritage of the sites
- having field trips to historical sites.

Research

Choose a historical site that you want to know more about. Interview some elders in your community. Find out from them what the area looked like when they were young and how people used it. Write a report about the way the area has changed.

Activity

Complete a field trip to a historical site or landmark, museum or archive. Write a reflective journal in which you imagine living in one of the places you have visited or read about. Imagine what life was like there and what your daily routine would be like. How different would it be from your routine today?

Case study

The Confederation Riots, Barbados, 1876

The internet is often the first place you go to if you want to research a topic. However, when you search on the web for a topic, you often come up with many different results. For example, if you were to search 'confederation riots 1876 Barbados' an internet search can show over 1000 results, such as:

- Encyclopedia.com gives a brief summary of the events.
- Google books: *Igniting the Caribbean's Past* by Bonham Richardson looks at the riot in relation to similar riots and unrest in the Caribbean region.

Other suggestions for sources you could use to research the Confederation Riots include:

- Visiting the The Barbados National Archives. You can find Parliamentary Papers for the period 1876–77 and the Minute Papers for the Colonial Secretary's Office for the year 1876. You can research how these papers reported the events.
- Reading history books in your local library and in school.
- Interviewing people in the community who may know about the Confederation Riots.

The internet is good place to research a topic, but you must make sure the information is from a trusted source.

Project

In groups, you are going to research the Confederation Riots of 1876.

Use primary and secondary sources to put together a brochure about the events of the riots. Use some of the ideas above for your research.

When you have gathered all the information together, write a fictional newspaper report of the events, using any photos and drawings that you have found. Write 150–200 words.

Then present your project to the class.

Key vocabulary

oral tradition

Historical events

We are learning to:

- examine the historical factors that have contributed to the social development of the region
- examine the impact of historical events such as slavery, indentureship and inter-island migration.

Impact of enslavement ≫

What was the impact on the communities in the Caribbean of some of these historical events that we have been looking at? For example, Trinidad and Tobago today is famous for its **racial** and cultural **diversity**, which means that people from many different backgrounds make up its population.

The origins of this can be traced back to the colonial era, with the arrival of enslaved Africans, and then later indentureship and inter-island migration. As a result, there are a large number of different languages and cultural traditions that come from countries all over the world. For example:

- Religion – practices that can be recognised in Obeah, voodoo and Shango.
- Language – the Caribbeans invented a common language. This led to the emergence of patois (a mixture of African, French, English and Spanish dialects).
- Food – for example, yam, cocoa, asham, fufu.
- Music – for example, Congo talking drum, abeng, xylophone, bamboo fife.

The pie chart shows the different ethnic groups that make up the population of Trinidad and Tobago today.

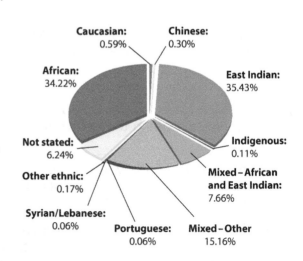

Caucasian: 0.59%
Chinese: 0.30%
African: 34.22%
East Indian: 35.43%
Not stated: 6.24%
Indigenous: 0.11%
Other ethnic: 0.17%
Mixed – African and East Indian: 7.66%
Syrian/Lebanese: 0.06%
Portuguese: 0.06%
Mixed – Other: 15.16%

Exercise

1. What does each number on the pie chart represent?
2. What are the two largest ethnic groups in Trinidad and Tobago?
3. Look back through this unit. How many of the ethnic groups came to Trinidad and Tobago through slavery or indentureship, and are they shown in the pie chart above?

Activity

Write a poem or short story describing some of the changes discussed in communities on this page.

Impact of indentureship >>>

Let us look at Trinidad and Tobago as an example. Indentureship impacted Trinidad and Tobago society demographically, economically and culturally.

- Demographically – by 1861, the total population of Trinidad was 50 per cent immigrants. Over time, this would have a significant impact on the cultural diversity of the island. As the immigrants began work on the estates, other immigrant groups moved into other work, such as shopkeepers and market gardeners, and professional jobs such as teachers, clergy and public servants.

- Economically – the sugar industry needed the additional labour. The immigrants helped to increase the number of workers on the estates, which eventually led to an increase in productivity and exports. After indentureship, the Indians also grew crops such as rice bodi and watermelons for domestic use. They also reared animals. Any surplus was sold in the local markets.

- Culturally – Trinidad and Tobago became more culturally diverse because of the movement of people; for example, there were different religions, languages and food.

Impact of inter-island migration >>>

Inter-island migration is the process of moving from one country to another country, for example from Grenada to Trinidad. After emancipation, people began moving within the Caribbean region in search of jobs and better working and living conditions.

For example, people moved from Grenada and St Vincent to Trinidad. They found employment as agricultural workers, domestic servants, store clerks and oil field workers.

One lasting effect of inter-island migration was the eventual formation of CARICOM in 1973, which allowed movement of people between CARICOM countries.

Project

In groups, discuss the impact that slavery, indentureship and inter-island migration had on your community. Use primary and secondary sources to research the different languages, cultures and traditions that are now in your community. Then write about 300 words and use images from the sources you have used.

Cane cutting in the Caribbean, circa 1930.

Exercise

4. In your own words, explain how indentureship had an impact on Trinidad and Tobago.

5. Explain the term inter-island migration.

Key vocabulary

racial diversity

Women and the community

We are learning to:

- compare and contrast the social development of various communities: emergent issues of gender.

Issues of gender

Life for enslaved African women in the 19th century was a very difficult and dangerous one. Initially, they were captured in their homeland in Africa and brought over to the Caribbean to work on plantations.

Once there, they would work in the fields, preparing the land, planting, doing the harvest, and transporting and milling the cane. Some worked as domestic staff in the plantation owner's house, but this was hard work too, and frequently the women were subjected to sexual abuse, often becoming pregnant by the master of the house.

After emancipation

After emancipation in 1838, the formerly enslaved people took up peasant farming. This was not easy work either, and sometimes women would have to work on other plantations doing manual work to supplement the family's income. Some women moved away from agricultural labour and opted to learn skills such as sewing and housekeeping to earn a living.

Woman carrying cocoa and nutmeg on her head, Grenada.

After indentureship

After indentureship, women continued to grow crops and rear animals, while others worked as cane cutters or labourers, and they would earn less than the men for doing the same work. Educational opportunities were few, though some women did take courses in dressmaking and making preservatives.

Exercise

1. In your own words, explain why life was difficult for women in the 19th century.

2. How did women who worked as peasant farmers supplement their income?

3. What subjects were open for women to study?

> ### Did you know...?
>
> In 1995, the United Nations (UN) Security Council stated that: "The equal access and full participation of women in power structures and their full involvement in all efforts for the prevention and resolution of conflicts are essential for the maintenance and promotion of peace and security."

Today, in most countries, women and men are equal under the law. They have the same rights, meaning there is what we call **gender equality**. But women and girls are still not treated as equals in all communities.

Many women are not allowed access to education and health care. They are often victims of domestic abuse and violence, sexual abuse, sexual harassment at work and the victims of human trafficking and crime.

Women bear most of the responsibilities relating to raising families and doing housework. Many are forced to work in informal jobs without benefits and security, because men are given preference in the formal employment sector.

However, education is widely available to girls in the Caribbean, and girls who attend school and university do well in their studies.

Today, there have been some changes in society that offer help and protection for women. These include:

- Women's rights – women now have much greater opportunities in education and employment, and they have laws to protect them against discrimination (for instance, the Maternity Leave Law, Grenada 1980) and laws to protect them in social and family situations (for example, the Domestic Violence Act, Barbados 2016).

- Greater educational opportunities – in the past, more money was invested in male education, but this has changed, with greater numbers of women moving into higher education.

- More women working – as opportunities have increased in education, so have the opportunities for educated women to work in roles that previously were reserved for men only.

Research

Find an organisation in your community that champions the causes of women. Research its role and activities, and write 150–200 words on its contribution to gender equality.

Exercise

4. Name three organisations in society today that offer help and protection for women.

5. Give five reasons why women are not treated as equals in some communities.

6. Do you think that gender issues only affect women, or do they affect everyone?

7. Do you agree or disagree with the United Nations' statement about gender equality? Explain your point of view.

Key vocabulary

gender equality

The need for reform

We are learning to:

- compare and contrast the social development of various communities: emergent issues of race.

The need for reform >>

The constitutions of the islands of the Caribbean are similar. They guarantee certain rights to citizens. The constitutions state clearly that rights are given to each citizen without discrimination due to race, origin, colour, religion or sex. The Caribbean has a long history of its citizens' fight for their rights.

Effigy of Guy Fawkes, Lewes, UK.

Bonfire Riots 1885, Grenada >>

On 5 November each year the British colonies commemorated the anniversary of Guy Fawkes. Guy Fawkes had attempted unsuccessfully to blow up the British parliament building in 1605. The anniversary was celebrated with bonfires and the making and burning of an effigy of Mr Fawkes.

This was a common celebration in Grenada. However, in November 1885 a law was passed prohibiting persons from lighting bonfires and discharging fireworks in the capital of St George's. It was felt that this was a fire hazard in a town of mainly wooden buildings.

The citizens of the town were not pleased with this law; they felt the government was trying to restrict their right to festivities and riots broke out. Bottles, stones, bricks and other missiles were thrown from houses into the streets, street lamps were broken and several police constables were severely injured. The police retaliated by arresting and beating a number of rioters. Today Guy Fawkes is still celebrated in Grenada, especially in the villages of Morne Jaloux and Mt Moritz.

Research

Using primary and secondary sources, research the 1951 uprising in Grenada. Use pictures and write 100–150 words.

Exercise

1. Explain in your own words why the government tried to prohibit the Guy Fawkes celebrations.

2 Explain in your own words the terms discrimination and race.

Case study

The 1951 uprising in Grenada

The working class in Grenada – mainly rural agricultural workers, road workers and urban shop clerks – were often treated unfairly with low wages and inadequate working conditions.

In 1950, Eric Gairy formed the Grenada Manual and Mental Workers Union. Hundreds of working-class people joined the union. The union demanded:

- increased wages
- holidays with pay
- sick leave with pay.

The estate owners and British colonial government ignored the demands.

Gairy called a general strike on 19 February 1951. It was the first general strike on the island and lasted for one month. The strike developed into an uprising or **insurrection**. Crops like cocoa and nutmeg were burnt and estate houses were looted and burnt. Gairy was arrested.

In the end Gairy was released and achieved the demands he requested. He formed a political party, the Grenada United Labour Party, and won Grenada's first election held under **universal adult suffrage** (one person, one vote).

Gairy had shown that the predominantly Black working class could demand changes from the predominantly White ruling class and succeed.

Questions

1. List the demands Gairy made to the estate owners and British colonial government.

2. Why do you think people were attracted to Gairy's trade union?

3. Create a timeline of the events in Grenada that we have just discussed. Add notes to your dates.

Sir Eric Matthew Gairy, former Prime Minister of Grenada

Did you know...?

Eric Gairy later became the father of independence in Grenada.

Key vocabulary

insurrection

universal adult suffrage

Society in the 20th century

We are learning to:

- compare and contrast the social development of various communities: emergent issues of class.

Unrest and strikes in the 1930s

Class is the division of people in a society into groups according to their social status, for example, upper class, middle class and working class. The 1930s saw a big change for the **working classes** in the Caribbean. From the early 20th century, the sugar industry had been in decline and, although other industries like tourism and oil were profitable, the wages of the working class were low. For example, the oil companies exploited their workers.

Workers were not allowed to strike, and very few workers had **political franchise** in the 1930s. In order to be eligible to vote for members of the Legislative Council, a person had to own property or have a high income. The interests of workers were therefore not represented in government.

Other factors also began to contribute to unrest among workers:

- There was a lot of unemployment and underemployment.
- **Trade unions** were not recognised.
- Wages were lower, but costs of living increased.
- Employers and colonial government officials still displayed racist and arrogant attitudes towards workers.

Workers wanted better working conditions, respect and the freedom to protest if necessary. This led to the development of trade unions and political parties. The laws were changed so that the rights of workers were respected and they had more freedom and protection. All of these factors eventually led to unrest in many other Caribbean countries. The timeline shows the events.

> **1935:** St Kitts – sugar workers strike for better wages
>
> ⌄⌄
>
> **1935:** St Vincent – demonstrations against increased customs duties
>
> ⌄⌄
>
> **1935:** St Lucia – dock workers strike
>
> ⌄⌄
>
> **1937:** Barbados – trade union leader deported, riot breaks out
>
> ⌄⌄
>
> **1937:** T.U.B. Butler organises strike at Trinidad Leaseholds Limited oilfields; strike spreads to other oilfields and becomes general strike; state of emergency declared
>
> ⌄⌄

Exercise

1. What factors contributed to the unrest amongst the working classes?

2. What did workers do in St Kitts in 1935?

3. Why do you think there was labour unrest in the Caribbean?

Trade unions

As a result of the unrest in the 1930s, and in particular the unrest in 1937, the British government conceded that the workers were being exploited by their employers. The British government then agreed that trade unions would be recognised.

The role of the trade unions was to be a strong 'voice' for the working class in the Caribbean, and would ensure that workers were paid and treated fairly.

Early trade unions included the Antigua Traders and Labour Union (1940), the Workers League, St Kitts (1940) and the Barbados Workers Union (1943).

Important early trade unions included:

- the Oilfields Workers' Trade Union (OWTU)
- the All Trinidad Sugar Estates and Factory Workers Trade Union (ATEFWTU)
- the Federated Workers Trade Union (FWTU).

In 1938, the Trinidad Labour Department was set up to mediate in disputes between the employers and the trade unions.

T.U.B. Butler (1897–1977)

Tubal Uriah 'Buzz' Butler, was a key figure in mobilising the oilfield workers in Trinidad to protest about their poor working conditions. Butler was born in Grenada; like many others, he was a product of inter-island migration and went to Trinidad in search of work in the oilfields.

He organised hunger marches in 1934 and 1935 and the first proper strike on the oilfields in 1935. Demonstrations were peaceful until the police tried to stop them. People were killed and injured, and Butler was arrested and imprisoned for two years in 1937. A few years later, he was arrested again after organising another strike.

Butler served as a member of the Legislative Council from 1950 to 1961. In 1970, he was awarded the Trinity Cross.

1938: Trinidad Labour Department established after investigations by British government into causes of unrest

1939: World War II breaks out

Project

The Trinidadian writer Samuel Selvon published a collection of short stories called *Ways of Sunlight* in 1957. The stories detail what it was like to live in 1930s multicultural Trinidadian society. Your teacher will help you either research about the book or find a copy for you. Read three or four of the stories and summarise what life was like in Trinidad.

Exercise

4. What role did T.U.B. Butler play in bringing about changes in Trinidad and Tobago in the 1930s? How important were these changes?

5. Do you think strikes and rebellions are the best way to bring about change in your country?

6. Add the most important dates from this period to your timeline.

Key vocabulary

class

working class

political franchise

trade union

The diversity of our community

We are learning to:

- value the diversity of various communities.

The diversity of communities

We have seen in this unit the impact slavery, indentureship and inter-island migration had on the economic, religious and cultural life of the Caribbean.

The immigrants who came to live in the Caribbean brought their own religions and cultural practices with them, which resulted in a **multicultural society**.

Today the Caribbean has become a place of great cultural diversity that we can value. Our people come from Africa, Europe and India, with many different ethnicities, languages, religions and cultural traditions.

Each community is different and depends on a number of factors, such as:

- its origin, history and location – for example, whether the community was set up after emancipation, after people had bought themselves out of indentureship or as a result of inter-island immigration
- characteristics of the community, such as its population and composition of ethnicity, religion, gender, age and language – for example, English, French, Creole, Spanish and Bhojpuri
- its settlement patterns and use of land – for example, how much of the land is used for housing, sugar cane, crops, pasture or not used at all
- economic and employment activities
- institutions and public services
- educational services – for example, some schools in some communities may be religious schools, such as Roman Catholic and Anglican
- cultural activities and traditions, including arts and music, cuisine and dress.

Local market, St George's, Grenada.

Activity

Create a mind map showing the different factors that make up a community. Add examples to each one.

Exercise

1. What three factors impacted on the economic, religious and cultural life of the Caribbean?
2. Name some of the nationalities that make up our region.

Religious practices ⟫

Trinidad and Tobago for example, is a multi-religious country, which means that there are many different religious practices in the country. The religious practices of a community are dependent on which religion the community follows. For example:

- Christianity celebrates Easter.
- Hinduism celebrates Diwali, Phagwa.
- Islam celebrates Eid al-Fitr, the Hosay Festival.

Cultural activities and traditions ⟫⟫

Each community has different traditions and festivals – for example, the religious festivals outlined above – but they can share non-religious festivals such as Indian Arrival Day, which commemorates the arrival of East Indian indentured labourers to work on the plantations (for example, celebrated in Trinidad on 30 May each year), and Emancipation Day, which commemorates the abolition of slavery (for example, celebrated in St Vincent and the Grenadines on 1 August each year).

Other diverse cultural aspects include:

- different types of cuisine (food), such as roti and curried mango (Indian), pelau (Spanish) and bamboo shoots and tea (Chinese)
- different types of traditional dress, such as the Indian sari
- music and dance – calypso, soca and rumba (all originating from Africa); dances like the Kuchipudi (Indian), lion and ribbon dances (Chinese), and African orisha dance movements
- folklore – stories about Anansi (originally from Africa) and Papa Bois (from French Caribbean culture).

Discussion

In pairs or groups, discuss the various activities and traditions that exist in Caribbean culture. Use the information on these pages and make a list of how many you have in your own community.

Carnival in Barbados.

Exercise

3. Name a religious festival celebrated by:
   a) Christians
   b) Hindus
   c) Muslims
4. Name five factors that help to explain why each community is different in the Caribbean.
5. You are going to do a project about your community. Take the five factors you identified in question 4, and write notes about what happens in your community in relation to these. You can add photos from the internet or your own drawings. Write about 300 words.

Key vocabulary
....

multicultural society

187

Development of industries

We are learning to:

- examine the historical factors that have contributed to the economic development of the community, introduction and development of industries, e.g. sugar, rice, cocoa, oil.

The sugar industry 〉〉

The sugar industry has a long history in the Caribbean. The timeline below summarises the key points:

- Sugar cane was planted in Barbados in 1627. By 1680 Barbados was a thriving sugar-producing colony.
- From 1783, French settlers planted more cane.
- By 1734 St Kitts followed with an agricultural industry which focused mainly on sugar cane cultivation.
- By 1764 Antigua was also producing sugar on a large scale.
- By 1795, Grenada's export of sugar to Britain surpassed that of its Windward Island neighbours
- After emancipation in 1838, sugar production dropped because of a shortage of labour and because the owners now had to pay wages to the labourers. This led to indentureship.
- When indentureship ended, the Indian immigrants left the big plantations to become small independent producers. From the mid 1870s onwards the islands of the Eastern Caribbean sought to diversify their economies and moved away from a total dependence on sugar. Crops planted included cocoa, bananas, arrowroot, coconuts and nutmeg.
- After World War I, sugar prices fell because of competition from sugar beet and cheap imports from Cuba and the East Indies.

Migrant workers cutting sugar cane on a plantation circa 1897.

Activity

Your teacher will organise a field trip to a museum or a sugar-producing estate. Before you go on the trip, work in groups and make a list of the questions you think you will be able to find answers to at the museum or sugar estate. Record your answers and use them to give feedback to the class after the trip.

Exercise

1. How did sugar farming change after emancipation?
2. Why did sugar production decrease after 1838?
3. Find three important dates in the information you have studied and add them to your timeline.

The cocoa industry »»

Cocoa was first introduced to Grenada in the late 1600s. By 1762 it was produced as a secondary crop, mainly in the hilly areas of the island like the parishes of St John and St Mark.

With the failing of the sugar industry by the 1860s, cocoa became the primary crop. By the 1890s cocoa accounted for 80 per cent of Grenada's exports and the country supplied 11 per cent of the world market.

The crop suffered a number of setbacks including an attack of the pink mealybug in the 1990s and Hurricane Ivan in 2004. Today cocoa is produced on a much smaller scale and is used mainly for the production of organic Grenadian chocolate bars.

Man preparing cacao beans.

The oil industry »»»

Some of the first oil wells in the world were drilled in Trinidad. When commercial production was established, petroleum replaced agriculture as the mainstay of the economy.

In the 1970s, sales of petroleum accounted for as much as 90 per cent of export earnings. Later, natural gas became more important than petroleum.

Diversification into the production of steel, petrochemicals and iron was made possible by the country's vast mineral resources.

Exercise

4. When was cocoa first introduced to Grenada?
5. List two setbacks faced by the cocoa industry in Grenada.
6. Where was oil first discovered and produced commercially?
7. Work in groups and research the crops grown after emancipation. Find out more about the production of cocoa.
   - Who were the cocoa farmers?
   - Where was cocoa exported?
   - How much was exported?
   - Where are Grenadian chocolate bars exported today?

   Find out about other crops, like coconuts, vegetables, arrowroot, bananas and nutmeg. Where were these grown? Were they exported or sold at local markets?

Life in the village and the city

We are learning to:

- compare and contrast the economic development of various communities, life in the village vs life in the city
- appreciate the history of their community
- use primary and secondary sources to create a digital story (narrative) about the community.

Economic development »

The Caribbean moved from an agriculture-based economy in the 19th century to focusing on other industries like oil and tourism in the 20th century. For example, Trinidad and Tobago moved from a sugar-based economy in the 19th century to an oil-based economy in the 20th century. This shift resulted in much of the population moving from a **rural** to an **urban** environment. This is known as **internal migration**.

In Trinidad the developing oil industry pulled many people to urban areas in search of work. Low wages in agricultural jobs, combined with the new oil industry and emerging jobs in construction and manufacturing, made the rural life less appealing.

A village is a man-made environment mostly made up of family homes, although it may have a small central area with some shops and community buildings such as a police station, clinic and church. In farming areas, a village may have only a few tarred roads. Jobs are more agriculturally based.

A city is a large settlement where people live and work and is made up of businesses such as shops, malls, industrial buildings such as warehouses and factories, and a transport infrastructure such as roads, train tracks, bus and train stations, airports, roads, harbour and port facilities. People often work in the city centre and live in the suburbs, so they have to commute to work by bus, car or train. Schools, health care and even entertainment are better in urban areas.

A view of the waterfront at Port of Spain, Trinidad.

Activity

Draw a mind map showing the differences between life in the city and life in the village.

Exercise

1. What are the two products that Trinidad and Tobago's economy has been (and is) based on?

2. In your own words, define the terms village, city and internal migration.

3. In your own words, explain the differences between a village and a city. Write about 100 words. A mind map may help you.

Life in the village and the city ▶▶▶

There are a number of differences between living in a rural community, such as a village, and in an urban area, such as a city. For example, in urban areas:

- There is better housing.
- Utilities, such as water and electricity, are better.
- There are more job opportunities.
- The transport infrastructure is better developed.
- There are better schools and colleges in urban areas.
- There are more health care facilities in urban areas.

There are some disadvantages to living in urban areas:

- Housing and everyday living costs are more expensive.
- Social problems such as teenage pregnancy, street children, substance abuse and child abuse occur in greater numbers in urban areas.
- There is more pollution than in rural areas.
- People don't know each other as well, there is less of a community feel, and people are less appreciative of community history and cultural heritage.

Friday night market, Gouyave, Grenada.

Project

You are going to do a project comparing life in a village and life in a city. Choose a village and city close to where you live. Think about some of the things listed above and do some research to compare what life is like. You should also consider economic and employment activities, how land is used and whether people are better off financially in a village or a city (think about how much people earn and how much they have to spend).

Use primary and secondary sources to help your investigation and, if possible, interview community members for their views on whether they would prefer to live in a village or a city. Use the internet, newspapers and magazines to illustrate your project. Use a table, like the one below, to compare your village and city.

When you have finished your research, write a reflective piece to answer the question "I would prefer to live in a village/city because..." Write about 250 words.

Village	City

Key vocabulary

rural

urban

internal migration

Questions

See how well you have understood the topics in this unit.

1. Match the key vocabulary word (i–v) with its definition (a–e).

    i) colonialism

    ii) colony

    iii) Crown Colony

    iv) indentureship

    v) emancipation

    a) gaining control over land in another country and exploiting its wealth

    b) the removal of restraint or restrictions on an individual or a group of people

    c) a country under the control of another country

    d) contract labour with harsh conditions

    e) a country ruled by the monarch of another country

2. What bill came into effect on 1 August 1834?

3. In your own words, explain some of the problems of the indentured labour system. Write at least 50 words.

4. After emancipation, why was there mass movement of the formerly enslaved people in the Caribbean?

5. Explain why agricultural diversification was good for the Caribbean.

6. Give five examples of a primary source.

7. What would you find in the Barbados National Archives?

8. What type of historical landmark is Nelson's Dockyard in Antigua?

9. Which historical site is being described?

    _____ was designed by British engineers and built by enslaved African people. The entire site covers approximately one mile. It is designated a UNESCO World Heritage Site.

10. How can we show respect for our historical sites?

11. Explain briefly what happened at the Bonfire Riots in 1885.

12. Name three trade unions that were formed in the Caribbean in the 1930s and 1940s.

13. Match these events with the dates.

    i) Strike on oilfields

    ii) T.U.B. Butler arrested

    iii) Hunger March

    a) 1934

    b) 1935

    c) 1937

14. Name three factors that help make each community in the Caribbean different.

15. Create a mind map or timeline which shows the history of the sugar industry in the Caribbean.

16. Create a mind map, or graphic organiser, which shows the differences between living in a rural community and living in an urban area.

17. In your own words, explain what happened during the 1951 uprising in Grenada. Write your account in the style of a newspaper report.

Checking your progress

To make good progress in understanding your community, check to make sure you understand these ideas.

Explain the role that colonialism and the existence of Crown Colonies played in the history of the Caribbean.

Explain the impact the transatlantic trade of enslaved people and emancipation had on the Caribbean.

Explain the path to unification within the Leeward Islands.

Name examples of primary sources.

Explain how the National Archives help to preserve the heritage of Barbados.

Create a brochure using primary and secondary sources on a topic.

Identify different types of historical sites in the Caribbean.

Examine the impact of enslavement, indentureship and inter-island migration on our community.

Examine how we value the diversity of various communities in the Caribbean.

Examine the historical factors that have contributed to the economic development of the community.

Name the industries which have contributed to the Caribbean's economic development.

Complete a project comparing life in a village and life in a city.

End-of-term questions

Questions 1–5 >>>

See how well you have understood the ideas in Unit 4.

1. Give examples of the following group types:

   a) social

   b) school

   c) religious

   d) sports

   e) charity and community

   f) cultural

2. Think of a group that you belong to. Write a short essay outlining the functions and characteristics of your group

3. Look at these characteristics of a primary group. What are the characteristics of a secondary group?

   a) They are small in size.

   b) The relationships are very personal and intimate.

   c) Contact often takes place, and is face-to-face.

   d) Each member often interacts with all the others.

   e) They create a sense of belonging and loyalty.

   f) Members are accepted because of who they are and what they are like.

4. What benefits are there if you belong to a group?

5. Explain the difference between these leader types:

   a) democratic leaders

   b) authoritarian leaders

   c) laissez-faire leaders

Questions 6–10 >>>

See how well you have understood the ideas in Unit 5.

6. Explain the terms government, constitution, democracy and referendum.

7. Write a short essay explaining the characteristics of a democracy and whether your country is a direct or a representative democracy.

8. Outline the reasons why we need a government.

9. Read 5.3. Imagine there was no government for one week in your country. Write a newspaper report of about 250 words, saying what you think might happen with no government.

10. Fill in the blanks in this diagram, which shows the structure of central government in the Caribbean.

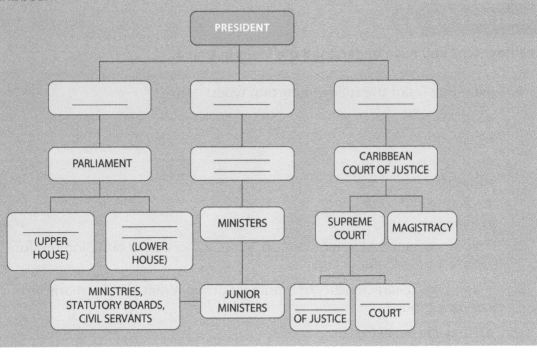

Questions 11–18 ≫

See how well you have understood the ideas in Unit 6.

11. Define the terms colonialism and Crown Colony, and explain how they relate to countries in the Caribbean.

12. Write a short essay explaining how indentureship started in the Caribbean. Outline the problems with indentureship that led to the end of the system in the early twentieth century. Write about 250 words.

13. Why was there mass migration of formerly enslaved people within the Caribbean in the aftermath of emancipation?

14. Explain the advantages of agricultural diversification in the nineteenth century in the Caribbean.

15. Give an example of a primary and a secondary source.

16. Explain why it is important to preserve historical landmarks and buildings in our community.

17. Read 6.8 and 6.9. Write a newspaper report that outlines the impact on Caribbean communities of some of the historical events described.

18. Explain the role of the sugar industry in the economic development of in the Caribbean.

Unit 7: Our heritage

In this unit you will find out »»

Our man-made and built heritage

- Our man-made and built heritage
  - ○ St George's Cathedral
  - ○ Fort Shirley
  - ○ places of worship
  - ○ civic and recreational buildings

Our physical and natural heritage

- The features of the Caribbean's physical heritage
  - ○ the ecological heritage of the Caribbean
  - ○ ecotourism and sustainability
- Biodiversity of the Caribbean
  - ○ flora: plants and flowers
  - ○ fauna: birds, mammals, reptiles, insects
- The significance of our physical/natural heritage
  - ○ wetlands, rainforests, coral reef, coastal areas, beaches, waterfalls
  - ○ World Heritage Sites: The Pitons, St Lucia; Brimstone Hill National Park, St Kitts
  - ○ conserving our resources

Our man-made and built heritage

We are learning to:

- define relevant terms and concepts: man-made heritage, built environment, built heritage
- describe the features in the environment that are part of our man-made or built heritage: historical sites and relics
- value the significance of our built or man-made heritage.

Man-made (built) environment

A **man-made** or **built environment** is one that has been built or made by people. It is an area where people live, work and enjoy themselves. For example, Bridgetown is a city. It is a built environment and so are other smaller villages and towns. Resources are needed to build these environments.

Bequia Island, St Vincent and the Grenadines

Man-made heritage

Your **heritage** is anything that is inherited from previous generations. All the people living in your country share a national heritage and people living in the Caribbean share a regional heritage. This is made up of our culture and history, as well as the natural and physical environment of our country and region. Our **man-made (built) heritage** is made up of those things which are part of our past, but which were built or made by man.

Heritage sites

A **heritage site** can have historical, cultural, social or physical significance. It can be a forest, a building, an island, a desert, a lake or even a whole city. For example, Morne Trois Pitons National Park in Dominica and Bequia in St Vincent and the Grenadines are heritage sites. Some sites are listed as World Heritage Sites by UNESCO. These are places that are considered to have special importance to humanity as a whole. These sites are protected and need to be looked after.

An angel in red, a unique stained glass feature of St George's Anglican cathedral, St Vincent and the Grenadines.

Exercise

1. In your own words, explain the terms 'built environment' and 'man-made heritage'.

2. Name two natural heritage sites in the Eastern Caribbean other than the ones we have already mentioned.

Some man-made buildings reflect our cultural heritage. Historic sites are places where aspects of our political, military, cultural or social history are preserved. There are laws to protect historical and heritage sites because of their special **value** to our community.

Historical sites may be buildings, landscapes or places with interesting structures or **relics**. Some countries have buildings that have been standing for thousands of years, such as the Mayan ruins in Central America.

Some historical sites include things left behind by people who lived in prehistoric times. They may include relics such as old pieces of pottery, bones, or paintings on caves and rocks. Some examples of famous buildings in the Eastern Caribbean include the following:

- St George's Cathedral in St Vincent and the Grenadines was rebuilt after the original structure was destroyed in 1780. The cathedral is the largest in the island and has a Georgian-style interior, nave and lower tower. Victorian-style transepts give the church the shape of the cross. Other features include a gilded wood chandelier and stained glass portraits of the crucifixion, and the Virgin Mary and St John above the high altar.

- Fort Shirley in Dominica is considered a very important site. The revolt of the 8th West India Regiment in 1802 occurred here, which led to British enslaved soldiers being freed. The fort discouraged French invasion of the island and several battles between the French and British naval forces occurred just offshore. It switched hands when the French controlled the island from 1778 to 1784 and was abandoned in 1854 when the fighting stopped. It has recently been restored.

Exercise

3. Why do you think the Eastern Caribbean does not have historical buildings from thousands of years ago?

4. Identify a historic building or site in your area. Make a note of:

   a) the name of the building or site

   b) what you know about it

   c) what it was originally used for and what it is used for now

   d) why you think it forms an important part of our heritage

Research

Find out which organisation cares for historical buildings in your country. For example, in St Vincent and the Grenadines it is the St Vincent and the Grenadines National Trust. For one historic site the organisation manages, find out:

- the name of the building
- when and where it was built
- the name of the original owners
- who owns it now
- what it is used for
- any interesting historical facts about the building.

Make a poster about one of the buildings, including any interesting stories or historical details about it and a detailed picture or drawing.

Key vocabulary
....

man-made/built environment

heritage

man-made (built) heritage

heritage site

value

relic

Places of worship

We are learning to:

- describe the features in the environment that are part of our man-made or built heritage: places of worship
- value the significance of our built or man-made heritage.

Churches ⟩⟩

Most religions expect people to gather at a central place of **worship**, where they may pray, give thanks, meditate or show their devotion in some way. Each religion has its own type of place of worship. A **church** is a Christian place of worship. The Roman Catholic tradition is known for its enormous cathedrals, designed to inspire an awareness of the great power of Christianity.

Roseau Cathedral, Dominica

The Cathedral of Our Lady of Fair Haven of Roseau in Dominica is an example of a striking Roman Catholic building. The original simple church structure dates back to 1730 and after a hurricane in 1816 destroyed it, a steeple, cathedral ceiling and crypt were added over the next 100 years to fulfil the needs of a growing number of parishioners. The current structure was completed in 1916.

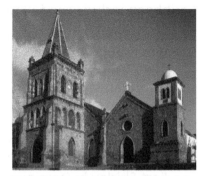

Roseau Cathedral, Roseau, Dominica

St John's Cathedral, Antigua and Barbuda

The original structure of this Anglican cathedral dates back to 1681. After an earthquake and rebuilding in 1746 and another earthquake, the current structure was built to withstand earthquake damage. It is known for its imposing baroque-style double towers and large bronze statues of St John the Baptist and St John the Divine at the southern gate. These statues were seized by the British from the French ship HMS *Temple* during wartime.

Almost all churches have a cross, the symbol of the Christian faith. Some churches have bells to let the community know it is time to come to church.

St John's Cathedral, Antigua, statues of John the Baptist and St John the Divine

Exercise

1. State two purposes that religious buildings serve.

2. What are some interesting features of St John's Cathedral, Antigua and Barbuda?

3. Research the history of a church in your country and write a short report of about 250 words.

A **mosque** is a Muslim place of worship. There are many mosques in the Caribbean, such as Kingston Mosque, Guyana, and Jumma Mosque, Barbados.

A **temple** is a more general name for a holy building or place of worship. Hindus, Jewish people and Buddhists all have their own types of temples, and some Christian churches are also known as temples.

Case study

The Nidhe Israel Synagogue, Barbados

This synagogue is one of the oldest in the western hemisphere, dating back to 1654 when Portuguese Jewish people from Brazil fled persecution to settle in Barbados. They brought with them technology that resulted in the introduction of the sugar industry to the island. One of the synagogue's key features is the 17th-century mikvah, a Jewish baptismal bath discovered in 2008 by archaeologist Michael Stoner. The synagogue is part of Historic Bridgetown and its Garrison, a UNESCO World Heritage Site.

Queenstown Masjid, Guyana

The Queenstown Masjid is a historic site and one of Guyana's oldest Islamic buildings, built in 1895. Building of the Masjid was led by Moulvi Gool Mohamed Khan, who noticed a steady increase in the Queenstown Muslim population who needed a place to worship. During the colonial era it served as a site where Muslims could meet openly for worship, manage their affairs and resources and organise various Islamic groups and associations. It was the home of the Young Men's Muslim Literary Society, formed in 1926, which was the first Muslim organisation to assume national status.

Questions

1. Where did the first Jewish migrants to Barbados come from and how did they benefit the island?

2. What is a mikvah?

3. Why was the Queenstown Masjid important for Guyanese Muslims?

4. Research the name of one Muslim, one Jewish and one Hindu place of worship in your country.

5. Do you attend a place of worship? If so, describe what it looks like, and the kinds of services you attend there, or have attended. If not, choose a place of worship you would like to attend, and explain why you would like to go there.

Project

Your teacher will arrange a visit to a place of worship. Write a profile about the place that you visit. Include these details:

a) the name of the place you visit

b) the year it was built

c) its history

d) its value to our heritage

Discussion

Do you think religions need places of worship? Why, or why not?

Key vocabulary

worship

church

mosque

temple

Civic and recreational buildings

We are learning to:

- describe the features in the environment that are part of our man-made or built heritage: civic buildings and recreation facilities
- value the significance of our built or man-made heritage.

Civic buildings ❯❯

A **civic building** is a large building, or group of buildings, which can be used for entertainment or business events, or which can be where the government carries out its work. Many of these government buildings are also historical sites because of their importance in the country's history. Some examples include:

- Government Headquarters, Basseterre, St Kitts, is the seat of the Prime Minister's office and other government ministries. The building was designed by architect Colin Laird and completed in 1965. It was extensively renovated, expanded and reopened in 1995 as the official government headquarters. The Treaty of Basseterre, which established the Organisation of Eastern Caribbean States (OECS), was signed at Government Headquarters in 1981.

Government Headquarters, Basseterre, St Kitts.

- The Courthouse, Kingstown, St Vincent, is where the nation's parliament meets and it also houses the law courts. In 1798 the British Assembly ordered the demolition of the existing French buildings that stood on the site, replacing them with a single, multi-use two-storey building. The current building is over 200 years old.

- Ilaro Court, Bridgetown, Barbados, is the official residence of the Prime Minister. Completed in the 1920s, its spacious gardens and striking gazebo are used to host social and cultural events of national importance.

- Government House, Morne Fortune, St Lucia, has been the official residence of the Governor General since 1979. The current brick structure was completed in 1895 after it was abandoned in 1865 and still plays a key role in the administration of the island.

Government House, Morne Fortune, St Lucia.

Exercise

1. What are civic buildings used for?
2. Create a timeline of the history of the civic buildings mentioned on this page.

Civic buildings can also be used for **recreation.** These are venues where people can go for relaxation and entertainment, including parks, sports centres, cultural venues, shopping malls, restaurants and cinemas. Citizens can even join in with cultural celebrations at these venues. Some examples include:

Pigeon Island National Park, St Lucia

- Pigeon Island National Park, St Lucia, is located on the northern coast of the island and is considered a cultural and historical landmark of the naval colonial history of the island. The 44-acre island is a naturally beautiful landscape dotted with the remains of old military buildings and a fort. Facilities at the park include an interpretation centre covering the island's history and restaurants featuring local cuisine. St Lucia Carnival and the St Lucia Jazz Festival are hosted here.

- Grenada National Stadium, Grenada, is a multi-purpose national facility. The National Cricket Stadium, which hosts international test matches, the National Athletic/Football Stadium, which is IAAF certified, and conference centre facilities are all found here. This venue hosted the 2016 Carifta Games, the 42nd Anniversary of Independence Celebrations and is the home of the Grenada Carnival, locally called 'Spicemas'.

- Peace Memorial Hall, St Vincent, is a performance arts and cultural venue with a history dating back to the 1950s. National performing arts competitions and showcases have been hosted here including the Bank of St Vincent Theatre Arts Festival. Other notable venues in St Vincent are the Arnos Vale playing field, Victoria Park and the recently completed E.T. Joshua Airport.

Activity

Choose a building that you believe is a particularly important part of our built heritage. Create a poster, flyer or brochure and accompany it with a short written piece (poem or prose) about its special meaning or value.

Exercise

3. Name any civic buildings found near where you live.

4. Do you have any recreation facilities in your area? Name any you can think of.

5. What kind of recreation facilities would you like in your area?

6. Prepare a two-minute oral presentation about the importance of public places and recreation facilities.

Key vocabulary

civic building

recreation

Our physical and natural heritage

We are learning to:

- define relevant terms and concepts: physical/natural heritage, indigenous, biodiversity, ecological, ecological sites and ecological heritage
- examine the features of the Caribbean's physical/natural heritage.

The features of the Caribbean's physical heritage

Our **physical heritage** is the part of our environment that is inherited from previous generations, is maintained in the present and will be passed on to future generations.

Our physical heritage is also part of the **ecosystem** of the Caribbean. Plants and trees have their own natural habitats, which means they grow easily in certain types of environment. Some plants are **indigenous,** meaning they are native to, or originate in, a particular region or country.

Indigenous flora refers to all natural vegetation in a particular area, such as trees and flowers, while **indigenous fauna** refers to all animal life in a particular area. The Caribbean has three main types of indigenous flora – the **wetlands**, **tropical rainforest** and the savannah.

Biodiversity is short for **biological diversity,** meaning a great variety of different forms of life. We can study biodiversity on many levels:

- **ecological diversity** – diversity of ecosystems, natural communities and habitats on planet Earth
- **species diversity** – variety of different species; for example Eastern Caribbean islands have a high biodiversity of butterflies
- **genetic diversity** – the variation in genetic material within a particular species or group, for example, trees.

The St Lucian warbler is endemic to St Lucia. This means it can be found nowhere else in the world.

Exercise

1. In your own words, define biodiversity, physical heritage and indigenous.
2. Explain what is meant by indigenous flora and fauna.
3. What are the three types of indigenous flora in the Caribbean?

Project

Create a poster with a photo/sketch of some of the indigenous flora and fauna found in your country. Underneath each photo or sketch note the scientific name, the common name and which ecosystem it can be found in. Are there any special laws to protect these plants and animals in your country?

Ecology is the study of the relationships between plants, animals, people and their environment. Our **ecological heritage** (the same as **natural heritage**) includes all elements of biodiversity, including plants and animals, and natural features.

Case study

Grand Etang Reserve, Grenada

Grand Etang is very ecologically diverse, as it features mountain, rainforest and wetland ecosystems. This means that animals and plants suited to live in any of these environments can all be found here. The reserve is also relatively isolated so human interference has not affected the balance of the ecosystem too much, which encourages species diversity. Hiking trails cross the reserve and birds like the Broad-winged hawk, Lesser Antillean swift and Antillean crested hummingbird can be found there due to the altitude. The reserve is government-run and protected, and is such an important part of the island's heritage that the Grand Etang Crater Lake is on the Grenadian coat of arms.

Grand Etang Reserve, Grenada, where mountains, rainforest and wetland meet.

Anguilla's Marine Parks

Anguilla's Marine Park System was set-up by the government in 1993 and is made up of five sites: Shoal Bay-Island Harbour, Little Bay, Sandy Island, Prickly Pear East and West, and Dog Island. These locations are close to land so they can easily be affected by human activity such as coastal construction, poor sewage management and boating. They are living ecosystems of reef-building coral and important habitats for fish species that support the fishing industry. Hawksbill and green sea-turtles also use these sites for nesting. These reefs protect the coastline. Anguilla is quite flat and small and sea swells due to bad weather are weakened by coral reefs so that beach erosion is reduced. Managing these parks balances their use for resources and tourism with sustaining them for future generations.

Questions

1. Why does Grand Etang Reserve have high diversity?

2. Give three reasons why marine park management in Anguilla is important.

3. In your own words, explain the term 'ecological heritage'. Give an everyday example.

Key vocabulary

physical heritage

ecosystem

indigenous

indigenous flora

indigenous fauna

wetlands

tropical rainforest

biodiversity (or biological diversity)

ecological diversity

species diversity

genetic diversity

ecology

ecological heritage/ natural heritage

ecological

Sustainability and ecotourism

We are learning to:

- examine the features of the Caribbean's physical/natural heritage: ecotourism and sustainability.

Sustainability ⟫

Sustainable activities do not damage the resources that make them possible. For example, if tourists visit a river and pollute or litter the environment, or remove fish, then they may destroy the natural environment for future generations. This type of tourism is unsustainable.

Ecotourism is a type of tourism that focuses on protecting the environment and local culture. Ecotourism means:

- travelling to undisturbed or unspoilt natural areas
- enjoying, studying or experiencing the natural environment without damaging it
- treating the environment responsibly and carefully
- benefiting local communities
- supporting conservation projects
- providing education to travellers and local communities.

Ecotourism in the Tobago Cays, St Vincent and the Grenadines ⟫⟫

The Tobago Cays is an important ecotourism site. This is a group of five uninhabited islands in the Grenadines archipelago: Petit Rameau, Petit Bateau, Baradal, Petit Tabac and Jamesby. These islands, along with the island of Mayreau and the extensive reefs around them, form the Tobago Cays Marine Park, which is a strictly protected and managed area.

There are restrictions against touching coral or removing any marine life, discharging wastewater from yachts anywhere in the park, bringing pets into the park, fishing or purchasing lobster out of season. Diving is only allowed with supervision from a registered local dive shop and the speed limit for sailing is 5 knots. The Marine Park Authority in Union Island is responsible for the day-to-day running of the park and enforcing regulations.

This is an example of ecotourism because tourists are made aware of their accountability and responsibility when visiting the area and must acknowledge the significance of the park's resources to the local community. In this way, they are best able to experience the park's attractions by listening to local expertise on the landscape, plants and animals.

Project

Design an **eco-friendly** hotel. Suggest ways to make your hotel eco-friendly in terms of its size, materials, style of design and the activities that it may offer.

Yachts in the Tobago Cays lagoon, St Vincent and the Grenadines

Research

Copy or trace a map of your country. Find the locations of at least three different ecotourism projects. Insert these on your map.

Ecotourism in Guyana ⟫

Guyana has the most potential for ecotourism in the Caribbean since it has the most diverse habitats and most biodiversity of all the countries in the region. A number of sites and attractions focus on ecotourism. Some of these are discussed here:

- Rewa Eco-Lodge: this site is located in central Guyana, where the Rewa and Rupununi rivers meet, in the Amerindian village of Rewa. Conservation International provided a grant for the creation of the eco-lodge in 2005. Guests can stay in a traditional hut called a benab or a cabin. Traditional meals are provided and traditional handicrafts can be purchased. Activities include wildlife-spotting on the river, trips to Corona Falls, hiking up Awaramie Mountain and dugout canoe visits to Grass Pond.

Traditional benabs at the Rewa Eco-Lodge, Guyana

- Arrowpoint Nature Resort: this site is located on the Kamuni River. Activities include bird-watching, caiman-spotting, fishing, forest hikes, swimming, kayaking and dining around the bonfire. Visiting the Amerindian village of Santa Mission is popular as tourists get to experience the way of life of indigenous people, including learning about traditional cassava-bread making.

- Surama Village and Eco-Lodge: this site is located in the Rupununi Savannah surrounded by the Pakaraima Mountains. This village features Makushi Amerindian culture, hospitality, food and crafts; guests live among the villagers. Activities include hiking the Surama Mountain, travelling the Burro Burro River, visiting Tiger Pond and open-air hammock camping at Carahaa Landing. The Iwokrama Canopy walkway is a nearby suspended walkway 30 m up and 154 m long. Tourists can walk around the jungle canopy to observe wildlife and plants while learning about the area from experienced guides.

Activity

Choose an ecotourism project in your country and do a case study on it. Find out where it is, the history of the project, the kinds of activities it offers, and which aspects of the environment it focuses on. Write up your case study in a booklet, providing pictures and information.

Exercise

1. In your own words, define ecotourism.

2. Do you think ecotourism is good for the Caribbean? Explain why/why not.

3. Compare and contrast ecotourism in the Tobago Cays with the Guyanese examples mentioned here.

4. Why do you think sustainable tourism is important in the Caribbean?

Key vocabulary

ecotourism

eco-friendly

Our indigenous flora

We are learning to:

- examine the features of Caribbean physical/natural heritage
- understand the biodiversity of the Caribbean's indigenous flora: plants and flowers.

Flora and **fauna** are the plants and animals that live in a particular place. The tropical climate of the Caribbean and its rich rainforests and wetlands are home to some of the most diverse plants and animals in the world.

Flora is a scientific word meaning plants. It includes all plant life – from tiny single-celled algae that live in water to the enormous ferns, bamboos and trees of our rainforests.

Fauna means animals. It includes all animals: mammals, birds, amphibians, reptiles and fish.

Tropical rainforest in St Lucia.

Diverse plant life

Mountainous volcanic islands usually have a high diversity of plant life. Dominica is a good example of this. It has 1226 species of plants. There are several reasons for this:

- Isolation – islands are surrounded by water on all sides. This makes them isolated environments where plants may evolve in ways not found in other places.
- Climate – The warm, wet tropical climate of the Caribbean is an ideal place for many different kinds of plants.
- Micro-habitats – The trees of the rainforest provide an environment that supports other types of vegetation, such as shrubs that live in the shade of the tall trees.
- Soil – Volcanic ash is an excellent fertiliser for soil. There is variation in soil quality from rich interior soil on volcanic slopes to poorer sandy soils and waterlogged soils on the coast.
- Location – When Caribbean islands rose from the sea, the landscapes were empty. However, closeness to South, Central and North America meant that plant species could arrive by sea or air to colonise these landscapes, causing a unique mix of plant species.

Flatter coral islands tend to have fewer different types of plant types.

Project

Choose three species of flora found in your country to research. Create a poster showing the three species, detailing their names, habitat, size, appearance and any other interesting details.

Plants in their natural habitat »

We have already seen that certain types of plants and trees have their own natural habitats, which means they grow easily in certain types of environment. Indigenous plants provide a good food source for indigenous animals, as they have evolved together in their environment.

Plants that grow naturally in an area are usually well adapted to the conditions of that area. For example:

- Plants that grow in a desert are adapted to surviving dry, hot conditions.
- Plants that live in wetlands are adapted to survive in lots of water and high salinity (salt levels).

The table below shows the vegetation of some of the habitats in the Caribbean.

Habitat	Vegetation
Savannah	Grasses, low shrubs
Rainforests	Tall trees, shrubs, creepers
Swamp	Dense mangrove trees and shrubs
Beach	Tall palm trees, grasses, short shrubs that do not require much water

Bromeliads take advantage of humid, shaded habitats, and some grow on other plants.

Coastal vegetation tends to be shorter and not as diverse since coastal sandy soil cannot hold water very well.

Research

In a scrapbook, collect pictures of the different types of flora that are indigenous to your country. Use magazines, the internet, newspaper or brochures. For each, write down its name, anything interesting about its appearance, where it can be found, whether it is a flower or a plant and any special facts about it.

Exercise

1. Explain the terms flora and fauna and give some examples of each that you see every day.

2. Explain in your own words three reasons why some countries have such a high diversity of plant life.

3. How many different types of plants do you think you see every day? Try counting them one day.

4. Why do you think a plant from the wetlands would not survive very long in the desert?

Key vocabulary

flora

fauna

Our indigenous fauna

We are learning to:

- examine the features of Caribbean physical/natural heritage
- understand the biodiversity of Caribbean indigenous fauna: birds and mammals.

Birds 》

Fauna are all the animals that live in a particular place.

Numbers of birds vary among the islands depending on the variety of habitats present for them to nest in and the availability of wetlands. Mangrove and sea-grass beds attract many birds because the shallow water is easier to fish in, while forests have lots of fruit to eat and rodents and insects to hunt. Because of the Caribbean's location, many birds come here when they migrate during the cold winter months.

- When it is winter in the northern hemisphere (October to March), birds migrate here from North America.
- Between May and September, many birds migrate from South America.

Indigenous bird species include the Grenada Dove, Barbados Bullfinch, St Lucia Parrot, St Lucia Oriole, St Lucia Black Finch, St Vincent Parrot, Whistling Warbler (St Vincent), Imperial Amazon and Red-necked Amazon (Dominica) and Barbuda Warbler.

Bird sanctuaries are special reserves that protect habitats that are rich in birdlife. They may offer tours, viewing points and educational tours.

There are many bird sanctuaries in the Caribbean, such as the Millet Bird Sanctuary, St Lucia; Mt Hartman National Park and Bird Sanctuary, Grenada; The Governor Michael Gore Bird Sanctuary, Grand Cayman; and the Guyana Botanical Gardens. However, there are also many other sites that are popular for bird-watching.

> **Did you know...?**
>
> According to the Society for the Conservation & Study of Caribbean Birds (S.C.S.C.B.) there are 770 species of bird in the Caribbean region (excluding Trinidad and Tobago), of which 148 are only found in the Caribbean, and at least 105 are found only on a single island.

The second largest frigate bird colony in the western hemisphere, located on the island of Barbuda, was devastated by Hurricane Irma in 2017.

Exercise

1. Suggest two reasons why the Caribbean has such a rich variety of bird species.

2. How does a bird sanctuary differ from any other bird-watching site?

Mammals

A **mammal** is any animal where the female feeds her young on milk from her own body. Examples of mammals include humans, dogs, lions, bats and whales (the largest mammal on Earth). Worldwide, there are over 5000 species of mammal.

The islands of the Caribbean have limited numbers of different land mammals. This is because unlike fish, birds or bats, mammals are less likely to reach an isolated island from a continent. The few species present probably evolved from a few individuals that were transported to the island after being stranded on driftwood or that were introduced by Amerindians and colonial visitors.

In fact, many island mammals have been driven to extinction due to the introduction of competing or predatory species like rats and mongooses, and by mass hunting, which causes the collapse of important food chains. For many of these extinct species, the Caribbean was the only place on Earth where they were found. One example is the Barbados Raccoon.

Some mammals, such as dolphins, live in water. The West Indian manatee, which lives in coastal wetlands, mangroves and rivers, is a highly endangered species. They used to be hunted, but they are now a protected species. Even though they are protected, they face danger from collisions with boats, getting tangled in fishing nets and loss of food due to water pollution. The biggest threat is the loss of the warm waters that provide their natural habitat. The Caribbean Monk Seal was a marine mammal that is now extinct due to hunting and overfishing.

Other mammals found on the Caribbean islands include:

wild goat	squirrel	cat
wild pig	grass mouse	mongoose
agouti	bat	raccoon
monkey	whale	deer
porcupine	dolphin	possum
tree rat	porpoise	armadillo

A West Indian manatee.

Activity

Look at the list of mammals. Find the names of the species of each mammal that can be found in the Caribbean. Collect pictures of as many of these as you can from the internet, magazines, newspapers or brochures. Write down any local names they may have, anything interesting about their appearance and where they can be found. For each type of animal find a species that isn't found in the Caribbean.

Exercise

3. In your own words, explain what a mammal is.

4. Why aren't there many different types of mammal on Caribbean islands?

5. How many different types of fauna do you think you see every day? Try counting them one day.

Key vocabulary

mammal

Our reptiles and insects

We are learning to:

- examine the features of the Caribbean's physical/natural heritage
- understand the biodiversity of Caribbean indigenous fauna: reptiles and insects.

Reptiles ❯❯

Reptiles include snakes, lizards, crocodiles, turtles and tortoises. They are **cold-blooded** animals that lay eggs and have dry, scaly skin. Amphibians – like frogs, toads and newts – are also cold-blooded animals that have a stage in their life when they can breathe underwater using gills.

Here are some species of reptile that can be found in the Caribbean:

> **Did you know...?**
>
> The world's smallest snake, the Barbados Threadsnake, is **endemic** (native) to the island of Barbados and was discovered to be a separate species in 2008.

Snakes	Lizards and iguanas	Frogs and toads
• Barbados Threadsnake • Barbour's Tropical Racer • Montserrat Worm Snake • Antilles Racer • Red-Bellied Racer • St Lucia Racer • Boa Constrictor • St Lucia Lancehead • Cook's Tree Boa • St Vincent Blacksnake • Grenadian Tree Boa • Cayman Dwarf Boa	• Panther Anole • Watt's Anole • St Lucian Anole • Barbados Anole • St Vincent Tree Anole • Puerto Rican Crested Anole • Martinique Spectacled Tegu • Dominican Ground Lizard • Green Iguana • Lesser Antilles Iguana • Blue Iguana	• Lesser Antilles Whistling Frog • Cane Toad • Cuban Tree Frog • Tink Frog • Red-snouted Tree Frog • Windward Ditch Frog • Highland Piping Frog

Exercise

1. Where have you seen the following types of animals?

   a) snakes   **b)** frogs   **c)** lizards

2. Do some quick research to arrange the list of reptiles in the table above into the following groups: native to the island, native to the region and not native to the region.

3. Make a list of some species of gecko and sea turtles found in the Caribbean.

Boa Constrictor.

An **insect** is a small animal that has six legs and a three-part body. Most insects have wings. Examples include ants, flies, butterflies, beetles and spiders. The tropical environment of the Caribbean supports many insects, including butterflies, beetles, ants, bees, wasps, dragonflies and damselflies, stick insects, katydids and crickets.

Insects aren't the only animals with many legs that can be found in the Caribbean; millipedes, centipedes, spiders and scorpions are also found here.

Case study

Insect hunter

Hi, I'm Adrian Hoskins: **entomologist** and natural history tour leader. My passion for butterflies and nature has taken me on many travels. I am from Britain but have always dreamed about visiting a tropical rainforest.

My wish to explore tropical places took me to Trinidad, where I was awestruck by the wonders of the rainforest. I saw my first morpho, daggerwing, glasswing, Heliconiinae and owl butterflies – species that I had dreamed about since childhood.

The hummingbirds and oropendolas, the haunting sound of cicadas, the high-pitched chirping of thousands of tiny frogs, and, best of all, my 'discovery' of the incredible moth *Siculodes aurorula* will stay in my mind until I die.

For the last 20 years I have been lucky enough to study and photograph the stunning butterflies of the rainforests, cloudforests and grasslands around the world.

I organise and lead butterfly-watching tours to many fascinating places.

Green iguana.

Blue Iguana.

Questions

1. An entomologist studies insects. What type of insect is Adrian Hoskins' special interest?

2. Why do you think he dreamed of visiting a tropical rainforest?

3. What was the name of the moth that Adrian found?

4. Which three types of habitat does he now visit in his work?

5. Choose three species of reptiles to research that are found in the Caribbean. Create a poster showing the three species, detailing their names, habitat, size, what they eat, and any other interesting details.

Key vocabulary

cold-blooded (of an animal)

endemic

insect

entomologist

Our wetlands

We are learning to:

- examine the features of the Caribbean's physical/natural heritage
- value the significance of our physical/natural heritage: wetlands.

Wetlands ⟩⟩

A wetland is an area of land that is regularly soaked with water. Wetlands link bodies of water (such seas and rivers) to the land. Coastal wetlands connect the land to the ocean. Inland wetlands fill with freshwater from rivers. Some wetlands have a mix of salty and fresh water called **brackish water**, depending on the tides. Wetlands such as Chancery Lane Swamp, Barbados and Central Mangrove Wetland, Grand Cayman, form part of our rich physical heritage.

Importance of wetlands ⟩⟩

- Stabilising water levels – Wetlands usually have many plants packed closely together. Their roots trap water from storm swells or high tides, preventing it from pushing too far inland, creating a protective **buffer** zone and reducing the destructive power of the water. This helps reduce land **erosion** as well.

- Cleaning water – When a river floods, the dirt from the land is trapped in the roots of wetland plants so that it doesn't reach the sea. In this way wetlands filter water. Some roots can even remove salt from water and chemicals can become trapped in wetland mud, so that the water is also more fresh and clean.

Mangroves are adapted to live in watery conditions.

- Habitats – The trees and water of wetlands provide places for fish, birds and other animals to live and feed. In fact, the shallow, murky water protects young fish so they can grow big enough to survive in the ocean or river.

- Human activity – People use wetlands for harvesting firewood, fishing, recreation and tourism. The farming industry relies on mangroves to help to ensure the balance of nutrients in the water and soil because they act as filters.

Exercise

1. What is a wetland?
2. Explain how wetlands can:
   a) protect the coast from erosion
   b) make water fresh and clean
   c) increase the number of fish on a coral reef
   d) be used to make money

Discussion

In groups, discuss whether tourism harms or helps the wetlands. How can tourism help to protect our natural heritage?

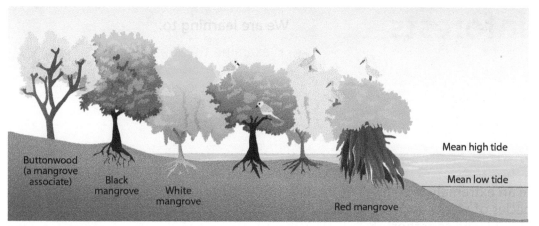

Different species of mangrove are adapted to live in different parts of the wetland. Red mangroves grow closest to the water, followed by white mangroves, black mangroves then buttonwood trees.

Mangroves »

Mangroves are trees that are specially adapted to live in wetlands.

- 'Prop roots' raise the trunk of the tree high out of the water so that changes in water level don't affect the main plant too much.

- Mangroves also have special roots that grow away from the main tree and grow upwards out of the mud. Regular roots can't breathe in waterlogged soil so these special roots breathe for the plant.

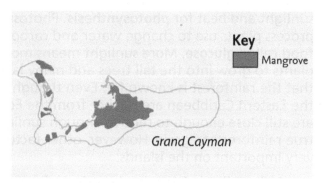

Distribution of mangrove vegetation in Grand Cayman.

- Seedlings of some mangroves grow roots while still on the tree. This means when they fall off they can grow into the mud immediately, so that when water levels change they do not get washed away.

Exercise

3. How are some mangroves able to breathe in waterlogged soil?

4. Why aren't mangrove seedlings washed away by the tides?

5. Look at the map of mangrove distribution in the Lesser Antilles.

   a) Which islands have no remaining mangrove vegetation?

   b) Are mangroves more likely to be found on the windward or leeward side of the islands?

   c) For Grand Cayman, explain why most of the mangroves are located in the island's large natural bay.

Key vocabulary

brackish water

buffer

erosion

Our rainforests

We are learning to:

- examine the features of the Caribbean's physical/natural heritage
- value the significance of our physical/natural heritage: rainforests.

Rainforests of the Caribbean

Rainforests have an extremely high level of biodiversity, with thousands of species of plants and insects, and hundreds of different animals all living together.

Guyana contains the best examples of true rainforest in the Caribbean. This is because Guyana is closest to the **Equator**, where the solar energy from the sun's rays is strongest. This is called **insolation.** This means the trees have plenty of sunlight and heat for **photosynthesis**. Photosynthesis is the process plants use to change water and carbon dioxide into food called **glucose.** More sunlight means more food for plants to grow into the tall trees and many layers of forest that the rainforest is known for. Even though the islands of the Eastern Caribbean are further from the Equator, they are still close enough to receive enough sunlight for some true rainforests to grow. However, other factors are also very important on the islands:

- Soil quality – plants need nutrients from the soil to make new leaves. Good soils like volcanic soil contain many nutrients.
- Rainfall – water is also required for photosynthesis to take place. Low rainfall means less glucose (food) for the plants, and less growth.
- Windward vs leeward – strong winds on the Atlantic (windward) side of islands means that trees may be shorter since the force of the wind makes growing upwards harder. The opposite is true for the leeward side.

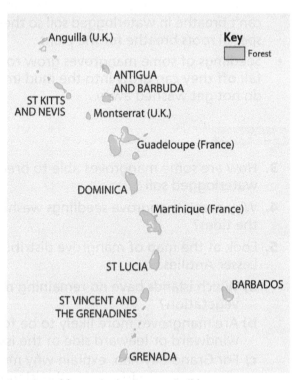

Location of forests in the Eastern Caribbean.

The forests in the Caribbean perform a number of important functions:

- Prevent erosion – The trees break the fall of the raindrops on their way to the ground, meaning their force does not break up the earth and soil. The root systems of trees act as filtration systems. Trees take up some pollutants through their roots. Some trees can actually break down pollutants such as solvents and pesticides.
- Flooding – The roots soak up water that would otherwise flood the area.
- Oxygen – Trees give out oxygen, so the proportion of fresh oxygen in the atmosphere is greater in forested areas.
- Air quality – Trees absorb pollution from the atmosphere, such as nitrogen oxide, carbon monoxide, ozone and other chemicals. They also reduce air temperature. Some pollutants, such as ozone, only form at high temperatures, so the lower air temperatures reduce the formation of these pollutants.
- Habitats – Many animals use trees for nesting, roosting and breeding. Trees next to watersheds provide protection for some water species. Tree debris such as leaf matter and chunks of broken wood get used by fish and other aquatic animals. Branches, leaves, fruit and flowers form part of the food webs of many ecosystems.
- Temperature – Trees provide shade along the banks of rivers and dams and release water in the form of water vapour through transpiration. This has a cooling effect on the temperature.

Research

The weather in a rainforest goes through a special daily cycle from morning to night. This cycle depends on the plants in the forest, but it includes changes in temperature, humidity and rainfall. Research the characteristics of this cycle.

Discussion

How many different types of forest tree can you list as a class? Are any parts of these trees used in your country for medicine, decoration or food?

Exercise

1. What is insolation and why is it important for rainforest growth?
2. Explain why Caribbean islands show a range of forest types instead of only true rainforests.
3. What functions do the rainforests in the Caribbean perform? What do you think would happen if there were no rainforests?
4. Write a letter to a newspaper about the importance of preserving the rainforests.

Key vocabulary
....

Equator

insolation

photosynthesis

glucose

Coastal areas and waterfalls

We are learning to:

- examine the features of the Caribbean's physical/natural heritage
- value the significance of our physical/natural heritage: coral reefs, coastal areas, beaches, waterfalls.

Coral reef »

Coral reefs are the sea's most diverse ecosystems. They support so much plant and animal life that they are known as the rainforests of the sea.

Coral reefs are highly valuable to life on Earth. They perform the following important functions:

- provide food
- protect shorelines
- provide jobs for people who work in tourism
- produce some kinds of medicines.

Some of the most threatened places around our islands are the coral reefs, which are endangered by global warming and pollution.

Coastal areas and beaches »

In the Caribbean, some of our greatest natural resources are our beaches. Beaches such as Dover Beach, Barbados; Dickenson Bay, Antigua; and Marigot Bay, St Lucia, are some of the main attractions to tourists. Together with our seas, rivers and coral reefs these are all resources that need to be protected.

Fishing beds »

Like many islands and coastal cities around the world, the Eastern Caribbean has a long history of fishing. Our waters are home to tuna, snapper, flying fish, kingfish, carite, croakers, bechine and shrimp.

However, fish populations all over the world are under threat.

This is because of:

- trawling
- overfishing
- pollution.

Did you know...?

One quarter of all species of sea animal depend on coral reefs for shelter and food, yet coral reefs cover less than 1 per cent of the Earth's surface.

Project

Research some of the different species of coral found in the Eastern Caribbean Sea. You may use books or the internet. Print or draw pictures of at least five different types of coral.

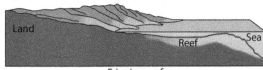

Fringing reef

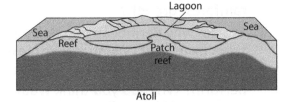

Atoll

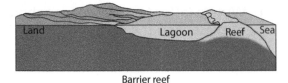

Barrier reef

Types of coral reef.

The physical environment of the Caribbean includes other fascinating features such as waterfalls. **Waterfalls** are places where rivers flow over a steep edge of a cliff or mountain. The sound and spectacle of falling water is a natural wonder for people all over the world. There are many waterfalls in the Caribbean, including Diamond Falls, St Lucia; Falls of Baleine, St Vincent; Victoria Falls, Grenada; and Kaieteur Falls, Guyana, which has a single drop of 741 ft, the tallest in the world.

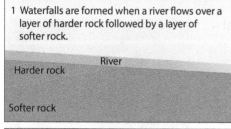

1 Waterfalls are formed when a river flows over a layer of harder rock followed by a layer of softer rock.

River

Harder rock

Softer rock

2 The soft rock orders more quickly forming a step in the river bed.

Harder rock

Softer rock

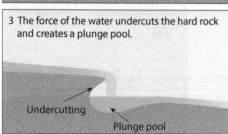

3 The force of the water undercuts the hard rock and creates a plunge pool.

Undercutting

Plunge pool

4 The hard rock is left overhanging and because it isn't supported, it eventually collapses.

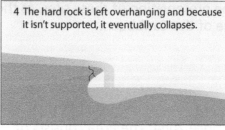

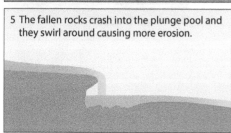

5 The fallen rocks crash into the plunge pool and they swirl around causing more erosion.

6 Over time, this process is repeated and the waterfall moves upstream.

Waterfall recedes upstream

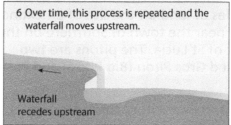

How waterfalls are formed.

Exercise

1. In your own words, describe why it is important to protect coral reefs.

2. What threatens the coral reefs?

3. Consider the diagram above; try to write a definition for each type of coral reef shown by describing its shape, distance from the coastline and other features.

4. Research a beach near you. Find out:
   - the size of the beach and who mainly uses it
   - facilities available to visitors
   - whether any environmental problems are facing the beach.

   Prepare a written report about this beach. Draw a map of your country and locate the beach on it.

Discussion

Are our beaches part of our heritage? If so, how should we protect them?

Key vocabulary

coral reef

waterfall

World Heritage Sites

We are learning to:

- examine the features of the Caribbean's physical/natural heritage
- value the significance of our physical/ natural heritage: World Heritage Sites.

Heritage sites ⟩⟩

A heritage site can have historical, cultural, social or physical significance. It can be a forest, a building, an island, a desert, a lake, or even a whole city. Some sites are listed as World Heritage Sites by UNESCO.

To date, in total 22 sites of historical and natural importance have been identified as World Heritage Sites in the Caribbean. The aim is to ensure the preservation of these sites, as they are part of the heritage of the Caribbean.

The Pitons, St Lucia.

Case study

The Pitons, St Lucia

The Pitons Management Area in St Lucia has been a World Heritage Site since 2004. The area consists of nearly 12 square miles of land on the site of an extinct volcano. The area is near the town of Soufrière on the south-western coast of St Lucia. The pitons are two mountain peaks called Gros Piton (Big Piton) and Petit Piton (Little Piton).

On both Gros Piton and Petit Piton, there are forests rich in flora and fauna. Gros Piton alone has 148 plant species, some of which are rare.

There are also 27 different species of bird, as well as rodents, opossums, bats, reptiles and amphibians.

The sea also forms part of the Piton Management Area. The sea has extensive coral reefs and many species of fish and other living organisms.

Questions

1. What type of heritage site are the Pitons?

2. How many World Heritage Sites are there currently in the Caribbean?

3. In your own words, describe which flora and fauna are at the Pitons.

Research

In groups, and using the internet, identify the 22 UNESCO World Heritage Sites in the Caribbean. In your findings, include the name of the site, the country and the year the site was awarded World Heritage status.

Case study

Brimstone Hill National Park, St Kitts and Nevis

Brimstone Hill National Park was established as a national park in October 1987, in recognition of its importance as a national cultural, historical and architectural resource. It was added to the UNESCO World Heritage list in 1999.

A single cannon was installed in 1690, and enslaved labour was used for the rest of the building process until it was completed towards the end of the 1700s. The buildings and walls are made of a volcanic rock called **basalt** and decorated with limestone elements.

The site features historic architecture dating from the 17th and 18th centuries, when colonialism and the rise of new societies in the Eastern Caribbean were at their peak. It was used until 1853, when it was abandoned.

The site is about 15 hectares, with Fort George, the main building, at its heart. There is also a 1.6 km buffer zone surrounding the site.

Facilities include a Visitor's Centre, and a Conference and Banquet Centre.

Adapted from: http://www.brimstonehillfortress.org/management_conservation.asp?siteid=8.

Brimstone Hill National Park, St Kitts and Nevis.

Questions

1. In your own words, explain why the Brimstone Hill National Park was set up.

2. Create a timeline for the Brimstone Hill National Park using the dates mentioned.

3. Work in pairs. Choose a heritage site in the Caribbean that tourists like to visit and use at least five different sources to research the site. Present your information on a wall chart. Your chart should have pictures and information arranged under these headings: location, historical background, importance and reservation.

Did you know...?

The Belize Barrier Reef Reserve system is a World Heritage Site. It is on the list of sites that are considered to be in danger. This means that extra attention must be paid to protect this site so that it may be preserved.

Project

You are the president of your school's Environmental Club. Create a five-step plan to prevent the extinction or destruction of a type of flora or fauna that is indigenous to your country and is part of our physical/natural heritage. Write a short essay outlining why you think the flora or fauna is in danger and the details of your five-point plan. Present it to your class.

Key vocabulary

basalt

Conserving our resources

We are learning to:

- examine the features of the Caribbean's physical/natural heritage
- value the significance of our physical/natural heritage: conserving our resources.

Conserving our resources 》

Why should we **conserve** our resources?

- Moral reasons – As human beings we have a moral obligation not to destroy other species or our environment.
- Ecological reasons – Plants provide food and shelter for animals, as well as resources for humans, such as wood. Animals provide food and help with natural cycles such as through pollination.
- Economic and scientific reasons – Medicines, foods and other products come directly from nature. If we destroy the environment, we reduce the chances of helping ourselves.

Water pollution.

In most parts of the world, the environment is harmed by air, land and sea **pollution**. Pollution can destroy habitats as well as fauna and flora. Most states have, therefore, set aside areas of land that are given special protection in order to allow the flora and fauna to survive. They have also brought in laws to protect forests and other environments.

Endangered habitats 》

Human activities easily damage and destroy natural habitats. An **endangered** natural habitat is one that is in danger of becoming destroyed or extinct, by human activities or other changes. When a particular type of habitat is destroyed, the plants and animals that live there lose their natural homes. These plants and animals may also become endangered or **extinct**. This is a great threat to the biodiversity of the planet.

Some threats to natural habitats include:

- land clearing and cattle grazing
- logging and deforestation
- global warming and climate change
- drilling for oil and gas
- overfishing.

Research

In a scrapbook, collect as many pictures of the different ecological sites in your country as you can. Use magazines, the internet, newspapers or brochures. Write down their names, where they can be found and any special facts about them.

Human activities cause many changes to the environment. We clear land in order to develop cities, roads, factories and other built environments.

What happens to animals and plants that used to live in a particular habitat when we clear it? Some species can migrate to other areas. Many others simply can no longer survive. When a whole species ceases to exist, we say it has become extinct.

A species is endangered if it is in danger of becoming extinct in the near future. Endangered species meet one of these criteria:

- Their habitat is about to be changed or destroyed.
- The species has been overexploited – for example, overfished or overhunted.
- Diseases or predators are causing the population to drop faster than the species can breed to replace it.
- Natural or human-made factors are affecting the species.
- The population is declining and scientists do not have enough information to know how many individuals are left.

In the Caribbean, we have several endangered species, including our leatherback turtles, hawksbill turtles and West Indian manatees.

Some of our endangered birds are the St Lucia parrot, St Vincent parrot and Imperial Amazon parrot. Some of the other endangered animals in the Caribbean include the Cayman Islands' Blue iguana and the Dominican Crapaud.

Baby leatherback turtles. Leatherback turtles are a vulnerable population. They nest on sandy Eastern Caribbean coasts.

Exercise

1. Name five threats to natural habitats.
2. Give three reasons why some species are in danger of becoming extinct.
3. Why do you think some habitats and species have become endangered?
4. Suggest three ways we can prevent more species from becoming endangered.

Key vocabulary

conserve

pollution

endangered

extinct (or extinction)

Questions

See how well you have understood the topics in this unit.

1. Match the key vocabulary word with its definition.

   i) man-made (built) heritage

   ii) man-made

   iii) built environment

   iv) heritage

   v) heritage site

   a) a place that has special historic, cultural or social value, usually protected by law in order to preserve it

   b) something that has been built or made by people

   c) features that belong to the culture of a society that were created in the past and have historical importance to that society

   d) buildings created by people which form an important part of our cultural history

   e) surroundings formed by structures made by people

2. For each heritage site below say which country it is found in and one interesting characteristic about it.

   a) St George's Cathedral

   b) Roseau Cathedral

   c) St John's Cathedral

3. Match these buildings to the description of what they are used for:

   i) Government House, Morne Fortune, St Lucia

   ii) Ilaro Court, Bridgetown, Barbados

   iii) The Courthouse, Kingstown, St Vincent

   iv) Government Headquarters, Basseterre, St Kitts and Nevis

   a) official residence of the Prime Minister

   b) houses the Court and House of Assembly

   c) the Prime Minister's office and government ministries are found here

   d) official residence of the Governor General

4. Explain the difference between flora and fauna.

5. Describe some marine ecotourism activities in Tobago Cays, St Vincent and the Grenadines, or forest ecotourism activities in the Guyanese interior.

6. True or false? Reptiles are warm-blooded and have dry, hairy skin.

7. Give three functions of the wetlands.

8. Why are coral reefs important to the islands of the Caribbean?

9. Explain in 100 words the important functions that the rainforests in the Caribbean perform.

10. What is a World Heritage Site? How many are there in the Caribbean?

11. Explain in no more than 50 words why, as a region, we need to conserve our resources.

Checking your progress

To make good progress in understanding different aspects of our heritage, check to make sure you understand these ideas.

Define man-made heritage and built environment.

Examine historical sites in the Caribbean.

Explain the significance of our built or man-made heritage.

Define physical and natural heritage.

Explain what is meant by indigenous flora and fauna.

Explain why sustainable tourism is important for the Caribbean.

Describe the ecological heritage of some Caribbean countries.

Name species of fauna that are indigenous to the Caribbean.

Create labelled posters showing the flora and fauna indigenous to the Caribbean.

Name features of the Caribbean's physical heritage.

Name World Heritage Sites in the Caribbean.

Explain why we need to conserve our resources.

Unit 8: Our environment

In this unit you will find out ⟩⟩

Physical resources and our environment

- Define relevant terms and concepts: exploitation
- Assess the impact of the use of natural resources on the environment
- Understand the effects of the use of natural resources on the environment
- Demonstrate concern for the impact of the overuse of natural resources on the environment
- Define relevant terms and concepts: sustainable use of resources
- Discuss CARICOM and OECS policies governing sustainable use of resources
- Understand policies on the use of natural resources
  - ○ Strategic plan for CARICOM 2015–19: Repositioning CARICOM
  - ○ OECS Sustainable Development Goals

Humans and our environment

- Discuss the reasons for changes in population distribution and density
  - ○ internal migration
  - ○ push and pull factors
  - ○ international and inter-island migration

Places and our environment

- Define tourism
- Identify tourism sites in the Eastern Caribbean
- Factors responsible for the development of the tourist industry
  - ○ natural factors
  - ○ human factors
- The advantages of tourism
  - ○ generation of income, job creation, promotes interconnectedness
  - ○ cruise tourism in the Eastern Caribbean: successes and advantages
- The impact of tourism on the environment
  - ○ water resources, land degradation, pollution, loss of land and habitats, climate change, damage to historical sites

Physical resources and our environment

We are learning to:

- define relevant terms and concepts: exploitation
- assess the impact of the use of natural resources on the environment.

What are natural resources?

Natural resources are materials that form naturally in or on the Earth. These include substances such as coal, oil and gas. Natural resources are considered very valuable and are sold between countries.

Many natural resources have to be **extracted** (taken out) from the Earth. Mining is a common way of extracting natural resources like coal, gold and tin.

Natural resources can be used as **raw materials** – that is, they are used to make something else. For example, trees are an example of a natural resource as they form naturally. Trees are also raw materials, because we can make paper, furniture and houses from them.

Mining is a way of extracting natural resources like coal, gold and tin from the ground.

Renewable and non-renewable resources

Natural resources can be both renewable and non-renewable.

- **Renewable resources** can be constantly replaced and will never be used up – for example, water and sunlight.
- **Non-renewable resources** cannot be replaced. Once they have been used up, they are gone for good – for example, **fossil fuels** such as coal, oil and gas. Non-renewable resources are often considered more valuable because they cannot be replaced.

An offshore oil rig.

Exploitation of our natural resources

Countries and companies can make a lot of money through the exploitation of natural resources. For example, countries such as Brazil have exploited their natural rainforests in order to make money.

However, this has come at the expense of the environment. Much of the deforested land is very poor quality now, and therefore is unsuitable for other industries, such as farming.

Activity

Choose one resource and produce a report of about 200 words. Show how its use has resulted in the destruction of the environment. Use the internet or magazines and add photos to your report.

The use and overuse of natural resources has many negative effects on the environment:

Natural resource	Impact on the environment
Coal	• Burning coal creates thick smoke that can **pollute** towns and cities. • Burning coal releases many dangerous gases into the atmosphere, such as sulphur dioxide. Large amounts of these gases in the atmosphere can be vary harmful, as they trap heat energy and can lead to climate change and global warming.
Oil	• Oil that is used to fuel vehicles and planes and to heat homes releases dangerous gases into the atmosphere such as carbon dioxide and carbon monoxide. These gases can lead to climate change and global warming. • Oil that is extracted from the Earth often results in oil spills, where oil leaks out into the sea. This can result in a significant loss of wildlife.
Gas	• Gas used to heat homes and create electricity can release large amounts into the atmosphere. This can lead to climate change and global warming.
Wood (forests/ trees)	• Destroying forests can lead to global warming, as there are fewer trees to breathe in the carbon dioxide and release oxygen. • Deforestation can affect the **global hydrological cycle (or water cycle)**, the continuous movement of water around the world. As there are lots of trees in rainforests, these areas contribute a lot of moisture to the atmosphere. • Trees are also able to **intercept** and store water, which is useful to prevent flooding. When large areas of trees are cut down, less moisture is put back into the atmosphere through transpiration, and flooding increases, as rainwater is not intercepted by the vegetation. • Deforestation can lead to **soil erosion** and loss of habitat and wildlife.

Key vocabulary

natural resource

extracted

raw materials

renewable resources

non-renewable resources

fossil fuels

pollute

global hydrological cycle (the water cycle)

intercept

soil erosion

Exercise

1. Define the term natural resources and give examples.

2. Explain the difference between natural resources and raw materials.

3. Explain the terms renewable resources, non-renewable resources and exploitation.

4. Choose two natural resources and explain how the use of them impacts the environment.

5. Can you think of any other natural resources that are exploited?

The overuse of natural resources

We are learning to:

- demonstrate concern for the impact that the overuse of natural resources can have on the environment.

The use of natural resources and global warming

The overuse and burning of fossil fuels such as coal, oil and gas, as well as destruction of rainforests, can lead to **global warming**.

- Coal has been used for many centuries and continues to be important today. Coal is mainly used for power and heating homes.
- Oil is used as a fuel, to power vehicles and planes. It is also used to heat homes.
- One of the main uses of gas is to create electricity.

When all of these fuels are burned, they release dangerous gases into the atmosphere. One of the most dangerous of these is **carbon dioxide**.

The burning of fossil fuels contributes to global warming.

Greenhouse gases

Carbon dioxide is a **greenhouse gas**. This means that it is a gas that forms naturally in the atmosphere.

Small amounts of greenhouse gases in the atmosphere are a good thing, as they keep the temperatures in the atmosphere warm enough to sustain human life. However, too many greenhouse gases is dangerous.

Too much carbon dioxide, methane, nitrous oxide and the other greenhouse gases in the atmosphere leads to an increase in global temperature, otherwise known as global warming.

Global warming can have very negative impacts on the environment, such as melting of glaciers, increase in sea levels, higher temperatures, drought and an increase in hurricanes.

> **Did you know...?**
>
> Although Eastern Caribbean countries do not contribute significantly to greenhouse gas emissions, the Eastern Caribbean region is among those most vulnerable to global warming.

Exercise

1. Give two examples of activities that lead to global warming.
2. In your own words, define greenhouse gas and global warming.

The use of natural resources and oil spills ▶▶▶

Oil forms underneath the surface of the Earth. In order to extract the oil, people drill into the large reservoirs of oil that are found underground, often under seas and oceans.

Oil is then transported to countries by pipeline or oil tanker. Every so often, it escapes from these pipelines and tankers, which leads to an **oil spill**. This can have damaging effects on the environment.

- When oil spills into seas and oceans, coastal vegetation such as mangroves is destroyed, as oil coats the vegetation. This destroys the habitats of coastal wildlife and can lead to loss of life.
- Many birds are killed by oil spills as oil coats their feathers, which prevents them from flying.
- Marine mammals such as whales and dolphins are killed. Oil clogs their blowholes, stopping them from breathing.

Trinidad and Tobago oil spills ▶

In 1979, Trinidad and Tobago suffered a severe oil spill after two tankers crashed 16 km off the coast of Tobago. This caused 280 000 tonnes of oil to leak into the Caribbean Sea.

During this oil spill, very little harm was caused to the environment, as most of the oil was burned off and therefore never reached the shore.

In 2013, Trinidad and Tobago suffered another accident when 11 oil spills occurred from a pipeline off the coast of Trinidad. The damage recorded included the following:

- Several kilometres of coastline were coated in oil.
- Coastal vegetation was destroyed by the oil.
- Many marine animals were killed.
- Many marine birds were killed.

The 2013 oil spill off Trinidad and Tobago.

Exercise

3. Where is oil found?
4. How is oil extracted from the Earth?
5. Give two examples of how oil damages the environment.
6. Explain briefly what happened in Trinidad and Tobago in 1979 and 2013.

Key vocabulary

global warming

carbon dioxide

greenhouse gas

oil spill

Sustainable use of resources

We are learning to:

- define relevant terms and concepts: sustainable use of resources
- discuss strategies that can assist with the conservation of our natural resources: CARICOM and the OECS.

Sustainable use of resources 》

Sustainable development is development that uses resources responsibly, without using them up or destroying them. Any form of economic development has negative impacts on the environment and its natural resources, as well as benefits for the wealth of the country.

Sustainable development and CARICOM 》》

In 2015 the Strategic Plan for CARICOM '2015–2019: Repositioning CARICOM', was published. The plan was built around the ideal of '**resilience**'. Resilience means that Caribbean islands should be able to recover quickly from problems. This plan aims to keep the development goals of the region on track. The plan does this by considering the resources the region has and the best way to use them to overcome challenges. One of these resources is the environment, and the plan states that CARICOM member states will focus on protecting and preserving the environment. The plan includes the following steps to build environmental resilience:

- focus on coastal zone management that considers marine biodiversity
- improved forest resource management
- studying how plans for land use will affect the environment, to reduce or avoid pollution
- using renewable energy and clean energy options (like solar power) wherever possible
- using the best technologies to monitor environmental changes so that countries can respond to these changes quickly.

Solar energy farm in St Lucy, Barbados.

Exercise

1. In your own words, define the term sustainable development.
2. What is the aim of the Strategic Plan for CARICOM?
3. How does the Strategic Plan for CARICOM work?
4. Name three strategies in the plan to help environmental resilience.

Sustainable development in the OECS >>>

The OECS follows a number of Sustainable Development Goals presented by the United Nations. Each goal is handled by OECS units that work to set up programmes to achieve them. Resource management is a main theme throughout these goals. The following OECS units handle some parts of sustainable development within OECS member states.

- The Climate Change and Disaster Risk Management Unit – climate change will increase risks to natural resources. Access to natural resources and their quality will be affected. For example, rising sea levels will reduce access to coastal land and reduce the quality of freshwater since seawater will mix with underground freshwater. This unit helps member countries get information to better manage the resources that are at risk from climate change.

- Sustainable Energy Unit – using renewable energy sources where possible and using non-renewable energy sources more efficiently is important in sustainable resource management. This means energy resources can provide more energy that is cleaner and lasts longer. This reduces the **carbon footprint** of each country. One of the aims of this unit is to provide the technology needed to use geothermal energy and solar energy. Providing information on the best building designs and practices that reduce energy waste is also a goal of this unit.

- The Ocean Governance and Fisheries Unit – the focus of this unit is maintaining marine ecosystems. Marine ecosystems are important for the economy, for example healthy coral reefs encourage tourism and commercial fishing. However, taking from these ecosystems must be balanced with how fast they can recover. This unit will be driven by scientific research on how much can be taken from the oceans without damaging the ecosystem. Laws can then be guided by this research.

Mining gold can bring profit but can damage forestry, land and water resources.

Research

Find out which ministry handles environmental management in your country. Write a brief summary of one ministry programme for sustainable use of land or forest resources and marine or water resources in your country.

Exercise

5. Which organisation do the OECS Sustainable Development goals come from?

6. List three OECS units that handle programmes on sustainable use of resources and explain how each works to help member countries manage their resources.

Key vocabulary

sustainable development

resilience

carbon footprint

Policies on the use of natural resources

We are learning to:

- discuss strategies that can assist with the conservation of our natural resources.

Policies on the use of natural resources in Trinidad and Tobago

Conservation is concerned with managing the use of natural resources. Conservation strategies allow people to use natural resources, but they only allow the use of some of the resources so that they are left for future generations.

National Integrated Water Resources Management Policy: Trinidad and Tobago

Coastal pollution is a big problem in countries like Trinidad and Tobago.

The National Integrated Water Resources Management Policy is a strategy in Trinidad and Tobago designed to assist with the conservation of the nation's water resources. Its focus is to put into place policies with regard to:

- the quantity and quality of water resources
- the effect of pollution on the nation's water resources
- **watershed degradation** – Trinidad and Tobago's forests protect water resources; deforestation, quarrying and forest fires have reduced the number of forests and therefore had an impact on the water resources
- increasing demand from the domestic and industrial sector.

The objectives of the National Integrated Water Resources Management Policy include:

- to protect and manage watersheds and wetlands as sources of water
- to ensure the fair and efficient allocation of water among all water users
- to promote public education and awareness, and wise use of water resources
- to promote the use of appropriate technologies to facilitate sustainable water resources management.

Exercise

1. In your own words, define the term conservation.
2. Name two concerns that the National Integrated Water Resources Management Policy focuses on.
3. Name three objectives of the National Integrated Water Resources Management Policy.

Research

Choose one of the agencies discussed and write two paragraphs on any aspect of the strategies they adopt to conserve natural resources.

National Forestry Policy of Trinidad and Tobago

The National Forestry Policy (2011) was produced to protect the loss of forests and degradation caused by a number of factors, including demand for housing and commercial activities, demand for timber, forest fires, quarrying, poor forestry practices, and poor legislation and enforcement.

The policy objectives are:

- to optimise the contribution of forest resources to livelihoods – cultural and spiritual/religious use, while ensuring sustainable use of forests, including extraction of timber and wildlife
- to protect native genetic, species and ecosystem diversity
- to maintain and enhance the natural productivity of forest ecosystems and ecological processes (watershed functions, etc.) to provide important ecosystem services.

The National Forestry Policy also aims to raise awareness of the economic, social and cultural values of forests.

Areas such as the Blanchisseuse Forest Reserve in Trinidad and Tobago are protected by the National Forest Policy.

Environmental Management Authority (EMA) of Trinidad and Tobago

The Environmental Management Authority (EMA) was set up in 1995 to educate the public about the nation's environmental issues through public awareness programmes.

The Environmental Management Authority also:

- makes recommendations for a National Environment Policy
- develops and establishes national environmental standards and criteria
- conducts analyses of air, soil and water, and helps with emergency pollution incidents.

Exercise

4. Why does Trinidad and Tobago need a policy on forestry protection?

5. Outline the policies of the National Forestry Policy.

6. Name two of the roles of the Environmental Management Authority.

7. Why do you think raising awareness of environmental issues is a policy of all of these organisations?

Key vocabulary

watershed degradation

Humans and our environment

We are learning to:

- discuss the reasons for changes in population distribution and density.

Internal migration »

Migration is the movement of people from one area, or country, to another. Internal migration is when a person moves within the same country and **external migration** is when a person moves between two different countries.

There are two types of internal migration: **rural–urban migration** and **urban–rural migration**. Rural–urban migration is the movement of people from rural areas to urban areas. Urban–rural migration is the movement of people from urban areas to rural areas.

Some reasons for rural–urban migration are shown below:

Push factors	Pull factors
famine/crop failure/ drought/natural disasters/war	better living conditions
unemployment and low wages	more jobs and higher wages
poor housing	good housing
lack of clean water	better access to clean water
lack of schools	more and better schools
poor health care facilities	more and better health care facilities
poor or no power supplies	electricity and power supplies
lack of services and amenities	more services and amenities

Some reasons for urban–rural migration are shown below:

Push factors	Pull factors
overcrowding	few problems of overcrowding
high crime rates	lower crime rates
unemployment	job opportunities in rural occupations
pollution	less pollution

Discussion

In groups, discuss what pull factors would encourage someone to move to the area that you live in.

Exercise

1. In your own words, define the terms migration, internal migration and external migration.

2. Explain the differences between a push and a pull factor.

3. Give reasons why people might want to move away from a rural location.

Project

Interview people from your neighbourhood who have moved into the area and find out why they moved. Write up a report listing the different reasons.

Push and pull factors ▶▶▶

People moving location are influenced by **push** and **pull factors**. Pull factors encourage people to move to new locations and are often for good, positive reasons.

Urbanisation ▶▶▶

In every country, there are some people who live in rural areas (the countryside) and others who live in urban areas (the towns and cities). There tend to be far more people living in urban areas than rural areas because there are more opportunities there, such as more jobs, better housing and better health care.

Cities such as Bridgetown, Barbados (110 000), St John's, Antigua (82 000) and Castries, St Lucia (70 000) have some of the highest urban populations in the Eastern Caribbean. Increasing numbers of people living in the cities is referred to as **urbanisation.**

Population density ▶▶

The term population density refers to the average number of people living in one square kilometre. We work out the population density so that we can understand how well populated an area is. It also allows us to compare one area with another.

Areas can have a high, moderate or low population density. A high population density means that there are many people living per square kilometre, while a low population density means there are few people living per square kilometre.

Unemployment ▶▶

When someone has a job, they are **employed.** When someone does not have a job, they are **unemployed.** Unemployment is a situation where a person in the labour force is capable and willing to work, but has not yet found a job.

If you are unemployed, it is very difficult. You will not earn any money, so will not be able to pay for things such as a house, car or sometimes even food.

Exercise

4. Explain the following terms: urbanisation, population density, employed and unemployed.
5. "Internal migration of any kind affects the population distribution within a country." Explain in no more than 100 words if you agree with this statement.
6. Write a short essay of 200 words on the reasons people change where they live.

Push factors
- Fewer jobs
- Lower wages
- Crop failure
- Limited educational opportunities
- Poor housing, services, facilities
- More crime – less safe
- Poor infrastructure

Pull factors
- More jobs
- Higher wages
- Fertile land
- More educational opportunities
- Better housing, services, facilities
- Less crime – feel safer
- Better infrastructure

Key vocabulary

external migration

rural–urban migration

urban–rural migration

push factor

pull factor

urbanisation

employed

unemployed

Regional migration

We are learning to:

- describe some effects of external migration
- describe international migration patterns
- discuss the history of inter-island migration.

External migration

Migration to countries outside the region has always been a way for Caribbean people to achieve **upward mobility**. Migrants may work for more money or a stronger currency overseas. This **remittance** money can be saved to return home and purchase land, build houses, start businesses, or support their family. Migrants may get access to training, education and skills that may not be available at home. This may mean migrants can find better jobs in countries they move to, or at home upon returning.

In the past, unskilled workers could migrate easily since many hands were needed to fill the labour gap and carry out basic jobs. Young, skilled and educated migrants are now preferred since their special skills and knowledge can benefit existing economic areas and create new ones, making the economy stronger. When these skilled and educated people leave, their home countries cannot benefit from their talents. This is known as a brain drain.

Agriculture is one industry which uses migrant workers through guest worker schemes.

Discussion

As a class come up with some reasons why people may migrate from international countries to live in the Eastern Caribbean.

International migration

In the 1950s migration from the Caribbean to former colonising countries like the UK and other European countries was at its peak. Caribbean institutions like schools, hospitals, transport and banking were modelled on those in European countries. Therefore, Caribbean people who were trained regionally could transfer their skills easily, and they could earn more money. At this time, these European countries welcomed migrants because there was rebuilding to be done following World War II, and there were not enough men of working age.

In 1962 The Commonwealth Immigration Act made it very difficult to migrate to the UK. At the same time North American laws made it easier for Caribbean migrants to enter North America since their migration to the UK showed positive economic

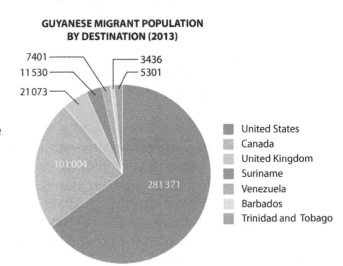

GUYANESE MIGRANT POPULATION BY DESTINATION (2013)

7401
11 530
21 073
3436
5301
101 004
281 371

- United States
- Canada
- United Kingdom
- Suriname
- Venezuela
- Barbados
- Trinidad and Tobago

effects. Canada and the United States had more land space to develop and wanted to improve their service industries. **Guest worker schemes** issued short-term and long-term work visas to Caribbean migrants. Jobs in the nursing, agriculture and hotel sectors were popular.

Inter-island migration 〉〉〉

Migration within the Eastern Caribbean has been driven by strong economies. Trinidad attracted migrants from the Eastern Caribbean in the 1970s because of the strength of Trinidad's oil-based economy. The success of Barbados' tourism and finance industries in the 1980s and 1990s meant the economy grew rapidly and attracted migrants from neighbouring islands. Similarly, the Bahamas, the Cayman Islands and Antigua attracted migrants due to the strength of their tourism, finance and off-shore industries.

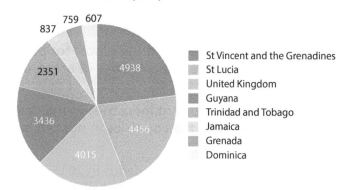

MIGRANT POPULATION IN BARBADOS BY COUNTRY OF ORIGIN (2013)

837 759 607
2351 4938
3436 4456
4015

- St Vincent and the Grenadines
- St Lucia
- United Kingdom
- Guyana
- Trinidad and Tobago
- Jamaica
- Grenada
- Dominica

Education encourages young people to migrate short-term to attend the University of the West Indies campuses in Barbados, Trinidad and Jamaica and other regional educational institutions.

When a country has a strong, growing economy it can attract workers from a few sectors:

- Plumbers, carpenters, masons and electricians as more homes, offices and factories need to be built.
- Highly paid professionals migrate because their skills are being underused at home, while there are opportunities for further promotion in growing economies.
- Artists, craftspeople and musicians migrate because people in growing economies have more money to spend on entertainment and recreation.

OECS member state citizens are allowed to migrate freely to take advantage of work opportunities. This promotes the sharing of knowledge, skills and training, and supports economies where there are labour shortages. This is important for regional integration. The Caribbean Single Market and Economy (CSME) allows free movement for some classes of workers including teachers, nurses, university graduates and media workers.

Project

Interview Caribbean nationals from other countries living in your neighbourhood. Find out the reasons why they moved and create a report listing the different reasons.

Exercise

1. Describe one negative effect and one positive effect of external migration.
2. What are two reasons why Caribbean international migration patterns changed in the 1960s?
3. What industries and countries have attracted inter-island migrants?
4. Explain why a growing economy attracts migrants.

Key vocabulary
....

upward mobility

remittance

guest worker scheme

Tourism in the Caribbean

We are learning to:

- define relevant terms and concepts
- identify tourism sites in the Caribbean.

Tourism ⟩⟩

Tourism is the practice of visiting places for pleasure. This might be visiting different countries or areas, or visiting specific sites of interest.

One of the most important industries in the Caribbean is tourism. For many of the countries in our region, tourism is crucial to the economy.

In the OECS countries and Barbados in 2016, 37.6 per cent of the population was employed in travel and tourism. Without our natural heritage, tourists would not visit the islands.

Sailing boats at Marigot Bay in St Lucia.

A **resort** is a place designed to offer visitors relaxing accommodation. A resort is usually a large hotel, or a type of complex, that offers accommodation, shops and leisure facilities such as swimming pools and restaurants.

Recently there has been a focus on ecotourism in the Caribbean, a type of tourism that allows tourists into a country or area but focuses on protecting the environment and local culture. Ecotourism means:

- travelling to undisturbed or unspoiled natural areas
- enjoying, studying or experiencing the natural environment without damaging it
- treating the environment responsibly and carefully
- benefiting local communities
- supporting conservation projects
- providing education to travellers and local communities.

Exercise

1. In your own words, define the terms: tourism, resort and ecotourism.
2. What percentage of the population of the OECS countries and Barbados works in the tourist industry?
3. Why is tourism important to the economies of many Caribbean countries?

Key vocabulary

resort

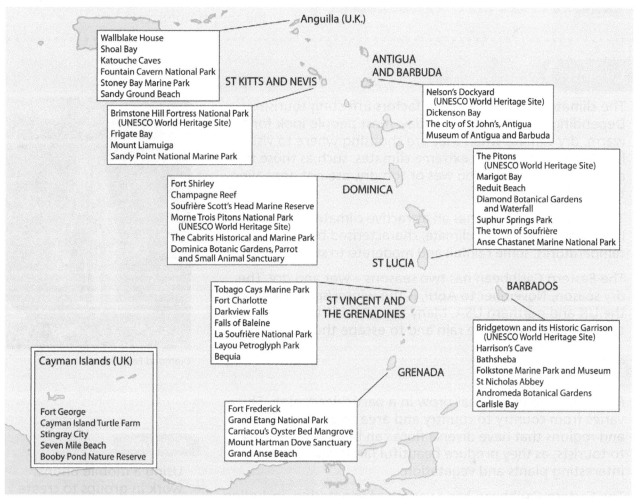

Tourist sites on Eastern Caribbean islands.

The map labels read:

Anguilla (U.K.)
- Wallblake House
- Shoal Bay
- Katouche Caves
- Fountain Cavern National Park
- Stoney Bay Marine Park
- Sandy Ground Beach

ST KITTS AND NEVIS
- Brimstone Hill Fortress National Park (UNESCO World Heritage Site)
- Frigate Bay
- Mount Liamuiga
- Sandy Point National Marine Park

ANTIGUA AND BARBUDA
- Nelson's Dockyard (UNESCO World Heritage Site)
- Dickenson Bay
- The city of St John's, Antigua
- Museum of Antigua and Barbuda

DOMINICA
- Fort Shirley
- Champagne Reef
- Soufrière Scott's Head Marine Reserve
- Morne Trois Pitons National Park (UNESCO World Heritage Site)
- The Cabrits Historical and Marine Park
- Dominica Botanic Gardens, Parrot and Small Animal Sanctuary

ST LUCIA
- The Pitons (UNESCO World Heritage Site)
- Marigot Bay
- Reduit Beach
- Diamond Botanical Gardens and Waterfall
- Suphur Springs Park
- The town of Soufrière
- Anse Chastanet Marine National Park

ST VINCENT AND THE GRENADINES
- Tobago Cays Marine Park
- Fort Charlotte
- Darkview Falls
- Falls of Baleine
- La Soufrière National Park
- Layou Petroglyph Park
- Bequia

BARBADOS
- Bridgetown and its Historic Garrison (UNESCO World Heritage Site)
- Harrison's Cave
- Bathsheba
- Folkstone Marine Park and Museum
- St Nicholas Abbey
- Andromeda Botanical Gardens
- Carlisle Bay

Cayman Islands (UK)
- Fort George
- Cayman Island Turtle Farm
- Stingray City
- Seven Mile Beach
- Booby Pond Nature Reserve

GRENADA
- Fort Frederick
- Grand Etang National Park
- Carriacou's Oyster Bed Mangrove
- Mount Hartman Dove Sanctuary
- Grand Anse Beach

Project

The map above shows some of the important tourist sites on Eastern Caribbean islands. For any two islands draw an outline map which shows:

a) a north arrow and scale

b) the capital city, airport and main harbour or port

c) the locations of each of the sites listed

For each site listed, write a short paragraph describing the site. Include interesting facts like the site's history, activities that can be done or wildlife that can be found there.

Development of the tourist industry

We are learning to:

- explain the natural factors that are responsible for the development of the tourist industry.

Climate »

The **climate** is one of the main factors affecting tourism. Depending on the type of holiday, most people look for a warm, dry climate when they are choosing where to visit on holiday. Countries with extreme climates, such as those that are too hot, too cold, too wet or too dry, are not appealing to tourists.

The Eastern Caribbean has an attractive climate for tourists. It has a tropical marine climate, characterised by warm temperatures, some rainfall and moderate to strong winds.

The Eastern Caribbean has two seasons – wet and dry. The dry season, November to April, is the winter/spring season in the UK and northern USA. Many tourists visit to enjoy warm temperatures with little rain and to escape the cold.

Diamond Falls, St Lucia.

Flora »»

Flora refers to plants that grow in a particular region. This varies from country to country and area to area. Countries and regions that have diverse flora can be more attractive to tourists, as they produce beautiful landscapes with interesting plants and vegetation.

The Eastern Caribbean has a variety of vegetation, including coastal mangroves, central rainforests and montane forests. These ecosystems attract people to the islands.

Activity

Using a mobile phone, work in groups to create a short video welcoming tourists to your island.

Exercise

1. Why is climate an important factor that influences tourism?
2. What characterises a tropical marine climate?
3. In your own words, define the term flora.

Activity

Write a short essay explaining why tourists should visit your island. Write about 100 words.

Fauna

Fauna includes all mammals, birds, amphibians, reptiles and fish that are found in a country or region. This may not be the most important factor affecting tourism. However, if a country has a large, varied fauna, it may be more appealing to tourists.

The most varied wildlife is found on volcanic islands. The chance to see, or swim with, nesting Green, Hawksbill or Leatherback sea turtles is particularly attractive to tourists. Rare bird species like the Grenada dove and St Lucia parrot, and butterflies are also a main attraction on the islands. Attractive fauna also include a variety of colourful species of reef fish and coral.

Shoal Bay, Anguilla.

Natural sites

Tourists visiting a country want to see the natural sites within the country. Some countries have many natural sites, such as lakes, beaches, mountains, coral reefs and forests, and these will all be appealing to tourists.

The Caribbean has an abundance of natural sites that are popular tourist destinations:

- white sand beaches of coral islands like Shoal Bay, Anguilla and Dickenson Bay, Antigua
- lakes such as Grand Etang Lake, Grenada and Freshwater Lake, Dominica
- waterfalls such as Dark View Falls, St Vincent and Diamond Falls, St Lucia.

Hiking is popular on volcanic peaks of mountainous St Kitts and Nevis. Nevis Peak, Nevis or Mount Liamuiga, St Kitts are crossed by hiking trails.

There are many tropical forests throughout the Caribbean that have an abundance of flora and fauna. The Cayman Islands and Barbados are popular for reef diving and snorkelling.

> **Did you know...?**
>
> Coral reefs are called the 'rainforests of the ocean' and the Caribbean has the highest level of coral reef diversity in the Atlantic Ocean.

Exercise

4. What does the term fauna mean?

5. What types of fauna can be found in the Caribbean? Name some which you have seen in your country.

6. Countries with plenty of natural sites can be more appealing to tourists. Why is this?

Key vocabulary

climate

Tourism and culture

We are learning to:

- explain the human factors that are responsible for the development of the tourist industry.

Natural factors make the region an attractive destination; however, human factors also attract tourists.

Social and economic stability

The islands of the Eastern Caribbean generally do not experience major social unrest such as wars or political strife, and crime rates are low.

Safety is always a major concern of tourists when choosing holiday destinations, so this makes the Eastern Caribbean attractive.

Social services such as hospitals, police, sanitation and transport are also easily accessible and are run using internationally accepted standards.

Amenities such as running water, telecommunications and electricity are also well maintained.

Tourists are accustomed to certain comforts and conveniences, and the availability of these in the Eastern Caribbean makes the region attractive.

Food is a cultural attraction in the Eastern Caribbean.

Heritage

The Eastern Caribbean has a rich and diverse heritage created by a mix of indigenous cultures, colonial rule and African ancestry. This means that in a relatively small space tourists can experience cultural experiences from many different parts of the world:

- colonial-era buildings such as forts, religious buildings and plantation houses are major attractions
- indigenous crafts and ways of life, both current and archaeological
- **creole languages** (created by mixing different languages) are all parts of Eastern Caribbean heritage which intrigue tourists.

Research

Write a recipe for the national dishes of five Eastern Caribbean islands including your own. Make sure you list the ingredients for each one.

Food and drink >>>

Each Eastern Caribbean country has a culinary culture based on:

- the use of local ingredients
- differences in popularity and availability of ingredients
- preferred cooking methods and...
- ultimately, taste.

Tourists appreciate the opportunity to try something different and unique. Many islands have developed tourism products based around food, for example the Barbados Food and Rum Festival and the Cayman Cookout. Tourists make it a point to try the local national dish on any island they visit.

Festivals >>

Eastern Caribbean festivals of music and dance are known for featuring local musical styles such as calypso, soca and zouk, and for featuring local and international artists.

Street parties such as Vincy Mas, Grand Kadooment, Antigua Carnival and St Lucia Carnival are popular for their relaxed atmosphere, where tourists and locals alike enjoy food, dancing and entertainment.

A number of events are scheduled around these parties such as calypso competitions and large outdoor markets selling local products.

People >>>

Eastern Caribbean people are known for their hospitality, approachability and friendliness. Tourists like to visit the area because of this. Caribbean people are aware of the importance of tourism to the economy and make an even greater effort to make visitors comfortable.

Project

Write a short report on the history of one festival, one archaeological site and one colonial site that attract tourists in your country.

Exercise

1. In your own words, describe why tourists find each of the following factors attractive in the Eastern Caribbean:

   a) social and economic stability
   b) heritage
   c) food and drink
   d) festivals
   e) people

Key vocabulary

amenities

creole language

245

Advantages of tourism

We are learning to:

- describe the advantages of tourism.

Generation of income ▶▶

There are many positive effects of tourism for a country or region. All countries are keen to develop their tourist industry, as it can generate lots of money for the country. This money can then be used to improve the services in the country, such as schools, hospitals, housing and communications. It also improves the standard of living of the people of the country.

If a country has a profitable tourist industry, many companies and businesses will want to invest there. When this occurs, more jobs are created – which helps with the problem of unemployment – and more wealth is produced for the country.

Tourism employs 37.6 per cent of the population and is well developed in the Eastern Caribbean. In countries with limited natural resources like oil, tourism is a major industry. It helps reduce dependence on agriculture. Barbados had 631 513 stay-over visitors for 2017, a record year, even though the population is only 285 000.

An increase in tourist numbers allows more people in the country to create small businesses of their own that cater to foreign visitors. This can help to tackle unemployment within Trinidad and Tobago.

Tourists who visit places such as the Botanical Gardens in St Vincent, contribute to the income of the island.

Job creation ▶▶▶

In Antigua and Barbuda, 19 500 people are employed in tourist-related industries. In St Lucia the figure is 36 000 and in Anguilla 4500.

Many jobs have been provided in the tourist industries, such as hotels, restaurants, cafés, entertainment facilities and other shops and services. This helps to tackle the high unemployment rates in the country.

Discussion

In groups, discuss the impact of tourism on the environment. Identify disadvantages as well as advantages, and then share your findings with the rest of the class.

Exercise

1. Why is the generation of income from tourism important to countries?

2. What types of jobs are created by tourism? Can you think of any more?

Key vocabulary

interconnectedness

multiplier effect

Interconnectedness is a geographical term that refers to countries being connected and is used to show how countries are connected in the world today.

Transport – Improvements in worldwide transport have made visiting foreign countries much more possible than previously. It is now possible to fly around the world in approximately 70 hours – almost three days. The Eastern Caribbean tourism industry is well developed and is one of the premier tourist destinations in the world. The Caribbean Tourism Organization is working hard to promote tourism in all Caribbean regions, focusing specifically on the importance of air transport as a means of allowing and supporting tourism in these regions.

Communications – Countries must make sure that there are good road, rail (where possible) and air networks in the country. Many countries now have international airports, big enough to accommodate large planes. For example, St Vincent has recently opened the Argyle International Airport, which replaces its previous, much smaller airport. Smaller islands can be reached by boat or smaller local flights. Development of roads is limited by the relief of the land in some countries.

Multiplier effect – The increased income generated by businesses associated with the tourism industry creates more wealth. More people are employed in the tourist sector and unemployment is reduced. Local people then have more spending power and are able to spend money in other shops and services, making these business owners wealthier. More and more money is then injected into the economy.

Other consequences of the multiplier effect include:

- transport improvements, such as building more main roads, as well as improving existing road networks
- improvements to schools and health care
- increased employment.

Tourists have the opportunity to interact with stingrays on a sandbar off Grand Cayman.

Exercise

3. In your own words, define the term interconnectedness.
4. Choose two advantages of tourism and state why they are so important.
5. Explain why tourism in the Caribbean is so important to the region.
6. Create a graphic organiser to show the advantages of tourism for the Caribbean.

Cruise tourism

We are learning to:

- describe the success of cruise tourism
- explain how cruise tourism is different from other types of tourism
- describe advantages of cruise tourism.

Cruise tourism development »

Cruise tourism developed as a strong industry for the Caribbean in the 1980s and now the Caribbean is the most popular destination for cruise vacations. The port a cruise starts from is called a **home port** and destination ports are called **ports of call**. The busiest home port for Eastern Caribbean cruises is San Juan, Puerto Rico, while Miami and Fort Lauderdale are also important. Ships sail between ports of call at night, and during the day passengers disembark to enjoy each destination. Destinations with cruise terminals receive more cruises.

Cruise ship docked at St John's, Antigua.

The Eastern Caribbean has been successful in cruise tourism because:

- it is close to the USA, the main cruise market
- there are colonial links to Europe so Europeans visit to experience a part of their country's colonial past
- each island has a unique character in culture, language and landscape, so tourists get a variety of experiences on one trip
- the islands are close together, so trips can be scheduled to visit one island every day.

The guest information booth at the cruise terminal in Bridgetown, Barbados.

Cruise vs long-stay tourists »»

- Cruise tourists spend one or two days while long-stay tourists usually spend a week or more.
- Cruise passengers spend less money on-shore since many of their needs, such as meals, are provided on the cruise ship. However, cruise tourists visit many islands and more islands benefit from each tourist's spending in one trip.
- Cruise tourists usually do not have enough time to participate in many different activities or see many attractions. Usually they invest in seeing one attraction and shopping, while long-stay tourists can see a variety of attractions.
- Cruise tourists prefer short tours, coastal activities and attractions close to the port or capital city, where transport back to port is easy and there is duty-free

Project

Write a list of cruise ships that visit your country. Find out where each ship's home port is and what other destinations they visit. On a map of the Eastern Caribbean draw a line representing each cruise. Use a different colour for each line. Add a key to your map.

shopping. Cruise ships follow very strict schedules, and cruise tourists are always concerned about having time to shop and make it back to the ship on time.

Advantages of cruise tourism ⟫⟫⟫

Employment and spending – Cruise ships employ some Caribbean citizens, providing training and skills development, and reducing unemployment. Cruise ships form links with local tour companies so they have guaranteed customers and income. Ships may resupply at ports of call, purchasing products from local businesses. Each individual visitor may spend less, but cruise ships bring many tourists at the same time so local businesses benefit from volume spending. Sellers of handicrafts and speciality foodstuffs (local spices, seasonings and sauces) and small-scale tour guides benefit most from this type of spending.

Taxes – Caribbean governments receive **head tax**, taxes paid by cruise lines for the use of port facilities, and taxes from large and small businesses that benefit from cruises.

Marketing – Cruise ships organise vibrant marketing campaigns that promote their Caribbean destinations. Cruise trips can be considered a type of window shopping for a future long-stay Eastern Caribbean holiday.

Discussion

As a class discuss the possible disadvantages of cruise tourism to the Eastern Caribbean.

**Cruise Line Expenditure ($US Millions)
Cruise Year 2014/15**

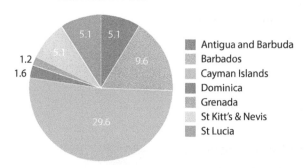

- Antigua and Barbuda
- Barbados
- Cayman Islands
- Dominica
- Grenada
- St Kitt's & Nevis
- St Lucia

Exercise

1. Why has cruise tourism been successful in the Eastern Caribbean?

2. Describe some differences between cruise and long-stay tourists.

3. Explain how cruises benefit the Eastern Caribbean economy.

Key vocabulary

home port

port of call

head tax

The impact of tourism on the environment

We are learning how to:
- discuss the impact of tourism on the environment.

Impact of tourism on the environment ⟩⟩

Tourism can bring many benefits to a country, but it can also have some negative effects on the environment. Negative effects will occur when the number of visitors is greater than the environment's ability to cope with these people.

Activities such as jet skiing can cause water pollution.

Water resources ⟩⟩

If a country has limited access to fresh water, many tourists visiting the area will need plenty of water for things such as swimming pools and showers and baths. This can lead to water shortages where there are already low water levels.

Land degradation ⟩⟩⟩

Land degradation is a process in which the quality of the land is reduced, either by extreme weather or human activities. One example is soil erosion, which can occur where there are large volumes of people walking in fragile areas. Soil erosion can occur in mountain and hilly regions, where tourists go hiking. The constant trampling over the vegetation causes it to die and the soil to wear away.

Pollution ⟩

All types of pollution are caused by tourists – air, water and noise.

- **Air pollution** is caused by air travel by foreign tourists. It is made worse by the extra vehicles on the roads.
- **Water pollution** can be caused by watersport activities on the lakes and seas, such as speedboating and jet skiing, and the disposal of sewage directly into the sea. This causes water pollution and poses a serious health risk. It also damages fragile environments like coral reefs.
- **Noise pollution** can be caused by planes and cars, as well as by recreational activities such as jet skiing.

Activity

Write a letter to the editor of your local newspaper, either condemning or supporting the development of a new tourist resort in your community.

Exercise

1. Explain how tourism can have a negative impact on the natural resources of a country.

2. What tourist activity can cause soil erosion?

Loss of land and habitats »»

In order to cater for tourists, large areas of land are lost to tourism:

- Farmland is replaced with large-scale holiday resorts and complexes.
- Coastal regions have hotels built on them.
- Communities may even make way for tourist facilities.

The environmental impact of this is substantial. Not only are large-scale tourist resorts and facilities unsightly, but coastal regions are often fragile environments and can be damaged by the large numbers of visitors. Wildlife and habitats may be badly affected or even lost completely.

Climate change »»»

Climate change is a major problem associated with tourism. The biggest environmental problem caused by tourism is the method of transportation. Most people visiting countries today tend to arrive by plane. Air transport is one of the largest generators of increased carbon dioxide in our atmosphere, leading to climate change and global warming. Some of the effects of climate change include:

- increased flooding
- more frequent and stronger hurricanes
- rising sea levels
- coastal erosion and damage to coral reefs.

Aeroplanes contribute to the build-up of carbon dioxide in the atmosphere.

Damage to historical sites »

As with any fragile environment, whether it is natural or man-made, an increase in the number of people visiting that place or area puts a huge amount of pressure on the attraction in question. Quite often historical sites of interest can be damaged by increased visitor numbers.

Organisations such as the Caribbean Conservation Association work with local governments to help create a greater awareness of the value of the Caribbean's natural resources.

Exercise

3. What are the main types of pollution?
4. What type of land is lost to make way for tourist resorts?
5. What is the biggest contributor to increased carbon dioxide levels in the atmosphere?
6. What are some of the possible consequences of climate change?

Key vocabulary

land degradation

air pollution

water pollution

noise pollution

climate change

Questions

See how well you have understood the topics in this unit.

1. Match the key vocabulary word (i–viii) with its definition (a–h).

i) natural resources	**a)** natural fuels such as coal, oil and gas
ii) raw materials	**b)** able to continue at the same level without destroying the resources it relies on
iii) renewable resources	**c)** when natural resources can be used to make something
iv) non-renewable resources	**d)** a naturally forming gas in the atmosphere
v) fossil fuels	**e)** materials that form naturally in or on the Earth
vi) greenhouse gas	**f)** natural resources that cannot be replaced
vii) global warming	**g)** an increase in global temperatures
viii) sustainable	**h)** natural resources that can be replaced

2. Complete the statements with the type of natural resource listed in the box.

gas	forests	oil	coal

a) Burning _____ creates thick smoke that can pollute towns and cities.

b) _____ that is used to fuel vehicles, planes and to heat homes releases dangerous gases into the atmosphere such as carbon dioxide and carbon monoxide.

c) _____ used to heat homes and create electricity can release large amounts into the atmosphere.

d) Destroying _____ can lead to global warming, as there are fewer trees to breathe in the carbon dioxide and release oxygen.

3. Explain the terms sustainable development and economic diversification.

4. Complete the flow diagram.

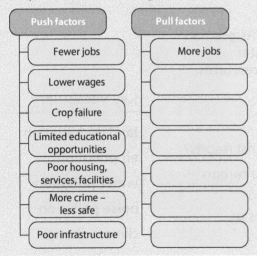

Push factors
- Fewer jobs
- Lower wages
- Crop failure
- Limited educational opportunities
- Poor housing, services, facilities
- More crime – less safe
- Poor infrastructure

Pull factors
- More jobs

5. Outline the policy objectives of the:

   a) National Integrated Water Resources Management Policy
   b) National Forestry Policy
   c) Environmental Management Authority

6. Draw an outline map of your country and label the location of four popular tourist sites.

7. On the map below, label the UNESCO world heritage sites with their names.

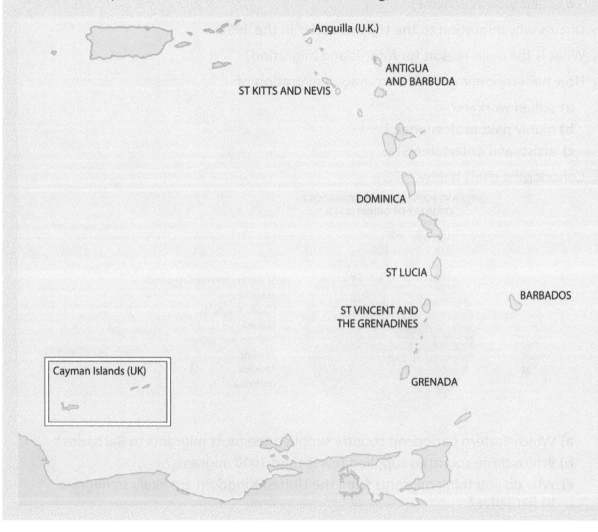

Anguilla (U.K.)

ANTIGUA AND BARBUDA

ST KITTS AND NEVIS

DOMINICA

ST LUCIA

BARBADOS

ST VINCENT AND THE GRENADINES

Cayman Islands (UK)

GRENADA

Questions

See how well you have understood the topics in this unit.

8. Describe what is meant by:

   a) upward mobility

   b) remittances

   c) brain drain

   d) guest worker schemes

9. Discuss why migration to the UK was easier in the 1950s.

10. What is the main reason for inter-island migration?

11. How has economic growth encouraged migration of:

   a) skilled workers?

   b) highly paid professionals?

   c) artists and entertainers?

12. Consider the chart below:

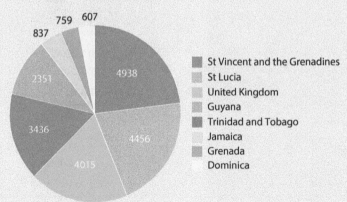

MIGRANT POPULATION IN BARBADOS BY COUNTRY OF ORIGIN (2013)

- St Vincent and the Grenadines
- St Lucia
- United Kingdom
- Guyana
- Trinidad and Tobago
- Jamaica
- Grenada
- Dominica

   a) Which Eastern Caribbean country supplied the most migrants to Barbados?

   b) Which three countries supplied fewer than 1000 migrants?

   c) Why do you think migrants from the United Kingdom are likely to migrate to Barbados?

13. Discuss why social and economic stability attracts tourists.

14. Why do tourists find Eastern Caribbean heritage intriguing?

15. Name two food festivals and two cultural festivals which attract tourists to the Eastern Caribbean.

16. Using examples say what is mean by a home port and a port of call.

17. Explain why cruise tourists prefer shorter tours and coastal activites.

Checking your progress

To make good progress in understanding different aspects of our environment, check to make sure you understand these ideas.

Define the term exploitation.

The effects of the use of natural resources on the environment.

Demonstrate concern for the effect of overuse of natural resources on the environment.

Define the term sustainable use of resources.

Discuss CARICOM and OECS programmes for sustainable use of resources.

Explain policies on the use of natural resources.

Discuss the reasons for changes in population distribution and density.

Explain how migration and urbanisation affect population distribution and density.

Discuss the history of international and inter-island migration.

Identify tourism sites in the Caribbean and discuss the natural factors that made regional tourism successful.

Explain the human factors that attract tourists to the region and describe the difference between cruise and long-stay tourists.

Discuss the advantages and the impact of tourism on the environment.

In this unit you will find out

Human existence

- Explain the term: human existence
- Explore the question "Why are we here?"
- Explain what makes us the same and what makes us different
  - what makes us unique and different
  - appreciate the differences that make us unique
  - similarities that allow us to grow together

Exploring values and virtues

- Explain the terms: values and virtues
- Explore why we need values and virtues
- Explain the impact of values and virtues on
  - decision making
  - responding to peer pressure
  - avoiding risky behaviour
- The qualities and importance of being virtuous
  - explore the qualities we need to show in our everyday lives

My place

- Describe our perception of ourselves within the family
  - my role in the family
  - where am I in my family?

Our faith community

- Belonging to a faith community
  - my life and faith
  - the faith community
  - families and religion
- The role of religion, faith tradition or belief system in personal character development

Human existence

We are learning to:

• define the term human existence.

Human existence refers to the questions: "Why do humans exist?", "Why are we here on Earth?", "What is our purpose?" and "What is the meaning of life?" The largest religious groups in the world – **Christianity**, **Hinduism**, **Islam** and **Judaism** – all look for answers to these questions.

Christianity 》》

Christians believe that each person is unique and that human beings are the highest form of life. They believe that their role in life is to take care of the world that God has created and to achieve this by:

St Gerard's Catholic Church, Anguilla.

• valuing and respecting all human life
• fulfilling their role in the family and in family life
• showing love, respect and kindness for all humankind
• recognising the difference between right and wrong
• caring for the world and its environment.

Hinduism 》》》

Hindus believe the aim of life is **moksha** (to be liberated) and that the path to achieving this is through spiritual effort, working selflessly for others and living a good life. Hinduism also teaches that its followers should worship God, help others, love their family and care for the environment. They achieve this by:

• valuing and respecting human life – all life is sacred
• not harbouring prejudice or discrimination
• fulfilling their role in the family and in family life
• believing that all races and religions are to be respected
• protecting and caring for the environment.

Activity

Look at the different ways Christians, Hindus, Muslims and Jewish people fulfil their role in life. Are there any that are common to all religions? If so, why do you think this is?

Exercise

1. Name the four major religious groups in the world.

2. In your own words, summarise what Christians and Hindus believe their role in life is. How is this achieved?

Islam >>

Islam teaches that worshipping God is the highest purpose of life. Muslims believe in a single god, called Allah, who has trusted life to them and that their aim is to live life well by following Allah's teachings.

The holy book of Islam is called the **Qur'an** and it teaches how Muslims must conduct themselves in their life:

- to value human life and to live a righteous life
- to uphold justice and to live a peaceful life
- to look after the young, care for the sick and look after the elderly
- to fulfil their role in their family
- to get along with other people and respect them as human beings
- to protect and care for the environment.

Muslims believe their holy book, the Qur'an, is a revelation from God.

Judaism >>>

Judaism teaches that humans are created in the image of God, and because humans share the same characteristics of God they share the same dignity and **values**.

Jewish people believe that a person is judged on how well they keep the laws and traditions of their faith, and that humanity's role on Earth is to carry out God's will. This is carried out by:

- recognising that all life is sacred and valuable
- living a moral life by following the Ten Commandments
- loving and serving God
- respecting, nurturing and caring for children
- fulfilling their role in the family and in family life
- protecting and caring for the environment.

We have seen that by following these belief systems (and others) people can find out what their role in life is and it can bring perspective on life. Therefore, a God or Gods, depending on your religious beliefs, give human life meaning.

Exercise

3. In your own words, summarise what Muslim and Jewish people believe is their role in life. How is this achieved?

4. For each religion discussed, create a mind map to help you understand the points raised.

Key vocabulary

human existence

Christianity (Christian)

Hinduism (Hindu)

Islam (Muslim)

Judaism (Jewish people)

moksha

Qur'an

values

Our uniqueness

We are learning to:
- explain what makes us the same and what makes us different
- develop an appreciation for the differences that make us unique
- celebrate the similarities that allow us to grow together.

What makes us unique and different ⟩⟩

Each person is **unique**, meaning we are special and different from everyone else. **Individuality** is what makes you different from others.

However, we all have **similarities** (things that are the same about us) and differences that define us as human beings, such as the colour of our eyes or being able to make people laugh.

We also have our own values (what we believe is important in life) and **ethics** (what we consider to be the right and wrong things to do). You may look and sound similar to other people in your family and in your community, but no one is exactly like you.

People have physical differences, for example, how tall they are, or what colour their eyes are. But looking at someone cannot tell us what they like doing, how they treat others or what their interests are. You may have this information, though, if you know the person.

To recognise people as unique individuals, we need to notice their

- actions – what kinds of things they do
- attitudes – how they approach their actions, and how they view themselves and others
- behaviours – patterns in what they do and how they do it.

Identical twins have the same physical characteristics.

Activity

Your teacher will put you in groups. Look at each other closely and write down the physical characteristics of everyone else in the group. Compare your answers with each other to see if you see each other in the same way. How have your friends described you? Do you agree with their description?

Exercise

1. In your own words, define the term unique.
2. Define the term ethics.
3. In pairs, look closely at each other. List two physical similarities and two physical differences you have.

Although people have physical differences and different actions, attitudes and behaviour we all share common characteristics with people. For example, we can share:

- Religious beliefs and traditions – the religious groups people belong to, their beliefs and religious customs. People practise a wide range of religions in the Caribbean.

- Ethnicity – if you have a shared ethnicity, you tend to have ancestors who came from the same place, and you may share traits of race, language or tribal background.

- History – we can share events and stories that shaped the lives of our ancestors and our nation.

- **Culture** – where all aspects of a society or group of people are brought together; for example, language, religion, arts, food and social custom.

- Language – the languages people speak, including creoles and dialects. Although the official language of many Caribbean countries is English, people often also speak their local creole or patois. These local languages can be a mix of African languages, English, French or Spanish.

- Customs – social, religious and national holidays and celebrations

- Arts – music, dance, stories, theatre and art

- Food – Caribbean cuisine can be a blend of African, Amerindian, European, Creole, Indian, Chinese, Spanish and Arabic influences, among others.

All of these factors help to unify us. Diversity (cultural, racial and religious) is something that we celebrate in the Caribbean. We all take part in festivals that celebrate other cultures and our similarities and differences.

Children at home in St George's, Grenada.

Exercise

4. Name the common characteristics that we can share in our community. Then, give an example of each based on your own community.

5. In groups, make a list of all the characteristics from the list above that you share; for example, the beliefs, customs, traditions of your family, the food you like, your favourite music.

Key vocabulary

unique

individuality

similarities

ethics

culture

Exploring values and virtues

We are learning how to:

- define the terms: values and virtues
- explain the relationship between belief systems and the development of values and virtues.

What are values?

Values are the moral principles and beliefs or accepted standards of a person or social group. Values are often shaped by the culture or society someone lives in.

Values can influence our decisions and can help us to decide what is right or wrong. Often our values change as we grow older. There are different types of values in our society:

- Individual values – these reflect how you live your life and the standards that you live by. Examples include being enthusiastic, kind, humble or creative.
- Relationship values – this is how you treat other people, such as your family, friends and classmates. Examples include being generous and trustful.
- Society values – these are the values that we would like society to follow. Examples include treating our elders well, being environmentally aware.

A value is not a 'thing', but more of a feeling or a way we feel towards other people and society in general. To have good values is to live a good and virtuous life, whereas to have bad values is to live a life that can lead you into trouble.

Values can also be taught. For example, in schools we are taught values and attitudes, such as respect for elders, honour for our father and mother, tolerance for each other's differences, curiosity about the world around us and appreciation for other cultures.

Values can also be spiritual and help us to maintain a religious outlook. For example, spiritual values help us to:

- establish a person's moral position
- encourage humane and selfless behaviour
- live a good life
- establish a good relationship with God
- have hope.

caring   confidence
courtesy
enthusiastic   creative
generous   excellence
helpfulness   honesty   honour   humble   justice   kindness   love   loyalty
purposefulness   reliability
reflectiveness
respect
responsibility   reverence
self-discipline
tolerance   service
trustworthiness   trustworthy
truthfulness

Activity

Look at the word cloud of values. Pick five of them which you feel describe your values and virtues and explain why.

What are virtues? >>>

Virtues are behaviours showing high moral standards. A person who is said to have good morals is valued as honest, respectful, kind and forgiving. A person who is said to have bad morals is often seen as the opposite of a morally good person. This person may be seen as dishonest or unkind.

There are four **moral virtues**, also known as the **cardinal virtues** in the Roman Catholic Church. All other virtues are based around these four virtues:

- Prudence – recognising one's moral duty and how to achieve that through good actions and behaviour; for example, seeing that it is wrong to steal a purse left on a bus, and finding its owner instead.

- Justice – being fair to everyone; for example, treating everyone in the same way no matter what they have done to you.

- Fortitude – showing courage, persevering and standing up to all the hardships that life may present; for example, overcoming an illness.

- Temperance – showing self-control and restraint; for example, not eating all the sweets at once, but eating only a few every day.

An example of self-control is when you choose the healthy food option and not the unhealthy one.

Why do we need values and virtues? >>>>

It is important for us to have values and virtues, as they help us in our personal development. They help us to:

- make moral judgments
- do what is good and promote the common good
- exercise reason and sound judgment
- form the basis on which our entire moral life or our human existence depends.

Discussion

In groups, discuss how relevant you think values and virtues are to your everyday lives.

Exercise

1. Define in your own words the terms values and virtues.

2. Explain in your own words the different types of values we can have in society, giving examples.

3. How do spiritual values help us to live our lives? Use your own words.

4. Explain why we need values and virtues and how they help us in our everyday lives.

5. Why is it important to develop good character?

6. Choose a virtue and explain how a person might develop it. Use the word cloud to help you.

Key vocabulary

virtues

moral virtues (or **cardinal virtues**)

Decision making

We are learning to:

• explain the importance of values and virtues in decision making.

Decision making 〉〉

Because you are a unique individual, and because everyone lives by a different individual **value system**, we all make different decisions. Some decisions are very easy to make, such as what clothes we are going to wear each day.

It is important that we make the right decision for the right reasons and to follow our own value system, rather than for the wrong reasons – for example, in order to please someone else.

When people are younger, other people (such as their mother or father) make decisions for them. As we get older, and have more freedom and responsibility, we will be faced with more situations in which we have to decide how to behave. Often we will need to make decisions based on our value system and on what is right and wrong.

Do not be forced to do something that you don't want to do – such as drinking alcohol.

Peer pressure 〉〉〉

Peer pressure is something that you will come across as you grow up. Your **peers** are people who are equal to you in some way, for example, in age, social status, interests or as members of the same class.

Peer pressure is when your peers try to influence you to do something that you do not want to do. They could be trying to get you to do something dangerous, harmful or illegal – for example, drinking, smoking, having sex, stealing, vandalising or hanging out with a bad crowd.

Peer pressure often happens in gangs, when people are too afraid to say no to the majority because they are scared of what will happen.

Exercise

1. Define the term peer pressure.
2. Explain why you should keep to your own values and not give in to peer pressure.

Responding to peer pressure

It is important that you be true to your values and not give in to peer pressure. You should not be afraid to say no. Here are some suggestions as to how to respond to your peers:

- The best way is just to say no. It can be difficult to say no the first time, but once you have said it, and you have stood firm with your beliefs, it sends out a message that you are not interested. This will help in the future because people will know that you can't be negatively influenced. It also helps you to take control.

- Think of the consequences. Think what the consequences will be if you do what your peer asks you to do. You could get in trouble with the police, make yourself ill, or hurt yourself or others. Think this through, then say no.

- Change the subject and walk away. One option is to make an excuse and say that you have to leave. You could say that your parents are expecting you home now, that you are tired and have to go home, etc.

You can do things to avoid the problem in the first place:

- Hang out with your true friends. Real friends won't ask you to do something they know will make you feel uncomfortable or put you in a dangerous situation. Spend time with your real friends and not other people just because you think they are 'cool'.

- Keep busy. Find other interesting activities with friends; perhaps join a sports club or a drama society. You could use your time to study to do better at school or help around the home more.

Finally, you can always ask someone else for advice. Talk to a friend – but make sure it is someone you really trust, or they might give you bad advice.

Do not be afraid to say "No!"

Activity

Using the information on this page, create a poster showing what you should do if pressure is being put on you to do something that you don't want to do. You can add photos or drawings. Show it to the rest of your class and share ideas.

Exercise

3. List some of the ways you can respond to peer pressure. Can you think of any other ways?

4. Why do you think you should hang out with your true friends?

5. What can you do to avoid being put in difficult situations?

Key vocabulary

value system

peers

peer pressure

Making the right decision

We are learning to:

- explain the importance of values and virtues in decision making.

Making the right decision ⟩⟩

We have seen that you will come across peer pressure as you grow up, and we have discussed ways to react when your so-called friends pressure you to do something that you don't want to do.

However, young people all over the world will always face many challenges. This is usually because of social problems in society and **risky behaviour** associated with those problems.

Risky behaviour is any action that can negatively affect your current or future wellbeing. Some behaviours can cause immediate physical injury (for example, drunken driving). Others can cause harm over a longer period (for example, smoking).

Substance abuse ⟩⟩⟩

Substance abuse can cause immediate as well as long-term harm. The most common substances that young people use and abuse are alcohol and cigarettes. Cigarette smoking can cause diseases such as lung disease and heart disease.

Drinking alcohol also causes long-term health damage, such as liver and heart disease, high blood pressure and cancer, and it weakens the immune system. It is also linked to more immediate dangers, such as car accidents, fighting and physical abuse.

Other substances include illegal drugs such as marijuana, heroin, cocaine, LSD and ecstasy. These can lead to serious health issues, both physical and mental. There is a risk of HIV from infected needles, and users often turn to crime to pay for their drugs.

In order to pay for their habit, drug users sometimes spend money that would otherwise be used for food and shelter for their family.

Substance abuse can lead to homelessness.

Exercise

1. What are the health risks associated with smoking?
2. What are the short- and long-term health risks associated with drinking alcohol?

Sexual behaviours ▶▶▶

During **puberty**, your body is rapidly producing hormones, which cause the development of your sexual characteristics.

Puberty is an important time in a young person's life, because people can make bad decisions during this time that will affect the rest of their lives.

Youths become more aware of their sexuality, and emotions run high especially in relation to the opposite sex. It is important during puberty that sex and sexuality are openly discussed and that ideas about it are shaped based on a person's cultural and religious background.

Awareness of the risks of sexual behaviour and making the right decision can help people choose safer and more responsible sexual practices.

Unprotected sex, which is sex without using a condom, can result in unwanted pregnancy. It can also result in the transmission of HIV, as well as other **sexually transmitted diseases** (STDs), such as genital herpes and warts, HIV, chlamydia, syphilis and gonorrhoea.

Promiscuous behaviour increases the risk of STDs as well as unwanted pregnancy. In the Eastern Caribbean, there are many cases of teenage pregnancy, as young men and women have unprotected sex.

If any of your friends, or anyone else, pressures you into taking drugs or alcohol – or if someone wants to have sex with you, but you don't – think of the advice we gave earlier:

- The best way is just to say "No!"
- Think of the consequences…
- Walk away.

Activity

In groups, create a poster that shows the consequences of a bad decision, and what happens after making a good decision. Choose a situation you all agree on.

Did you know…?

Puberty usually starts between ages 8 and 13 in girls, and between 10 and 15 in boys.

Exercise

3. Why is puberty an important time in relation to sexual health?

4. True or false? Awareness of the risks of sexual behaviour and making the right decision can help people choose safer and more responsible sexual practices.

5. What are two consequences of unprotected sex?

6. If you find yourself in a situation where there is 'risky behaviour', what should you say to yourself?

7. In groups, discuss the importance of values and virtues when making the right decision. Consider why it is important to make the right decision and why you should learn to do this at an early age.

Key vocabulary

risky behaviour

puberty

sexually transmitted diseases (STDs)

Qualities of being virtuous

We are learning to:

• discuss the qualities of a virtuous individual.

The virtuous life ⟩⟩

What sort of **qualities** should a virtuous person have, why should we practise virtues, and how should these be applied to our everyday lives?

The qualities and importance of being virtuous ⟩⟩⟩

Virtues can be seen as the basic qualities that we need for our wellbeing and happiness as we make our way through life. Living a virtuous life will help us to:

• strengthen our relationships with friends, family and the community
• achieve goals, whether they are short-term goals like helping an elderly person to tidy their garden, or long-term goals such as getting good marks at school
• achieve happiness in our lives.

One key quality needed to help you achieve these aims is **perseverance**, the ability to keep trying no matter how many failures you may have – for example, spending more time working hard and persevering to pass your exams, rather than being on social networking sites all day and night.

There are many other qualities a virtuous person can have. Some of them are in the word cloud.

Studying hard for your exams will bring rewards.

acceptance caring cleanliness compassion confidence considerate courageous creative determined discipline encouragement enthusiastic friendly gentle gracious grateful helpful honest humble kindness loyal modest patient persevere truthful responsible trustworthy reliable

Exercise

1. Explain in your own words what being virtuous means.
2. What three things will living a virtuous life help us to achieve?
3. What do you think is meant by the expression "If at first you don't succeed, try, try, try again"?

Did you know...?

Every year, 2 October is International Day of Non-Violence – named in honour of Mahatma Gandhi.

In some countries, almost everyone speaks the same language, or follows the same religion, or comes from the same ethnic group. Most countries have a mix of different groups of people. People form groups by ethnicity, religion, culture or language.

Case study

Qualities in our everyday lives

A Every Saturday Akeel would visit his elderly neighbour Mr Cooper to tidy up the yard and his house.

B Marcus and Matthew are classmates and are good friends. One day, Matthew saw that Marcus was upset about something but wouldn't say what the matter was. Matthew made sure that he looked after Marcus during the school day.

C Alijah was going home from school one day when he saw a purse lying on the roadside. When he looked inside the purse, he saw a lot of money, but also the address of the owner. Alijah took the purse back to the owner, who gave Alijah a small reward for bringing the purse back.

D Wilfred loved playing cricket but he found it difficult to get a place in the school cricket team. Wilfred decided to practise his bowling a little every night, and after a few weeks of practice he finally got in the team. He is now one of the first names on the team sheet.

E Mr Archer was the leader of the local youth group. When the funding for the group was withdrawn, he was worried that the local children would have nowhere to go and would perhaps fall into bad company. He decided to fund the youth club himself. When the local council found this out a few months later, they started up the funding again. Mr Archer didn't mind helping in this way and didn't want anyone to know he had done this.

Questions

1. Look at each scenario and identify one (or more) of the virtues shown in the word cloud.

2. Explain why the virtues you have identified were shown in each scenario.

3. Why do you think Mr Archer (in E) did not want it to be known he had helped out the youth group?

4. In which scenario is loyalty shown?

5. Which scenario demonstrates perseverance?

Research

Research the life of Mahatma Gandhi, who lived a virtuous life. Gandhi lived his life on the principles of love, self-sacrifice, acceptance and peace. Find out how he became the 'Father of the Nation' to India and why he preached the importance of peaceful protest.

Mahatma Gandhi.

Key vocabulary

qualities

perseverance

My place in my family

We are learning how to:

• describe our perception of ourselves within our family.

My role in the family ⟩⟩

We have seen in Book 1 that each member of a family plays a role in their family. A role is a pattern of behaviour that comes from your position in the family. For example:

• A parent's role is to take care of the children and make decisions for the household.

• Grandparents provide support for the parents.

The children's role in a family is to:

• show respect for their parents

• help with household chores

• care for siblings and elderly family members

• attend school and take responsibility for their studies

• ensure that they do not waste family money or possessions.

Along with your role in the family come responsibilities – the things we are expected to do as part of our role. Examples of responsibilities in a family might include:

• earning money and paying bills

• buying food and clothing

• preparing food and cooking

• cleaning the house, doing the laundry, drying and folding clothes

• tidying bedrooms and bathrooms

• doing your homework

• taking care of the youngest in the family

• taking care of the elderly in the family.

We all have a role in our family.

Exercise

1. What is the role of children in a family?

2. Look at the list of responsibilities in a family. Which of these should children do?

3. Look at the list you have created from question 2. Which of these responsibilities do you carry out at home?

In many families, children take on one of four main roles according to where they are in the family. They may be:

- the hero or achiever – often the eldest child in the family
- the scapegoat, who is blamed for things that go wrong – often the second or third child in the family
- the invisible one who feels like they are not noticed – this, too, is often the second or third child in the family
- the mascot/clown, who makes everyone laugh or smile – often the youngest child in the family.

The list and the table below summarise how children can feel about their position in the family. Remember that everyone is unique and different, and there are different situations in every family, so this might not apply to every family.

Discussion

In groups, discuss where you think you are in your family, according to the table. Do you think people describe you as shown in the table, and do you feel on the inside as the table suggests?

Type	Hero	Scapegoat	Invisible one	Mascot
Age position	Usually the oldest	May be the second or third child	May be the second or third child	Usually the youngest
At school	Achiever; high grades	Rebellious; may sometimes fail	Quiet and shy	Popular or joker
Others may describe them as…	A leader Lucky Talented Serious Mature Successful	Tough Angry Naughty Not as successful as the hero	A loner Shy Withdrawn Quiet	Easygoing Relaxed Energetic Cute Funny
On the inside, they may feel…	Lonely Scared "I'm never good enough."	Left out Misunderstood Lonely "I don't get enough attention."	Different Like an outsider "No one notices me."	Afraid Anxious "I wonder if I'm crazy."

Exercise

4. What are the four main roles that children can take on within a family?

5. According to the table, if you were the oldest child in a family, what type would you be?

6. What type do you think you are? How do you feel about this?

My life and faith

We are learning how to:

- explain how we perceive ourselves in terms of belonging to a faith community
- describe the role of our religion, faith tradition or belief system in personal character development.

My life and faith

We have seen how people practise a wide range of religions in the Caribbean. Catholicism is the most popular form of Christianity, but there are also Pentecostals, Evangelical and Full Gospel Christians, Anglicans and Baptists. Citizens of Caribbean countries also include Hindus, Muslims and Jewish people.

When members of each religious group act in their day-to-day life according to their religious teachings, they set a good example to motivate others to act righteously. For example, if members of the Roman Catholic faith act in their everyday life according to the teachings of Jesus Christ, they inspire people to behave in the same way.

Hindus offering morning prayer in Georgetown, Guyana.

The faith community

Most religions have a **belief system**, which is a set of beliefs or stories that are held by many people, such as how and why we were created, what happens after death and rules or principles about how to lead a good life on Earth. They also have their own daily, weekly and annual customs, practices and traditions, which help shape their everyday lives. When a group of people share a particular set of beliefs it is known as a **faith community**.

Families and religion

Religion has an important part to play in family life:

- Christianity teaches that relationships in a family should be loving, respectful and positive.
- In Hinduism, parents should love their children and provide for them physically, emotionally and spiritually; children should honour their parents.
- In Islam, family is central – each family member has a role to play.
- In Judaism, the family is at the heart of the community and is built on strong moral and ethical values.

Research

Research the religious history of your family. See if you can find out how long your family has followed your faith. Have they always gone to the same place of worship? Has anyone made any special contribution to the faith or place of worship? You could create a timeline or a family tree to show their involvement.

The role of religion in personal character development

Socialisation, along with learning about our culture, beliefs, traditions, morals and values, helps us as we grow up and develop. By being a part of a faith community, you will develop a sense of identity and belonging, which will guide you as you come to find your place and purpose in the world.

Religion is closely associated with finding meaning in the world, and being part of a faith community will help us to:

- nurture and satisfy children's needs by:
  - providing love, peace and security
  - engaging in play, exploration, humour, hope and wonder
  - encouraging them to take part in and contribute to the spiritual and social wellbeing of their family, friends and community
- be aware that there is a wider world
- meet new friends and help other people
- become spiritually aware (of whichever religious faith we follow)
- deal with social issues such as truancy, crime, sexual health, drinking, smoking, drugs and antisocial behaviour
- shape people's moral character and help to develop a sense of responsibility
- build a network of kind and respectful relationships – a community of friends and a network of support.

Religion plays an important role by helping us to form social relationships; promoting wellbeing and identity; and increasing our sense of purpose, meaning in life and service towards others. We can understand ourselves and how we connect to the wider world better.

Project

In groups, review the material in this chapter and then research the role of religion or belief systems in personal character development. Do you think religion has a role to play in what your character is like? Do you think religion has influenced your life so far? Why is having a religion or a belief system a good thing?

Exercise

1. Explain the terms belief system and faith community.
2. What will happen if each day you act according to the religious teaching that you follow?
3. Write a list of five things that being part of a faith community can help you achieve.
4. Think about the faith community that you belong to and consider the daily, weekly and annual customs, practices and traditions that are part of that community. Complete a 'Me Chart' that shows what role and contribution you make within the community in terms of faith.
5. Why do you think being part of a faith community is so important to your personal development?

Key vocabulary

belief system

faith community

socialisation

Questions

See how well you have understood the topics in this unit.

1. Match the key vocabulary word with its definition.

   i) human existence

   ii) dignity

   iii) values

   iv) unique

   v) individuality

   vi) similarities

   vii) virtues

   a) things that are the same in some ways

   b) the qualities that make a person different from others

   c) the need and right to honour and respect

   d) what we believe is important in life

   e) behaviours that show high moral standards

   f) the only one of its kind; unlike any other

   g) why people are here on Earth or the purpose and meaning of life

2. Name four ways in which Christians believe they can achieve their role in life.

3. Name four ways Hindus believe they can achieve their role in life.

4. Name the three ways we can recognise people as unique individuals.

5. Match these different types of values we have in our society to their definitions and examples.

Types of Values	Definitions of Values	Examples of Values
Individual values	These are the values that we would like society to follow.	Examples include being generous and trustful.
Relationship values	These reflect how you live your life and the standards that you live by.	Examples include how to treat our elders and be environmentally aware.
Society values	This is how you treat other people, such as your family, friends and classmates.	Examples include being enthusiastic, kind, humble, creative.

6. Explain in your own words your understanding of the four moral virtues, and give one example of each:

   prudence

   justice

   fortitude

   temperance

7. Name four ways in which the holy book of Islam, the Qur'an, teaches Muslims how they must conduct themselves.

8. Match the key vocabulary word (i–iv) with its definition (a–d).

   i) Christianity

   ii) Hinduism

   iii) Islam

   iv) Judaism

   a) means 'submission to the will of Allah'; Muslims believe in a single god, called Allah

   b) the religion of the Jewish people

   c) belief in the teachings of Jesus Christ

   d) belief that the aim of life is moksha

9. Draw a poster to show ways you can respond to peer pressure. Use these headings as a starting point and add your own ideas to each one:

   The best way is just to say no

   Think of the consequences

   Change the subject and walk away

10. Name some of the risky behaviours that we should avoid, and why.

11. This word cloud shows some of the virtuous qualities a person can have. Take three of these words and write a sentence for each one, describing how you can show this virtue in your everyday life.

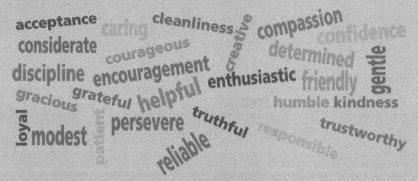

12. Name four ways in which Jewish people can carry out the will of God on Earth.

13. Explain why religion has an important part to play in the family life of Christians, Hindus, Muslims and Jewish people.

Checking your progress

To make good progress in understanding different aspects of your personal identity, check to make sure you understand these ideas.

☐ Explain the term human existence.

☐ Consider the question "Why are we here?"

☐ Give examples of how different faith communities conduct their lives.

☐ Explain in your own words the terms values and virtues.

☐ Explain why we need values and virtues.

☐ Explain the importance of values and virtues in decision making.

☐ Give examples of the role of children in a family.

☐ Give examples of different responsibilities we have in our family.

☐ Consider our role within the family.

☐ Explain in your own words the role of the faith community.

☐ Explain the role religion plays in family life.

☐ Identify how being part of a faith community helps us to lead a better life.

End-of-term questions

Questions 1–7 >>>

See how well you have understood the ideas in Unit 7.

1. Explain the difference between man-made heritage, built environment and built heritage.

2. Explain what a civic building is, and its function. Name some examples in your country.

3. Match the terms (i–iii) with the definitions (a–c):

   i) ecological diversity

   ii) species diversity

   iii) genetic diversity

   a) variety of different species, for example a great biodiversity of butterflies

   b) the variation in genetic material within a particular species or group, for example trees

   c) diversity of ecosystems, natural communities and habitats on planet Earth

4. Name three national parks, or protected areas, that are found in the Eastern Caribbean.

5. Write a short essay outlining some of the ecotourism projects that can be found in the Eastern Caribbean. Write about 150 words.

6. Explain how the physical features, flora and fauna of your country contribute to your nation's national heritage.

7. Write a letter to a newspaper explaining why mangroves should be protected.

Questions 8–14 >>>

See how well you have understood the ideas in Unit 8.

8. Write a short report outlining how the overuse of coal, oil and gas affects the environment.

9. Explain the role of the following organisations who assist with the conservation of our natural resources.

   a) CARICOM

   b) OECS

10. Give reasons for the following:

    a) push factors for rural–urban migration

    b) push factors for urban–rural migration

    c) pull factors for rural–urban migration

    d) pull factors for urban–rural migration

11. Explain the difference between these terms: migration, internal migration and external migration.

12. Explain the factors that are responsible for the development of the tourist industry in the Caribbean.

13. Write an essay in which you describe the advantages of tourism.

14. What impact does tourism have on our environment? Write a report outlining all the issues, and consider whether tourism is a good or bad thing for the Caribbean region.

Questions 15–20 〉〉〉

See how well you have understood the ideas in Unit 9.

15. Explain, in your own words, the term human existence.

16. Explain how Hindus achieve moksha.

17. Name the three ways that we can identify someone as being unique.

18. Read 9.2. Name five common characteristics that we can share with other people in our community. Give an example of each.

19. Match the terms (i–iii) with the definitions (a–c):

i) individual values

ii) relationship values

iii) society values

a) these are the values that we would like society to follow. Examples include treating our elders well; being environmentally aware.

b) these reflect how you live your life and the standards that you live by. Examples include being enthusiastic, kind, humble, creative.

c) this is how you treat other people, such as your family, friends and classmates. Examples include being generous and trustful.

20. Look at the word cloud of some of the qualities a virtuous person can have. Pick three words and give an example of how you can apply these qualities in everyday life.

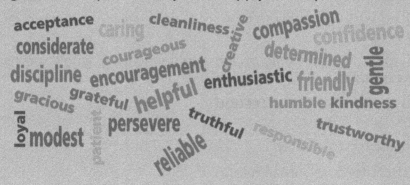

Glossary

abolish/abolished when a system has been put to an end

accountable to be responsible for something

air pollution substances found in the atmosphere that are harmful or dangerous

amenities useful or pleasant facilities or services

Amnesty International an organisation whose work is to secure the release of people imprisoned for their beliefs, to ban the use of torture, and to abolish the death penalty

anarchy when the absence of a government causes a breakdown of law and order in a society

annotate to write brief notes on a map or diagram

appoint to formally assign someone to a job, role or position

appreciation recognising someone's positive qualities or contributions

arable farming the growing of crops

associate professional someone who works supporting a professional worker

associated state Anguilla, Antigua, Dominica, Grenada, St Kitts-Nevis, St Lucia, and St Vincent and the Grenadines had the status of associated states

authoritarian leader someone who controls everything in a group or organisation rather than letting people decide for themselves

authority the power or right to give orders and directions to others, to make decisions and to enforce those decisions

basalt a type of black rock produced by volcanoes

bay an area where the coast curves inland

beach an area of sand or stones that have been deposited along the coastline

belief system a set of stories about things, such as how and why we were created and what happens after death

belonging to feel accepted or part of a group

bitcoin a system of open source peer-to-peer software for the creation and exchange of (payment in) a certain type of cryptocurrency; the first such system to be fully functional

bicameral system a Legistalture made up of two houses

biodiversity (or **biological diversity**) the great variety of life forms on Earth

brackish water a mixture of salty and fresh waters found in wetlands

brain drain the problem of highly skilled people leaving a country to find opportunities elsewhere

budget the amount of money that is available to spend

buffer a barrier to prevent damage

Cabinet part of the Executive, consisting of a Prime Minister and Ministers

calypso a song about a current subject, sung in a style which originally comes from the West Indies

candidate a person who seeks election

cape (or **headland**) a narrow piece of land that extends into the sea

capital city the urban area where the government is based

carbon dioxide a gas produced by breathing out, and by checmical reactions

carbon footprint a measure of the amount of carbon dioxide released into the atmosphere by a single endeavour or by a company, household, or individual through day-to-day activities over a given period

career a job or profession that someone works in

Caribbean identity the idea of what it means to belong to the Caribbean region

CARICOM The Caribbean Community

Carifesta Caribbean Festival of Arts

census a way of collecting information about the population of a country by asking questions about each household

chairperson someone who leads the council

charismatic authority power that comes from one's exceptional personality or character, or powers of persuasion

Chief Minister leader of the winning political party in an election

choropleth map a map that shows the population density of a country or area

Christianity people who believe in the teachings of Jesus Christ

church a Christian place of worship

cite to say where you found information

citizen someone who is a member of a country and who has certain rights in that country, but also has duties towards that country

city a large town, with a large population

civic building(s) a large building, or group of buildings, which can be used for entertainment, business events or are places where the government carries out its work

class the division of people in a society into groups according to their social status, for example upper class, middle class and working class

classification a system of organising information

climate the average weather conditions over a period of time

climate change the change of the Earth's temperature and weather patterns as a result of increased carbon dioxide in the air

coast/coastline an area of land beside the sea

cockpit cone-shaped hills with steep sides and deep holes in them

cold-blooded (of an animal) having its temperature rise and fall depending on the temperature of its environment; unable to produce its own body heat

colonialism gaining control over land in another country and exploiting its wealth

colony a country under the control of another country

committee a group of people selected or elected to do a particular job

communications transport facilities, such as roads, railways, ports and airports

communist someone who believes in communism

commute the journey you make between home and your place of work

competition when two or more people try to achieve the same thing

compromise where people accept an outcome which is different from what they want, because of circumstances or because they are thinking of other people's wishes

conservation/conserve protecting, restoring and preserving something

constituency an area in a country where voters elect a representative to a local or national government body

constituency council the council which presides over a constituency

constitution the principles and laws by which a country is governed

constitutional monarchy a country that has become independent from the colonial power

contract a legal agreement, usually between two companies or between an employer and employee, which involves doing work for a stated sum of money.

contribution something someone can do to make a product or make it successful

controlling when someone tries to get people to behave in a particular way, for example their behaviour

cooperation working together

coral reef a long, mass of coral which lies just below the surface of the sea

council an administrative body in local government

councillors people who are elected to serve in local government on councils

crater lake a volcanic crater which has filled with rainwater

creole language a language that has developed from a mixture of different languages and has become the main language in a particular place

Crown Colony a country ruled by the monarch of another country

cultural awareness the understanding of the differences between people from different countries or other backgrounds, especially differences in attitudes and values

cultural background the beliefs and traditions that a group of people share

cultural bonds cultural ties that bring people together

cultural diversity a wide range of customs, traditions and beliefs in a society

cultural heritage the cultural traditions that we have inherited from past generations

culture the customs, arts, shared language, history and ideas of a group

deforestation the removal of trees and vegetation to create open spaces for human activities

democracy a system of government in which a country's citizens choose their rulers by voting for them in elections

democratic leader someone who discusses issues as a group and accepts those decisions

dignity the sense that you have of your own importance and value, and other people's respect for you

diplomatic someone who is careful about what they say without offending anyone

direct democracy a political system which allows citizens of legal voting age to establish rules and laws

direct services where a service is sold directly to customers for their individual benefit

diverse having variety and differences

diversification increasing and varying the types of something; for example, farming and agriculture practices

diversity a range of things that are very different to each other

doline a shallow usually funnel-shaped depression of the ground surface formed by solution in limestone regions

dot map a map that shows population distribution and population density

drainage the process by which water is carried away from an area

dyad group of two

eco-friendly not damaging to the environment; sustainable

ecological involved with or concerning ecology

ecological diversity the variety of different habitats, ecosystems and life forms on Earth

ecological heritage/natural heritage all elements of biodiversity, including plants and animals and their natural features

ecology the study of the relationships between plants, animals, people and their environment

ecosystems a system formed by an environment and the living and non-living things within it

ecotourism tourism that does not damage or destroy the natural environment or local culture

elect to choose

election a process during which voters choose candidates by voting for them

elector a voter or person who has the right to vote in an election

Electoral College the members of the Senate and the House of Representatives who elect the President of the country

electorate people who are registered to vote in an election

elementary occupations low-skilled work made up of simple tasks

eligible someone who is allowed to do something, for example vote in an election

emancipation the removal of restraint or restrictions on an individual or a group of people

employed when someone has a job

employee someone who is paid to work for someone else or a company

employer a person or organisation that employs people

employment the fact of having a paid job

endangered in danger of extinction

endemic native to a particular country or region

enslaved person someone who is made the property of another person and has to work for that person

entomologist someone who studies insects [entomology is the study of insects]

Equator The Equator is an imaginary line around the middle of the Earth at an equal distance from the North Pole and the South Pole

erosion the process of wearing away the land

ethical conduct a set of moral principles people live by

ethics what is morally right and wrong

ethnicity features that belong to the culture of a society that were created in the past and have an historical importance to that society

Executive the branch of government that makes policies and coordinates the work of different government branches

expenditure the amount of money spent on something

exploited/exploitation the overuse of something

external migration when a person moves between two different countries

extinct/extinction the process where an animal or plant species disappears forever

extracted taken out

faith community when a group of people share a particular set of beliefs

fauna animals and wildlife that are found in a country or region

fault a large crack in the surface of the Earth

field observation/fieldwork the action of looking around you and noting interesting things that you see, such as high points of land, valleys or rivers

field sketch a diagram that you can draw to show the main features of a landscape

financial stability the prudent use of financial resources to meet future goals over an extended period without becoming indebted

first-past-the-post system (FPTPS) a way of counting votes in which the candidate with the most votes wins

flora plants that grow in a particular region

focused having or showing a clear and definite purpose

formal group a group that has written rules, a clear division of work and power, and procedures for replacing members

formal savings where savings are put into commercial banks and other commercial organisations

forum a place, situation or group in which people exchange ideas and have discussions

fossil fuels natural fuels such as coal, oil and gas

free trade trade which allows people to buy and sell goods freely, without restrictions

friendship a relationship between two or more friends

function the purpose of a particular thing or person

gender equality equal treatment, opportunities and rights for men and women

genetic diversity the variety within a particular species

global hydrological cycle (the water cycle) the constant movement of water around the Earth

global warming an increase in global temperatures

glucose a type of sugar that gives you energy

governance the way in which an organisation, or a country, is run

government a group of people, usually elected, who have the power and authority to manage the affairs of a country

Governor an official who is appointed to govern a country

Governor-General a person who is sent to a former British colony as the chief representative of Britain

Governor-in-Chief head governor

greenhouse gas a naturally forming gas in the atmosphere

group cohesion a group's ability to stick or stay together and last

group a group is made up of two or more people who do things together to achieve their common goals

growth poles areas of development

guest worker scheme a scheme through which a person, especially one from a poor country, lives and works in a different country for a period

habitat a home for a plant or animal

hamlet a very small village with a few houses

head of state (President) ceremonial head of state

head tax taxes paid by cruise lines for use of port facilities, and taxes from businesses that benefit from cruises

heritage features that belong to the culture of a society that were created in the past and have an historical importance to that society

heritage site a place that has special historic, cultural or social value, usually protected by law in order to preserve it

hierarchy a system in which people are ranked according to their status or power

hills high points of land which are less than 600m above sea level; hills are usually formed by glaciation

Hinduism belief that there is a universal soul called Brahman; this universal soul can take the form of many gods and goddesses

historical site a place that has special historical, cultural or social value, usually protected by law in order to preserve it

home port the port from which a cruise starts

honest someone who tells the truth or deceives anyone

honesty telling the truth and not trying to decieve anyone

hot spring a natural spring of mineral water at a temperature of 21°C (70°F) or above, found in areas of volcanic activity

House of Representatives the lower house of Tobago's Parliament

human environment the area where humans live and work

human existence the existence of humans, why they are here on Earth or their purpose and meaning of life

human resources people and their knowledge, abilities, experience and talents

human rights the basic rights which all people should have, for example the right to liberty, equality, respect, freedom of expression

humanity the characteristic or quality of being kind, thoughtful and sympathetic towards others

hurricane an extremely violent wind or storm

hydrological cycle another name for the water cycle

ICT skills the ability to use a computer or smartphone to find information and to share it with other people

identity the way you think about yourself, the way the world sees you and the characteristics that define you

immigrant a person who has come to live in a country from some other country

immigration the migration of a person or group of people into a country where they were not born in order to settle or reside there

income the amount of money a person (or business) earns

indentured/indentureship contract labour with harsh conditions

independence when a country is free from outside control

indigenous native to, or originate in, a particular region or country

indigenous fauna indigeneous animals

indigeneous flora indigeneous flowers or plants

indirect services where a service is sold to many customers at the same time

individuality the qualities that make a person different from others

industrial estate an area where many industries and factories are found in one place

industry economic activity based on manufacturing goods and processing materials

informal group an informal group does not have written rules or objectives or a strict hierarchical structure

informal savings where savings are put into non-commercial organisations

inhumane extreme cruelty

insect a small animal that has six legs, a three-part body and often has wings

insolation the quantity of solar radiation falling upon a body or planet, esp per unit area

insurrection a violent action that is taken by a large group of people against the rulers of their country, usually in order to remove them from office

integration joined together or working cooperatively as a single unit

integrity someone who is honest in their principles

interact people spending time together or working together

intercept to stop, deflect, or seize on the way from one place to another; prevent from arriving or proceeding

interconnectedness a geographical term that refers to countries being connected and how countries are connected in the world today

internal migration when a person moves within the same country

Islam the religion of Muslims

jointed marked with constrictions, at which the stem breaks into separate portions

Judaism the religion of the Jewish people

Judiciary the branch of government that makes sure that laws are enforced

justice administering the law in a fair way

karst denoting the characteristic scenery of a limestone region, including underground streams, gorges, etc

labour force the part of the population that is able and available to work

laissez- faire leader someone who lets the group make its own decisions, in its own way

land degradation the reduction in quality of the land either by extreme weather or by human processes

landmark a building or a feature which is easily noticed

lava field a vast plain stretching from inland to coast formed when lava flows cooled and hardened

law and order when the majority of people in a country respect and obey the laws of the society or country in which they live

leader an individual who influences the behaviour or actions of another person or who directs and guides a group towards decisions

leadership when a leader (or leaders) influences a group to achieve a common objective

leadership qualities personal qualities that help a person to lead others

Legislature the branch of government that makes laws

Lietenant-Governor an official elected by the Canadian government to act as a representative of the British king or queen in a province of Canada

limestone is a whitish-coloured rock which is used for building and for making cement

linear settlement houses and other buildings are built in lines, often along a road or river

livestock farming the rearing of animals

local government the part of the government that looks after government functions at local level

local government officer an employee of a local council

lumber trees or large pieces of wood cut from trees

majority rule and minority right a democratic system in which the majority should not take away the rights of the minority

mammal any animal where the female feeds her young on milk from her own body

manager someone who is responsible for running part of, or all of a company or business

mangroves a tree whose roots are above the ground and grow along coasts or on the banks of large rivers

man-made (built) heritage buildings created by people which form an important part of our cultural history

man-made features features created by humans such as buildings, roads, ports and airports

man-made/built surroundings formed by structures made by people

mayor the head of a city or borough

mediate someone who tries to settle an argument between two opposing sides

medicinal properties having healing properties

Member of Parliament someone who represents their constituency in Parliament

merengue a Caribbean dance in duple time with syncopated rhythm performed to such music

migration the temporary or permanent movement of people from one place to another; reasons can include 'pull factors' such as for work, education and change of location

Ministers the leaders of the government ministries (departments)

Ministry a government department which deals with a particular thing or area of activity

mitigate to make something less unpleasant, serious, or painful

modern states countries with modern systems of government

moksha the Hindu goal of becoming one with Brahma, and release from the cycle of reincarnation

monarchy a system where a state can be headed by a monarch or sovereign

money the coins and notes that you use to buy things, get paid by your employer or have in your hand

monoculture where a country uses most of its agricultural land to plant one main crop on a large scale

moral virtues/cardinal virtues the four virtues the Roman Catholic church ask people to follow

mosque a Muslim place of worship

mountains high points of land which are higher than hills (above 600m) and are steeper; mountains are the result of tectonic activity

mouth the place where a river meets the sea

multicultural society a society consisting of many cultures

multiplier effect refers to increased spending made possible from an injection of money from a new source

municipal associated with or belonging to a town or city which has its own local government

national identity a sense of who you are and that you are part of a country

nationalist connected with the desire of a group of people within a country for political independence

natural disaster a natural event which causes a lot of damage and kills a lot of people

natural hazard a natural process that can have negative effects

natural resource something that forms naturally or on the Earth and that we use for other purposes

need something that you need to survive or for your well-being

needs planning identifies future needs and the source of the future income to pay for these needs when they arise

noise pollution harmful levels of noise

non-confrontational where someone does not show aggression or is not hostile or threatening

non-renewable resources natural resources that cannot be replaced

nucleated settlement houses and other buildings are grouped together around a central point, such as a church

oil spill when oil escapes from a pipeline or tanker

on-the-job training training that a worker gets while they are working

oral tradition where information is passed from generation to generation through the spoken word

outstanding something that is very impressive or remarkable

Parliament a law making agency where a country's laws are decided

parliamentary monarchy a country which has a parliament and a monarch as the head of state, for example Barbados

pastoral farming a form of agriculture which rears livestock only and not crops

patriotic feeling of strong support and love for your country

patriotism showing a deep love for, and devotion to, your country

peasant farming the small-scale rearing of livestock, growing of vegetables and ground provisions, and the cultivation of crops such as corn, cocoa and bananas, primarily for consumption by the farmer and their family, with any remaining produce able to be sold at market

peer pressure when someone does something because their peers are doing it, but don't necessarily want to do it

peers people who are the same age or status as you

per capita per person

perimeter the outside edge of an area of land

permanent work/worker full-time employment or to be in full-time employment

permeable if a substance is permeable, something such as water or gas can pass through it or soak into it

perseverance the ability to keep trying no matter how many failures you may have

photosynthesis if a substance is permeable, something such as water or gas can pass through it or soak into it

physical features hills, mountains, rivers, lakes and other features of the landscape

physical heritage the part of our physical environment that is inherited from previous generations, such as oceans, mountains, forests and wetlands, and is maintained in the present and will be passed on to future generations

plains large areas of flat land

planters people who own or manage plantations in tropical countries

political franchise suffrage, the right to vote in an election

pollute to contaminate, as with poisonous or harmful substances

pollution when something is introduced into the natural environment which has a harmful effect and damages the natural surroundings and the flora and fauna that live there

population the total number of people living in a specific geographic area at a particular point in time

population density the average number of people living in one squared kilometer

population distribution how the population is spread out

port of call a place where a ship stops during a journey

power control and authority over people and their activities

precautionary need money needed for unexpected events

Premier leader of the government of a country

preserve/preservation maintaining an original state

President ceremonial head of state

pride a sense of respect you have for your country

primary groups a small group in which people frequently interact (often daily), know each other very well, and can depend on each other, for example a family

primary industry an industry that harvests raw materials or is involved in the extracting and developing of raw materials

primary source a document or object created at the time

Prime Minister political leader and head of the government

principles a rule or idea that explains how something works

professional someone who works in a job which involves a special skill or they have had special training

proportional representation a system of voting in which each political party is represented in a parliament or legislature in proportion to the number of people who vote for it in an election

psychologist someone who analyses and studies human behaviour

psychology the study of the human mind

puberty the period of physical development during which adolescents begin to develop sexually until they are capable of sexual reproduction

pull factor something which encourages a person to move to an area or location

push factor something which encourages a person to move away from an area or location

qualities the characteristics that someone or something has

quaternary industry an industry that provides knowledge and ideas

Qur'an the Muslim holy book

racial diversity when people from many different backgrounds make up a population

rational-legal authority a form of leadership in which people come to positions of power through a fair system of rules and laws

raw materials when natural resources can be used to make something

recreation when people go to particular facilities or places for leisure or relaxation

recreational facilities services that offer opportunities for people to enjoy themselves

referendum a vote by the eligible voters of a country on a single law or question and accept or reject an idea or law

reforestation the planting of trees over an area which used to have forest on it

reggae a type of West Indian popular music having four beats to the bar, the upbeat being strongly accented

reliability/reliable someone who can be trusted

relic an object surviving from an earlier time that tells us something about our history

relief the height and shape of the land

remittance a sum of money that you send to someone

renewable resources natural resources that can be replaced

representative democracy political system in which people elect people to represent them in government and govern the country on their behalf

Representatives members of the House of Representatives

republic a type of government in which the leaders and government are elected by the citizens of the country

resilience the ability of an ecosystem to return to its original state after being disturbed

resort a place where people go on holiday

respect/respectful due regard for someone or something

responsibility/responsibilities job or task we are expected to complete or the things we are expected to do as part of our role responsible if you are responsible for something, it is your job or duty to deal with it and make decisions relating to it

retrieve to find information online

revenue income

rights moral principles or norms that describe certain standards of human behaviour

risky behaviour actions that can negatively affect a person's wellbeing

river a long stretch of freshwater that flows towards the sea

role a part we play in relation to others or a pattern of behaviour that comes from your position in the family

Rule of Law the principle that no one is above the law

rural places which are located in the countryside, away from towns and cities

rural areas villages and hamlets with not many services

rural-urban migration when people move from rural areas to urban areas

salary a payment made to a worker by an employer at regular intervals for work done

sales industry professions dealing with selling on behalf of a company

sanctions a form of punishment, used to make sure that group members follow the group rules

sanitation having a clean supply of water and good sewage system

savannah a grassland or plain with few trees or a large area of flat, grassy land

saving(s) money that has been put aside or money that has been saved up

scattered/dispersed settlement pattern houses and other buildings are spread far apart over a large area

search engine a tool that allows you to search for information on the internet by entering keywords

secession when a country, or a group, separates from a larger group

secondary groups large groups which are not as close or intimate as primary groups, for example a sports club

secondary industry an industry mostly involved in processing and manufacturing or manufacturing industries which make products from raw materials

secondary source a document created after an event took place

self-employed providing one's own work or income, without an employer

Senate the upper house of Parliament, made up of Senators

Senator member of the Senate

service industry a company or business who provides a service but does not produce physical goods

services public utilities and facilities that are provided for settlements where people live

settlement a place where people settle down and live

settlement pattern the shape of the settlement

sexually transmitted diseases (STDs) diseases which are carried in the blood, semen and other body fluids, or in the genitals, which are transmitted through sexual intercourse

similarities things that are the same in some ways

slaves people who are the property of another person and have to work for that person

social group two or more people who work together to achieve a common purpose or goal

socialisation how we interact and communicate with others and how we form relationships

soil erosion the wearing away of topsoil

source the place where a river starts

species a type of animal or plant

species diversity varieties of species

speculative need money held in a different form, for example a house, which can later be converted into money

standard of living the level of comfort and wealth that a person or family may have

structure the way something is made, built or organised

suburban relating to a suburb

sustainable development development of a country that uses natural resources in a way that allows them to grow back or be replenished

sustainable/sustainability something that can be continued without destroying the resources that make same level without destroying the resources it relies on

symbol a sign or image that is used to represent something

technician someone whose work involves using technical equipment at a skilled level

tectonic plate large pieces of the Earth's crust

temple a holy place used by people of a particular religion, such as Hindus, Jewish people or Buddhists

temporary work/worker short-term employment or to be engaged in short-term employment

tertiary industry/sector an industry that provides services or service industries which sell manufactured goods or involves providing services and making goods available to customers, like banking for example

tertiary workers those employed in an industry that provides services or service industries which sell manufactured goods or involves providing services and making goods available to customers, like banking for example

tolerance acceptance of views, beliefs or behaviours that are different from one's own

tourism the business of travelling on holiday and visiting places of interest or services provided for people on holiday

town urban area of up to 100 000 people, smaller than a city

trade union an organised group of workers which protects their interests and rights

traditional authority a form of leadership in which people come to a position of power through traditions or customs, because it has always been that way

transaction need money to make everyday purchases

transatlantic slave trade, transatlantic trade of enslaved people the buying and selling of enslaved people, specifically involving the forced removal of African people from their homeland and their transportation across the Atlantic Ocean to the Caribbean, to work predominantly on sugar plantations

triad group of three

tropical forest/tropical rainforest a forest situated between the Tropic of Cancer and Tropic of Capricorn

underemployment the state of having work that does not fully use one's skills or abilities

unemployed/unemployment when someone does not have a job or the state of not having work

unicameral system a Legislature made up of one house

unification the process where two countries, or more, join together

unique the only one of its kind; unlike any other

United Nations an organisation whose role is to encourage international peace, co-operation, and friendship

unity being joined together or in agreement

universal adult suffrage this means that each adult person has one vote

universal resource locator (URL) The address of a website

universal suffrage the right of all adults (with minor exceptions) to vote in elections

unskilled workers workers who have no formal training, education or skill

upward mobility the movement of an individual, social group, or class to a position of increased status or power

urban belonging to a town or a city

urban areas towns and cities with many services

urbanisation increasing numbers of people living in the cities

urban-rural migration when people move from urban areas to rural areas

value how important or useful something is

value system a series of values by which people choose to live

values what we believe is important in life

village a settlement of between a few hundred and a few thousand people or a small community in a country area

virtues a quality which someone has which is thought to be morally good

volcanic cone very tall peaks created by volcanoes

volcano a mountain from which hot melted rock, gas, steam, and ash from inside the Earth sometimes burst

votes the ballot of voting papers on which you choose your candidate in an election

voting the person with the most votes gets the position of authority

wages a payment to a worker for work done in a particular time period

want something that you would like to have, but is not essential

water cycle the process through which water moves between the Earth's surface and places underground and the atmosphere

water pollution substances found in water bodies such as lakes or seas that are harmful or dangerous

waterfall where water falls over the edge of a steep cliff

watershed degradation Trinidad and Tobago's forests protect water resources; deforestation, quarrying and forest fires have reduced the amount of forests and therefore impacted on the water resources

wetlands a land environment that is regularly soaked with water, where the land connects with a river or sea

work ethics the rules and standards of conduct that are acceptable in the workplace

working class the group of people in a society whose work usually involves physical skills, who do not own much property and who have a relatively low social status

worship to show respect to a god by, for example, saying your prayers

zouk a style of dance music that combines African and Latin American rhythms and uses electronic instruments and modern studio technology

Index

Index

Index

Acknowledgements

The publishers wish to thank the following for permission to reproduce photographs. Every effort has been made to trace copyright holders and to obtain their permission for the use of copyright materials. The publishers will gladly receive any information enabling them to rectify any error or omission at the first opportunity.

(t = top, b = bottom)

p4t Tim Graham/Contributor/Getty Images, p4b Salim October/Shutterstock, p8 Sirtravelalot/Shutterstock, p9 Elena Elisseeva/Shutterstock, p10 YAY Media AS/Alamy Stock Photo, p11 Burlingham/Shutterstock, p12t Elena Elisseeva/Shutterstock, p12b ,Sirtravelalot/Shutterstock, p13 T photography/Shutterstock, p14 Tony Watson/Alamy Stock Photo, p15 Thomas Imo/Photothek/Getty Images, p16 iofoto/Shutterstock, p17 michaeljung/Shutterstock, p18 Jenny Matthews/Alamy Stock Photo, p19 michaeljung/Shutterstock, p20 Chris Howes/Wild Places Photography/Alamy Stock Photo, p21 Ethel Wolvovitz/Alamy Stock Photo, p22 Pete Oxford/Danita Delimont/Alamy Stock Photo, p23 Sundlof - EDCO/Alamy Stock Photo, p24t M.Sobreira/Alamy Stock Photo, p24b Anton_Ivanov/Shutterstock, p26t Kenneth Man/Shutterstock, p26b Lena Ivanova/Shutterstock, p28 AugustSnow/Alamy Stock Photo, p30 WAYHOME studio/Shutterstock, p32 PeopleImages/Getty Images, p33 Radovan1/Shutterstock, p34 sirtravelalot/Shutterstock, p40 blickwinkel/Held/Alamy Stock Photo, p41 Michael DeFreitas Caribbean/Alamy Stock Photo, p42 Alistair Ruff/Alamy Stock Photo, p43 Prisma by Dukas Presseagentur GmbH/Alamy Stock Photo, p44 mauritius images GmbH/Alamy Stock Photo, p45 Michael Runkel/robertharding/Alamy Stock Photo, p46t GoodMood Photo/Shutterstock, p46b HECTOR RETAMAL/ Staff/Getty Images, p48 Keystone Pictures USA/Alamy Stock Photo, p49 Keystone Pictures USA/Alamy Stock Photo, p50t Allstar Picture Library/Alamy Stock Photo, p50b Allstar Picture Library/Alamy Stock Photo, p51t Stacy Walsh Rosenstock/Alamy Stock Photo, p51b SEAN DRAKES/Alamy Stock Photo, p52t Ebet Roberts/Contributor/Getty Images, p52b Gijsbert Hanekroot/Contributor/Getty Images, p54 David Redfern/Staff/Getty Images, p60t Alexander Markelov/Shutterstock, p60b Mark Waugh/Alamy Stock Photo, p62t Juneisy Q. Hawkins/Shutterstock, p62b Richard Whitcombe/Shutterstock, p65 Photovolcanica.com/Shutterstock, p66t mangojuicy/Shutterstock, p66b Stephen Robertson/Shutterstock, p67 Ramunas Bruzas/Shutterstock, p68 Alexey Boldin/Shutterstock, p69 Walshphotos/Shutterstock, p70 Inga Locmele/Shutterstock, p71 Rasstock/Shutterstock, p73 Charles Wollertz/Alamy Stock Photo, p74t stormarn/Shutterstock, p74b Ryan Heffernan/Aurora/Getty Images, p77 Charles Wollertz/Alamy Stock Photo, p78 22August/Shutterstock, p79 Stocktrek Images, Inc./Alamy Stock Photo, p80 Sean Pavone/Shutterstock, p81 Fotoluminate LLC/Shutterstock, p82 EQRoy/Shutterstock, p87 KishoreJ/Shutterstock, p91 a-plus image bank/Alamy Stock Photo, p92 Shanna Baker/The Image Bank/Getty Images, p93 Matyas Rehak/Shutterstock, p94 photosounds/Shutterstock, p95 Kletr/Shutterstock, p96 Matt Propert/National Geographic Creative/Alamy Stock Photo, p97 shipfactory/Shutterstock, p98 Anton_Ivanov/Shutterstock, p100 Angela N Perryman/Shutterstock, p101 Meryll/Shutterstock, p108t Tim Graham/Contributor/Getty Images, p108b Salim October/Shutterstock, p113 Helene Rogers/ArkReligion.com/Alamy Stock Photo, p114 dbtravel/dbimages/Alamy Stock Photo, p118 wavebreakmedia/Shutterstock, p119 Helene Rogers/Art Directors & TRIP/Alamy Stock Photo, p120 Michaeljung/Shutterstock, p121 Zimmytws/Shutterstock, p123 Georges De Keerle/Contributor/Getty Images, p124 Christian Black/Alamy Stock Photo, p127 Stuart Burford/Alamy Stock Photo, p132 photka/Shutterstock, p134 Dexter Communications Inc, p136 JUAN BARRETO/Staff/Getty Images, p137 Lisa S./Shutterstock, p138 Park Dale/ Alamy Stock Photo, p144 Stocksnapper/Shutterstock, p146 Graham Mulrooney/Alamy Stock Photo, p148 Sean Drakes/LatinContent/Getty Images, p149 REUTERS/Alamy Stock Photo, p150t Sergey Komarov-Kohl/Alamy Stock photo, p150b EQRoy/Shutterstock, p152 awsome design studio/Shutterstock, p154 Yuriy Boyko/Shutterstock, p155 https://www.varietybarbados.org, p156 nito/Shutterstock, p162 Fox Photos/Stringer/Getty Images, p163 Hulton Archive/Stringer/Getty Images, p165 Culture Club/Contributor/Getty Images, p167 Public Domain, p168t flowerphotos/Alamy Stock Photo, p168b The Granger Collection/Alamy Stock Photo, p170 Heritage Images/Contributor/Getty Images, p171 BANANA PANCAKE/Alamy Stock Photo, p172 Steven Wright/Shutterstock, p173t SOTK2011/Alamy Stock Photo, p173b National Archives of Trinidad and Tobago/Natt.Gov.tt, p174t Jon Arnold Images Ltd/Alamy Stock Photo, p174b Graham Mulrooney/Alamy Stock Photo, p176 robertharding/Alamy Stock Photo, p177 Duplass/Shutterstock, p179 Print Collector/Contributor/Getty Images, p180 Paul Thompson Images/Alamy Stock Photo, p182 Jenny Matthews/Alamy Stock Photo, p183 PA Images/Alamy Stock Photo, p186 Nick Hanna/Alamy Stock Photo, p187 Avalon/Photoshot License/Alamy Stock Photo, p188 Hulton Archive/Stringer/Getty Images, p189 CKP1001/Shutterstock, p190 Altin Osmanaj/Alamy Atock Photo, p191 Nature Picture Library/Alamy Stock Photo, p198t B. Campbell65/Shutterstock, p198b V. J. Matthew/Alamy Stock Photo, p200t Rolf Richardson/Alamy Stock Photo, p200b Nik Wheeler/Alamy Stock Photo, p202t Graham Toney/Alamy Stock Photo, p202b Dennis MacDonald/Alamy Stock Photo, p203 Tim Wright/Alamy Stock Photo, p204 FLPA/Alamy Stock Photo, p205 Claudio Bruni/Alamy Stock Photo, p206 Larwin/Shutterstock, p207 Les Gibbon/Alamy Stock Photo, p208 Michele Falzone/Alamy Stock Photo, p209t Efrain Padro/Alamy Stock Photo, p209b robertharding/Alamy Stock Photo, p210 John Cancalosi/Alamy Stock Photo, p211 Reinhard Dirscherl/WaterFrame/Getty Images, p212 Eric Isselee/Shutterstock, p213t Wade Eakle/Lonely Planet Images/Getty Images, p213b Frontpage/Shutterstock, p214 Joost van Uffelen/Shutterstock, p220 LatitudeStock- TTL/Gallo Images/Getty Images, p221 Przemyslaw Skibinski/Shutterstock, p222 Soundaholis studio/Shutterstock, p223 Daniel Just photography/Shutterstock, p228t straga/Shutterstock, p228b Lukasz Z/Shutterstock, p230 Danicek/Shutterstock, p231 Think4photop/Shutterstock, p232 Milan Portfolio/Shutterstock, p233 Kakteen/Shutterstock, p234 WaterFrame/Alamy Stock Photo, p235 Henner Damke/Shutterstock, p238 Jon Nicholls Photography/Shutterstock, p240 Mooredesigns/Shutterstock, p242 Alicia Dauksis/Shutterstock, p243 Photostravellers/Shutterstock, p244 mirtmirt/Shutterstock, p246 M. Timothy O'Keefe/Alamy Stock Photo, p247 Jo Ann Snover/Alamy Stock Photo, p248t Roman Stetsyk/Shutterstock, p248b RaksyBH/Shutterstock, p250 puksamran/Shutterstock, p251 sharply_done/istock/Getty Images, p258 Stock Connection Blue/Alamy Stock Photo, p259 Marvin del Cid/Moment/Getty Images, p260 Fotostudio de Oude School/Moment/Getty Images, p261 FRUMM John/hemis.fr/Hemis / Alamy Stock Photo, p263 Iuliia Iun/Alamy Stock Photo, p264 FabrikaSimf/Shutterstock, p265 DOUG RAPHAEL/Shutterstock, p266 Novikov Alex/Shutterstock, p268 Jupiterimages/Stockbyte/Getty Images, p269 GL Archive/Alamy Stock Photo, p270 Juanmonino/iStock/Getty Images, p272 PRAKASH SINGH / Staff/Getty Images.